Street Criers

A Cultural History of Chinese Beggars

HANCHAO LU

Stanford University Press
Stanford, California
2005

Stanford University Press
Stanford, California

Printed in the United States of America on acid-free, archival-quality paper

Library of Congress Cataloging-in-Publication Data
Lu, Hanchao.
   Street criers : a cultural history of Chinese beggars / Hanchao Lu.
      p.   cm.
   Includes bibliographical references and index.
   ISBN 0-8047-5148-X (cloth : alk. paper)
   1. Beggars—China.   2. Beggars—China—History—19th century.
3. Beggars—China—History—20th century.   4. China—Social conditions—
19th century.   5. China—Social conditions—20th century.   I. Title: Cultural
history of Chinese beggars.   II. Title.
HV4610.A4L79 2005
305.5′69′0951—dc22   2005009127
Original Printing 2005

Last figure below indicates year of this printing:
14   13   12   11   10   09   08   07   06   05

Typeset by G&S Book Services in 10.5/12.5 Bembo

For Linlin, Frederic, and Jeffrey

Contents

Illustrations and Tables

HUMAN HISTORY has been written mostly by intellectuals and by and large on subjects related to the powerful, the well-known, or the privileged. Until recently, the common people have not been among the most popular topics in historical writing, although in any given time and place they composed the majority of any society. Even less on the agenda were the disadvantaged, whose lives and experiences, with a few noticeable exceptions, had typically fallen into oblivion. Recent scholarship has significantly altered this situation. Vigorous accounts of the lives of the unknown and energetic debates in the fields of socioeconomic history and cultural studies have diversified academic approaches and enhanced our knowledge of human experience. It is my hope that the present work can contribute to the great enterprise of bringing the obscure and disadvantaged to record.

This study is about beggars' culture and the institution of mendicancy in China from late imperial times to the end of the Republican era, with a reference to the resurgence of beggars in the post-Mao era. Among the topics discussed are the concepts and practices of mendicancy, organized begging, state and society relations as reflected in the issue of poverty, public opinion about beggars and the various factors that contributed to almsgiving, the role of gender in mendicancy, and so on. Panoramically, we will see that the culture and institution of Chinese mendicancy, which had their origins in earlier centuries, remained remarkably consistent through time and space.

In virtually all cultures—and the Chinese is no exception—a socioeconomic gulf separated street people from mainstream society and beggars were generally stigmatized. However, mendicancy constituted a culture in China that was more complex than just a mere tale of social outcasts. The social role of Chinese beggars overlaps with an extraordinary range of others. Mendicancy by definition is asking for alms without payment or recompense, but Chinese beggars frequently offered makeshift services while they were begging. An authentic beggar could be now and then a true street entertainer of various sorts: singer, dancer, acrobat, snake charmer, monkey trainer, and on festivities, a "pageant" player. More than occasionally he or she could also perform as porter, errand runner, door guard, fortune-teller, storyteller, prostitute, barber, mourner-for-hire, debt-collector-for-hire, night watchman, or even police officer and picket. Beggars typically were not criminals, but swindlers, thieves, and gangsters were not uncommon among them. Knights-errant and town eccentrics were also found in the ranks of mendicants and, in fact, such characters became favorite topics of both popular readings and literati writing. Thus the notion of mendicancy in China was richly ambiguous and ingeniously connotative.

Moreover, there were perennial and lively interactions between the world of beggars and mainstream society. Major historical characters and cultural icons in China belonged not just to the more "regular" society but were shared with the underclass and indeed they frequently became a prominent part of the subaltern culture. The reverse was true as well. Through creative imagination, beggars' culture also had a profound influence on mainstream society, ranging from public opinion on poverty, morality, and individuality to practical application of the culture in daily life such as in cuisine and child rearing. A "culture of poverty" (to use Oscar Lewis's phrase) was never a prevailing phenomenon in China. Instead, there was a culture *on* poverty in China that engaged both mainstream society and the subaltern culture of the mendicants. No matter how much of an outcast a beggar was in late imperial and modern China, he or she might never completely lose his or her place in society and culture. The culture of other vagrants—from medieval European Gypsies to contemporary North American tramps and hoboes—may find echoes in the world of Chinese beggars, yet rarely in history did beggars occupy such a prominent and colorful niche in a nation's culture as they did in China.

But such conspicuousness should not be interpreted as meaning Chinese mendicants had a better life than that of vagabonds elsewhere. On the contrary, the richness of the culture of Chinese beggars was largely a result of sheer poverty and incredible misery. That culture, which arose from destitution, was an artifact of the human will to live. As the impoverished vagrants received little or no assistance from the state, by begging and applying an extraordinary variety of begging techniques, they were forced to make the whole of society accountable for their misfortune in order to live. And, with little social assistance, the destitute organized themselves after a certain fashion to assure some degree of security and fairness within the group and to increase their chances of survival outside it. Thus, paradoxically, the most scattered and rootless people were at the time extremely well organized, and the most vulnerable social group could transform its poverty and adversity into "ammunition" and make the entire society vulnerable to its grievances. In the process, various types of exoticism and mannerisms associated with beggars came into being.

A major challenge to writing on mendicancy is that beggars, like all subaltern groups, seldom write about themselves and, other than telling of their bitter life for the purpose of appealing for alms, beggars tend not to talk about their experiences. Researchers therefore have to rely heavily on the narratives provided by outside observers, to which biases were almost inevitably attached. A remedy for the dearth of beggars' self-portraits is to carefully look through and compare a variety of other canvases, including sociological surveys, governmental reports, eyewitness accounts, personal reminiscences, missionary reports, literary notes, and, of course, beggars' own words and ditties. The ubiquity of beggars in early twentieth-century Chinese cities had prompted some social-minded individuals and institutes to investigate and write on the subject. For instance, an investigation of 700 beggars in Shanghai conducted in the early 1930s left a valuable unpublished field report, which has been extensively used in this study. The Culture and History Institutes (*Wenshi ziliao guan*) that were widely established in China in the 1950s–60s are a unique source for social and cultural history, with a mine of published and unpublished firsthand sources on the underclass and underground society across the nation. The opening of a number of archives and the recent boom of the publishing business in China have made some previously rare materials more accessible. With due awareness of the political motivation and, more recently, commercial drive behind the availability of some of the materials, researchers may find that more balanced sources for writing on the urban underclass are encouragingly increasing in number.

Academic writing can be a lonely endeavor. Fortunately, we live in a world where scholarly communications are vibrant and often cross cultural and national boundaries. Parts of this study were presented at the annual meetings of the Association for Asian Studies (2002) and the European Association of Chinese Studies (2000) and urban and Chinese history conferences held in Changchun, Lyon, and Los Angeles. I would like to thank the conference organizers and panel commentators, particularly Kathryn Bernhardt, Christian Henriot, Philip Huang, Perry Link, Kerrie MacPherson, and Richard J. Smith. The *Journal of Social History* published a small portion of this study (fall 1999), and I received encouraging words from Philip Kuhn and Dorothy Solinger that had more impact on this work than they might have guessed. The East Asian Institute of the National University of Singapore, headed by Wang Gungwu, granted me a visiting fellowship for 2000–2001 that allowed me to concentrate on research and writing. The Georgia Tech Foundation generously supported my research trips to China, which proved to be tremendously beneficial to this project. Ming-te Pan, Douglas Reynolds, and Qin Shao, among others, cheerfully shared their study and research materials with me. Richard Gunde, whose generosity has been noted in numerous author's acknowledgements in the China field, once again helped me with his insights and unfailing moral support. At Stanford University Press, senior editor Muriel Bell and her associate Carmen Borbón-Wu, and senior production editor Judith Hibbard, have been a constant source of guidance and assistance for this project. I also wish to express my gratitude to two anonymous readers for the press, whose comments have significantly improved the final version of this work.

Hanchao Lu
Atlanta, Georgia
May 2004

Street Criers

China at the Turn of the Twentieth Century

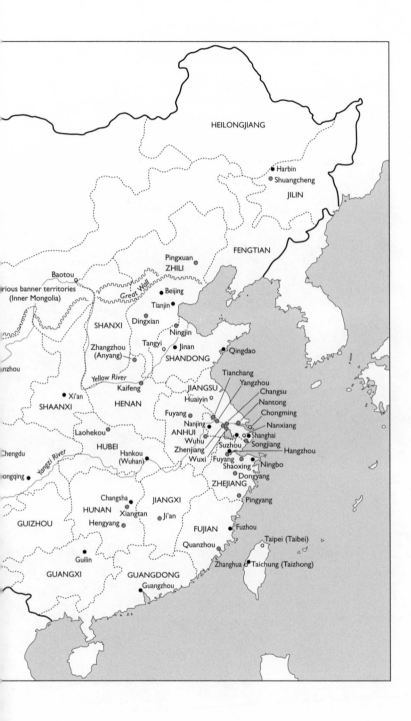

Introduction

MENDICANCY IS ONE of the oldest social phenomena in human history. The Chinese word for "begging" appeared as early as the eighteenth century B.C., in oracle-bone writing, and continued to be used in the literature of the Bronze Age.[1] Records describing begging in public appeared in Chinese documents as early as the third century B.C.[2] The modern Chinese word for "beggar" (*qigai*) first appeared no later than the early years of the Song dynasty (960–1279).[3]

Like many other seemingly all too clear and familiar terms that are actually hard to define, the word "beggar" can imply many things. It does not, in other words, necessarily refer simply to a person who "begs" for a living. The anthropologist David Schak has succinctly summarized the situation:

> The term *beggar* and its Chinese equivalents are quite nebulous in the way they are used by both Chinese and Westerners who have written on the subject, despite the fact that in both languages the equivalent words have relative clear primary denotation. Thus . . . one will see references to "beggars" who work, entertain, perform services, extort, coerce, steal, and even rob.[4]

This is of course not to suggest that the term is misleading. Rather, it accentuates the diverse ways street people struggled for survival in the grim social environment of modern China. It is this subject that forms the primary focus of this study. As we shall see in the following chapters, the manifold manners in the world of mendicants did not prevent them from being identified, either by the general public or by themselves, as beggars.

Time and Space: The Boundaries of This Study

The culture and institution of Chinese mendicancy remained remarkably consistent throughout time and space. The temporal boundaries of this study are marked by the establishment of the People's Republic in 1949 on one end and by the early nineteenth century on the other—a conventional periodization for "modern China"—but much of the beggars' culture in this period had its origins in earlier centuries. Because of the murky nature of the world of beggars, dates of certain cultural artifacts and events related to mendicancy cannot always be specified, but virtually all sources indicate the subaltern culture and customs of the nineteenth century had ancient roots. More specifically, many of the institutions of and concepts regarding beggars can be traced back to the thirteenth century, when vibrant trade and material growth led to a higher degree of commercialization than China had ever before experienced. Beggars were both victims and beneficiaries of this development. Over time, beggars increasingly became a more visible part of Chinese society and by the last imperial dynasty, the Qing (1644–1911), throughout the country mendicancy had long been an established, albeit despised, profession. The ubiquity of begging continued to 1949. The urban reform and Republican revolution of the early twentieth century did not fundamentally change the institution and its culture.

Geographically, this study encompasses dozens of localities across the nation, from the traditional heartland of Chinese civilization on the banks of the Yellow River to the less sinicized Mongolian and Manchuria frontier, from the coastal Yangzi valley in the east and the Pearl River delta in the south to the deep hinterlands near the Tibetan plateau. In terms of China's urban hierarchy, these widely scattered places encompassed everything from small rural towns to major metropolitan cities, including in between county seats, regional hubs, and provincial capitals (see Map). In virtually all things related to mendicancy, from the concept of beggary, to public opinion on beggars, to the ways and techniques of begging, to beggars' organizations and the way Chinese officials coped with them, the similarities across the country greatly outweighed the differences. Ever since G. William Skinner's call for regional studies, a main trend in research on China has been to emphasize local history and regional differentiation. Given the size of China and the diversity and complexity of its culture and society, research with a local focus is certainly appropriate. Much of this study is indeed based on local findings. However, we shall see that shared characteristics of Chinese beggars across the country overshadowed regional variation and provided mendicancy with a remarkable degree of cultural homogeneity.[5] In that sense, micro studies can contribute to a macro perspective on China as an essentially unified cultural entity.

The Subaltern and the Mainstream

The living conditions of Chinese beggars, who perhaps more than any other group suffered from the widespread poverty in modern China, were disheartening. It usually took an effort for outsiders to comprehend how beggars in China managed to consider themselves clothed when they only had a few rags to hang on their body, how their hovels could make a dwelling

Beggar of the Loong-Hwa Pagoda
Der Bettler der Lang-Chua Pagode
Le Mendiant de la Pagode de Loung-Houa
Il mendicante della Pagoda di Lang-huà
Нищий отъ Луль-Хуа народы

FIGURE I.   An old beggar in front the Longhua Temple in southwest Shanghai—from a postcard of 1908. The extremely shabby clothing of Chinese beggars often made Western observers wonder what the original form of the attire was and how panhandlers managed to keep the tatters hanging together. In the foreign community in the late nineteenth and early twentieth centuries, Chinese beggars frequently became the subject of postcards, reflecting their exotic image in the Western mind. SOURCE: *Jiumeng chongjing,* a postcard collection of Fan Lin and Bei Ning compiled by Chen Shouxiang.

for humans, and how they could survive on the meager and miserable food they ate (Figure 1). A British observer in the mid-nineteenth century commented that compared with the Chinese beggar, the "English mendicant is . . . a royal personage, who dresses magnificently and lives luxuriously."[6] This is by no means an exaggeration: all too often the suffering of beggars, especially child waifs, ended only when their lives ended. The bulk of roadside corpses daily picked up by the police on winter mornings, a notorious early twentieth-century street scene in major Chinese cities, consisted of beggars.

The penury, nevertheless, did not prevent a free flow of culture from both directions between the underclass and the society above it. Although street beggars were generally stigmatized and were separated from mainstream society by a huge socioeconomic gulf, their interactions with mainstream society were spontaneous, recurring, and frequently lively. Major characters in the Chinese cultural pantheon, including gods, emperors, paladins, heroes, and what might be called cultural icons and celebrities, belonged not just to the more "regular" and "decent" society outside the world of mendicants, but were in their own right also a prominent part of the subaltern culture of mendicants. Through creative imagination and self-willed faith, they were invited into beggars' dens to serve as their "patron saints," to be welcomed as the forefathers of their calling, and to preside over the rituals of their guilds. In a way, Chinese beggars had a stubbornly upbeat faith, believing in their own version of the dictum that "all men are created equal" and seeing their plight as a temporary downturn in the long journey of human life.[7]

Mainstream society was not unsympathetic to this view. Compassion for beggars was a universal feeling across time and space. Public sympathy for street people was the main motive for almsgiving and sometimes worked against indifferent state policies toward, in William Wilson's phrase, the "truly disadvantaged."[8] But rarely in history did beggars occupy such a prominent and colorful niche in a nation's culture as they did in China. The contempt of the general public for beggars is readily taken for granted, but evidence that contradicts this assumption cannot be easily dismissed. Conventional wisdom, often reflected in religious allegories and folktales, took beggary to be an outcome of failure in life and sometimes a result of a moral defect. But it also frequently took mendicancy as a role model, and sometimes even as a dynamic, of the individual striving to climb up the social ladder. Rising from beggary was not fictitious or the sensational plot of a popular drama, it was a moral. True stories of dramatic social mobility were of course rare, but they did exist and were conspicuous and influential. The concept of poverty, at least to the popular mind most of the time in Chinese history, was therefore more an issue of "moral philosophy" than of "political economy."[9]

Also, in a culture that had little sense of anything like the Christian notion of original sin, mendicancy was taken as an atonement for one's trespasses unconsciously accumulated in daily life. Self-imposed suffering as a beggar, or just to symbolically "take a meal that comes from hundreds of households," could be perceived as a way to redeem oneself from evil spirits or to escape from looming misfortune. Moreover, the very fact that aged mendicants had survived incredible miseries was taken as evidence of their fortitude or even their invincibility in the face of ill fortune, and that invincibility was thought to be transferable to protect others. In other words, in an ironic way the most vulnerable part of society was sometimes seen as secure and invulnerable. This might be seen as dialectical logic in quotidian life, although it was expressed in a superstitious fashion.

There were yet other similar ironies regarding mendicants. For instance, the most helpless people, whose very survival depended on alms from strangers, were considered capable of communicating with the most powerful supernatural deities. During the Chinese New Year's celebration, to take an example, beggars were seen as messengers of the God of Fortune. To arrogate and alter Oscar Lewis's phrase, "culture of poverty," there was a culture *on* poverty in China that engaged both mainstream society and the subaltern culture of the beggars. And, if the culture of poverty theory inclines to blame the disadvantaged for being caught in a vicious circle of self-destruction, then the culture on poverty in China, as far as the beggars were concerned, cherished the hope of social advancement and valued the exertions attached to it—no matter how remote the real chances of upward mobility might have been.[10]

State and Society

In spite of the general tolerance of and compassion for beggars, and even fantasy about them, little was done to help them other than offhanded almsgiving on the street. Government-sponsored charities for beggars were recorded as early as in the fifth century, and periodic charities for vagrants provided by religious institutions and local communities were also common and customary. By the seventeenth century, government-sponsored poorhouses were established at the county level.[11] But inadequate budgets and general mismanagement made them ineffective in coping with the everlasting and mounting problem of poverty. Typically, despite China's pervasive indigence, a county with hundreds of thousands of people only had a single poorhouse, with the capacity to shelter a couple dozen inmates, and soup kitchens, if available, only opened during the very cold months. The situation was best described by the Chinese saying, "To extinguish a cartload of burning firewood with a cup of water."[12] Government policies toward mendicancy were indifferent and impotent, and mostly consisted of, to apply another Chinese aphorism, "Waging war on paper."[13] Often, official charities ended up being little more than a political showpiece of the state or a gesture of its good will.

Any discussion of government policy toward beggars touches upon, in a singular way, the character of the state. The Chinese state up to modern times was frequently regarded as, and also officially proclaimed itself to be, Confucian, which meant, among other things, a characteristic emphasis on moral leadership of the authorities and active political participation of the literati elite. Yet time and again the nature of Chinese authorities could also be quite Taoist, in averring that human societies had their own natural course of development that required little governmental, or even human, intervention. "I do nothing and people transform themselves," the Taoist sage Laozi proclaimed. "I enjoy serenity and the people govern themselves."[14] It is common knowledge that until the early twentieth century the Chinese state had never effectively penetrated below the level of the county, which by the nineteenth century had an average population of a quarter million and was officially governed by one single magistrate, who "was so overburdened with a wide range of vaguely prescribed duties that he had little time or facilities to do any of them well, if indeed he had the intention or capacity to do so at all."[15] A 1919 reference book on China summarized the situation:

> The government in its relation to the local districts was until very recently governed by the '*laissez faire*' principle long ago enunciated by Laotze [Laozi], which says, 'Govern a big nation like frying a small fish.' Such a condition obtains not only in the country but in cities as well. The existence of the various guilds testifies to the fact that people in various walks of life have learned to manage their own affairs, free from governmental control or interference.[16]

Although the picture depicted in this passage needs careful scrutiny (as academic works in recent years have quite successfully done), the statement is essentially accurate. The beggars' world seemed to corroborate the dicta that composed the basis for the Taoist political philosophy. For centuries Chinese beggars had shown great resilience in their struggle for survival under circumstances where social welfare and governmental programs were either hopelessly impotent or in some cases totally absent. Instead, mendicancy, with its often ingenious techniques and methods, gradually constituted a profession, and the spontaneously formed and autonomously run beggars' guilds that were crucial to that profession came to provide an institutionalized way for the myriad urban poor to survive with little or no help from the state.

As the state had no adequate measures to cope with the problems of poverty, the most unfortunate could only survive by appealing to the entire society to respond to their misfortune. The theme for the destitute was the simplest one. It was the most primitive and straightforward yet profoundly sacred human desire: to live. An ancient Chinese tale recorded in *The Book of Rites* (*Liji*) tells how a starveling refused to accept food delivered to him with contempt, preferring to die with integrity than survive in humiliation. The story was such a classic that a maxim derived from it entered the popular discourse.[17] But the very fact that this allegory had a lofty moral reveals the sheer reality that the great majority of people might have appreciated the starveling's integrity but could not emulate it. When facing a life-or-death choice, nearly all people follow their basic instinct to seek survival first. As the Chinese political philosopher and statesman Guanzi (Guan Zhong, ca. 725–645 B.C.) stated in the seventh century B.C., "Full granaries make proper manners; sufficient food and clothing sustain the sense of honor and shame." This observation on human nature has been frequently quoted ever since.[18] Unfortunately, in modern China, granaries were often empty and daily necessities were scarce. The only thing the destitute could sell was the one thing that the proud starveling refused to give up: human dignity. However, once the threshold was stepped over and dignity was no longer a concern, ostensibly powerless street people could be quite intimidating.

The historian Philip Kuhn suggests that Chinese beggars persisted in their way of life because "they had the power to make the public fear them," and he specifies "contamination" and "ritual sabotage" as the weapons of the "social terrorism of beggars" in Qing society.[19] David Schak reduces the great variety of begging methods in premodern China to three broad categories: positive appeals and tactics, by which beggars maximized and exhibited their pitifulness (in particular, their physical handicaps) to arouse human compassion; remunerative appeals and tactics, by which beggars provided some service (such as performing certain functions at wedding and funeral ceremonies) for alms; and negative appeals and tactics, by which beggars deliberately made themselves a nuisance and then asked a potential almsgiver to pay them to leave.[20] Although the last category is the closest to Kuhn's "social terrorism of beggars," the other two could also easily fit it: the presence of a miserable beggar was itself a "contamination" and to refuse a beggar's service in a life-cycle ceremony often meant the ceremony would be sabotaged by a huge crowd of unruly beggars.

The so-called social terrorism of beggars, which was made possible and enhanced by beggars' guilds, was in a way forced upon paupers. With little or no assistance from the state, they could only organize themselves in a certain fashion to assure some degree of security and fairness within the group and to increase their chances of survival outside it. In this respect, a beggars' guild was not unlike other social groups in China, such as trade organizations, native place associations (*tongxianghui*), professional societies, and the like, which existed to secure autonomy in their own domains in order to promote their members' interests—which in some cases, such as beggars', was sheer survival—in an increasingly competitive urban world.

Beggars' guilds (or, as they were often derogatorily called in Chinese, *bang* or gangs) were both spontaneous and officially acknowledged. To a great extent beggars' organizations not only dovetailed with the state's goal of containing its vagrant population, they cost the government little. The beggars' guilds had different degrees of effectiveness across the nation, but they all shared what might be called a control-and-concern dualism over their members. The guild contained the local beggars in its turf, constrained them to follow its rules and customs, and protected their interests with organized acts and collective undertakings. By the nineteenth century, such beggars' guilds were ubiquitous in China and had proven to be more successful than any government program in coping with the street people. Thus this institution endured the great political upheavals of the late Qing and Republican period and survived until the early 1950s.

A Break or Continuity?

An obvious question concerning the continuity of the institution of mendicancy was the impact on beggars brought by the late Qing and early Republican reforms. Before the 1911 revolution that ended China's two-millennia-long monarchy and after, many cities carried out reform programs aimed at building a modern municipal administration. One of the primary targets of the reform was street beggars. In theory at least, begging and vagrancy were no longer "legal" or "legitimate" as they had been in the past, and beggars were now subject to arrest and periodic police "sweeps." Recent studies of Chinese urban history have shed considerable light on the changing view on beggars and new municipal measures to cope with them in the first few decades of the twentieth century.

Kristin Stapleton's work on the interior city of Chengdu offers the best case to date of how the late Qing reform led by local progressives effectively changed the street scene in a big city. For a while early in the twentieth century the government programs on poverty seemed so effective that beggars, who numbered an estimated twenty thousand, disappeared from the city.[21] Di Wang's monograph on street culture in Chengdu further delineates the picture with remarkable vividness.[22] Zwia Lipkin also gives a detailed account of how the Nationalists, after establishing Nanjing as the national capital in 1928, were propelled by the desire to create the image of a modern society under the new regime and fought with the problem of beggars.[23] Similar battles were engaged, as Kwan Man Bun has related, in the northern city of Tianjin, where beggars were one of the primary targets of the self-appointed champions of modernity in the first half of the twentieth century.[24] These municipal programs were a part of China's struggle at the time for national salvation through modernization. The exertions against beggary based on the Western (and therefore perceived as "modern") notion of vagrancy and mendicancy being illegal could be taken as evidence of a change in the concept of beggars in Chinese society in the early twentieth century.

But one must not overstate the effects of the reforms. Although begging might have been "legal" or tolerated in pre-twentieth-century China, it was always seen as a threat to orderly society and thus was subjected to official supervision and containment. The state's intention was to contain beggars, in a way not unlike putting offenders into some form of custody in the Western legal tradition. The Qing government, for instance, had a detailed plan to enroll beggars in the *baojia* neighborhood mutual responsibility system in order to contain and regulate them. Frequently, government poorhouses or similar institutions acknowledged by local officials were intended more to detain beggars than to feed them. Long before the modern urban reforms, in some cases street people were asked to turn themselves in to county poorhouses, and those who did not avail themselves of this refuge were condemned as "bad characters," apprehended, and severely punished.[25]

Moreover, the discrepancy between China and the West regarding public opinion and government policy toward beggary may not be as definite as we have previously thought. It is an oversimplification to say mendicancy was legitimate in China while illegal in the West. In early modern England, for instance, there were officially licensed beggars, an institution based on the notion that these paupers were the deserving poor. In practice, the authorities were never able to truly distinguish the genuinely needy from fraudulent beggars, with the result that mendicancy often remained in limbo between lawful conduct and illegal activity.[26] Almost exactly the same concept, practice, and dilemma were observed in eighteenth-century France, where legislation on beggars seems to have been intended more to create a "spirit of laws" than to be enforced.[27] In America during the Great Depression of the 1930s, the indigent licenses to beg were issued in New Jersey in lieu of relief.[28]

On the other hand, beggary in pre-twentieth-century China was never seen as truly legitimate and the government frequently, although with little success, tried to cope with it through legal action. This was because, as in the West, beggary was seen as symptomatic of a bad government. "Roads should be empty of beggars, and should there be any, it will be considered the fault of the chief minister," stated the Chinese classic of politics, *Guanzi*. This saying was quoted with approval time and again for more than two thousand years.[29] In a way, the modern urban reforms regarding mendicants were a legacy of such thinking. Only it now had a new momentum or impulse, for street beggars were frequently cited by Westerners as a symbol of China's backwardness and the incapacity of its government. Sweeping a city free of street people was taken as a mark of progressiveness and modernity. But the notion was not much different from that expressed by Guanzi (the supposed author of the book of the same name) who lived two centuries before Socrates.

Most of all, while early twentieth-century urban reform made considerable progress in terms of "modernity" in some Chinese cities, it had its obvious limits. Its programs were frequently short-lived and abortive; the reform regarding beggars was perhaps the least successful.[30] China at the time was crisis-ridden and ravaged by devastating wars, foreign aggression, revolutions, famines, and natural disasters (for instance, there were seventy-seven recorded major natural disasters in the period 1911–37).[31] Charities and workhouses, both privately run and government sponsored, were at times set up to assist the poor, but like their predecessors, they were far from adequate. In particular, government programs for beggars were insufficient and, perhaps in most cases, worse than those in the Qing period. As a result, mendicants and the institutions and culture associated with them persisted. Taking Chengdu as an instance, reform in the first decade of the twentieth century won considerable praise. The city was extolled by some Western observers as "the cleanest . . . and probably . . . the most progressive and enlightened of any purely native city" in China. In particular, the official program on street people was applauded as a "magnificent triumph," "entirely" successful, and even a "revolution."[32] Yet, as we will see, Chengdu in the succeeding Republican era remained a city swarming with beggars and had some of the most active mendicant gangs in the country. Other cities that undertook similar urban reforms experienced similar results. To take China's most modern city, Shanghai, as an example, in the late 1920s and early 1930s it had only two workhouses for vagrants, with a capacity of sheltering 700 inmates, while the city had about 25,000 beggars at the time.[33] "As far as beggars are concerned," wrote a Shanghai policeman in 1936, "all that worries the authorities in the International Settlement is that they should be expelled, forcibly if necessary, and driven into Chinese Territory."[34] The policy was criticized on the Chinese side as "draining the water into other people's fields," and the "clean up" turned out to be a classic Shanghai street scene of a marathon between the police and the beggars, but nothing was really done to cope effectively with the problem.[35]

Thus, the often momentary reforms and superficial government programs left the problem of mendicancy most of the time unattended to and the only practical measure, the semi-official acknowledgement of beggars' organizations, persisted. As David Buck points out, "A beggar contingent organized under a leader was a regular feature of Chinese cities."[36] This remained as true in the Republican period as during the Qing. In large cities, beggars were subject to arrest when occasional campaigns against vagrancy were in full swing, but nonetheless they were typically omnipresent. The most conspicuous indication of the power of beggars' guilds was the so-called beggar tax, protection fees guilds demanded from local stores (and sometimes also residences) in exchange for being exempted from harassment. The practice survived urban reforms and continued through the Republican period.

A contemporary author commented on the continuity of the beggar tax after the 1911 revolution:

> Ever since the founding of the Republic, there has been one reform after another. On the surface, it seems that the practice of using beggars for official work has ended; in reality, however, the beggar taxes did not disappear with the monarchy. Beggars are still collecting taxes under official sanction, which shows just how deep are the roots of the old ways and how tenacious they are.[37]

It was only because of the state's extremely rigid control and unprecedented penetration into society after the Communist revolution that large crowds of beggars and their organizations generally disappeared from Chinese cities.

This study therefore does not treat the early twentieth century reforms, either before or after the 1911 revolution, as a prominent landmark that signaled drastic changes in the world of mendicants. Rather, with due sensibility to the impact of these reforms on beggars—which were mostly temporary or insubstantial—I have chosen to see the late nineteenth and early twentieth centuries, in particular as far as the culture of beggars is concerned, as essentially one time period.

Finally, beggars and poverty are always associated, if not indeed entirely inseparable. Although this study is mostly about beggars' struggles and protests, their rackets and wangles, their politics and resistance, and the culture behind their institutions, it must always be remembered that the people brought under our microscope were constantly living in penury and misery. Because of the obviously inferior social status of this group, discussions of beggars, even if one is sympathetic, can easily slip into elitist prejudice. Beggars, perhaps more than any other subaltern group, seldom talk about their true lives, much less write about them. Although every effort has been made in this study to utilize firsthand surveys and investigations and, whenever possible, to hear about beggars in their own voices, most of the materials used in this work were inevitably written or passed on by people who lived outside the world of beggars. Therefore, as we witness some of the less known and more intimate aspects of Chinese beggars' lives, we must not lose sight of the basic fact that the plight of these people in general was real and formed the basis of their common identity—that they were beggars.

CHAPTER 1

On the Rivers and Lakes

CHINESE MENDICANTS possessed some distinguishing incongruities that made them more than a bunch of vagabonds who begged on the street. They were paupers who took mendicancy for a living, yet in soliciting alms they verged on providing a variety of performances and services. They were generally regarded as homeless, yet most of them kept close family ties and many had a place they could call home. As a group, they came from a predominately rural background, yet their profession as mendicants was clearly seen as an urban calling. By all means they were subaltern to mainstream society, yet they had a recognizable influence on higher culture. These paradoxes had complex origins, but most of all they were derived from an intangible yet actual world known in Chinese as the *jianghu*.

Defining the Subaltern

IN THE REALM OF JIANGHU

The Chinese word *jianghu*, literally meaning "rivers and lakes," is a popular metaphor referring to an unorthodox, adventurous, and somewhat mystical world. The expression was coined in *Shiji* (*Historical Records*), a classic completed by Sima Qian (ca. 145 B.C.–?). Primarily a history, *Shiji* is a rich mine of standard speech, and a source of numerous classic proverbs, literary allusions, and idiomatic expressions that have been commonly used for more than two millennia in China. In one of *Shiji*'s sixty-nine biographies, Sima Qian records that Fan Li, a shrewd politician who lived at the end of the chaotic Spring and Autumn period (770–476 B.C.) when rival kingdoms were constantly at war with each other, "took a flat-bottomed boat and floated along rivers and lakes (*jianghu*)" to retreat from politics after he had helped the King of Yue (whose state was located in what is today the Shao-xing area of Zhejiang Province) to defeat the King of Wu (today the Suzhou area of Jiangsu Province).[1] Fan Li's retirement from politics was strategic, and "floating along the rivers and lakes" only led to his success in another realm: business. He was to become the richest man in the country. More-over, he left a long-lasting mark on Chinese culture: the byname he adopted while doing business, Tao Zhugong, entered the Chinese lexicon as a syn-onym for "wealth." More profoundly, the word *jianghu* went beyond its lit-eral and geographic meaning to suggest retreat and living in seclusion, with the implication that a retiree in the world of the jianghu cherishes the hope or determination expressed in the words "I shall return."[2] I may also add that the Chinese, inhabitants of an essentially continental nation, were inclined to take "water" ("rivers and lakes" surely belong to that category) as a sym-bolically alternative world to the more familiar and conventional earth-bound one.[3] Confucius once said, "I will get in a rowboat and float about on the sea if the Way [Confucian doctrines] cannot prevail."[4] This, one of Confucius's most frequently quoted adages, indeed expressed a sentiment similar to Fan Li's "floating along the rivers and lakes."

By late imperial times, the word *jianghu* had gone beyond its initial im-plication of retreat and exile to become an idiomatic expression liberally used to mean a world that diverged from mainstream society, living in an unorthodox way, enjoying adventures far from home, and what can be called the culture of subalterns. Derived from these connotations, jianghu had also become a broad category referring to the world embodied in va-grants of all sorts, including itinerant entertainers, quacks, swindlers, charla-tans, tramps, hoboes, "knights-errant," and so on. While the term has been used in a derogatory sense most of the time—which is not at all surprising since the great majority of people lived more conventional lives and shunned the unorthodox—it can have some positive implications such as openness, forthrightness, and gallantry. It was said, in a metaphorical way, that people in the world of jianghu took "rivers" as their eyes, thus they had broad vi-sion, and they took "lakes" as their months, thus they had the gift of gab. Sharp eyes and a glib tongue qualified a person to venture into the world of "rivers and lakes," a place full of challenges and uncertainties.[5]

Almost as if to form a pair, the people who lived in or were associated with the world of jianghu were called *sanjiao jiuliu* (literally, "three religions and nine sects"). The term originally referred to the three major religions or schools of thought in China (Confucianism, Taoism, and Buddhism) and nine groups of people based on their beliefs (Confucians, Taoists, the Yin-Yang technicians, the Legalists, the Logicians, the Mohists, the Political Strategists, the Eclectics, and the Agriculturalists). The divisions among these groups originated in the late Zhou period (770–221 B.C.), China's most vibrant age of philosophy. Over the years the idiom "three religions and nine sects" had become a term, used in a somewhat disapproving tone, to refer to people of various trades or people of all walks of life. And, from this original "nine sects" developed another set of nine groups known as the "lower nine" (*xia jiuliu*), including pickpockets, go-betweens, swindlers, entertainers, servants, runners, peddlers, prostitutes and, not surprisingly, beggars.[6]

THE PURPORT OF "BEGGAR"

The fundamental notion of the beggar in China differs little from elsewhere in the world. A person who takes mendicancy as a way of life is a beggar. Nearly all beggars are paupers who are unable or, in some cases, unwilling to work for a livelihood and therefore depend on the generosity of others for a living. But to the public mind beggars also include vagrants who provide some—often unsolicited or even unwanted—service in exchange for alms. The latter category can be quite inclusive, exceeding the conventional demarcation that sees the beggar as a person asking for alms without offering anything in return. Frequently, street entertainers, itinerant fortune-tellers (especially if they were blind), quacks (itinerant herbalists), and night watchmen were regarded as sorts of mendicants.

There are at least four Chinese terms (*qigai, taofan, jiaohuazi,* and *biesan*) that are commonly translated as "beggars." Two of them (*qigai* and *taofan*) are straightforward, that is, each has a literal meaning that connotes a "begging person." The other two (*jiaohuazi* and *biesan*) need some explication and interpretation, for neither of them literally means "beggar" or can be remotely related to that meaning, albeit they were most commonly used in that way. The standard term for "beggar" is *qigai* (sometimes abbreviated as *gai*), a rather literary term and one that remains a formal expression.[7] A much more common term was, and still is, *taofan* (begging for rice; or more generally, begging for food), an expression that best captures the essential needs of the street poor. This vernacular name for beggars was long known to foreign observers, as Walter Mallory, the secretary of the China International Famine Relief Commission, quite correctly noted in the early 1920s: In China "beggars are referred to in colloquial idiom as 'food wanters'; and they all provided themselves with pails or bowls in which they can receive the refuse from the table of the well-to-do."[8]

Beggars were also known as *jiaohuazi,* or simply *huazi* (that is, omitting the first character, *jiao*), an expression associated with the Buddhist notion of "teaching and converting" (*jiaohua*). Wandering monks or mendicant friars described their seeking alms with the euphemism *jiaohua* or "teaching and converting." These monks were virtually beggars, at least for the period they were "teaching and converting." But their religious mission set them apart from regular almsmen and the general public usually did not regard them as beggars. However, no later than the early seventeenth century, the homophone *jiao* ("crying" or "shouting") had replaced the original *jiao* ("teaching") to create the term *jiaohuazi*, which was used exclusively to re-fer to "beggars." Although the term does not literally mean "beggar" at all, by modern times it was used nationwide to label beggars, and few people knew or ever bothered to ask its origin.[9]

Another word for beggar, *biesan*, which was particularly common in Shanghai and elsewhere in the lower Yangzi River valley region, had a much shorter history, for it originated in pidgin English. "Empty cents" was an ex-pression coined by Shanghai compradors to mean "one who has no money." Through mispronunciation, the word "empty" became *biede*, "cents" be-came *shengsi*, and "empty cents" became *biede shengsi*, which, in Shanghai, was a synonym for "there is not a single penny in his pocket." The expres-sion *biede shengsi* was simplified into *biesan* to mean beggar.[10] Here, the first character, *bie*, means shriveled and blighted, and the second character, *san* (three), was often used in slang to refer to vulgar figures.[11] Once combined, these two originally unrelated Chinese characters convey a graphic image of a wretched-looking vagabond who lives by begging or stealing. Like other slang expressions that often have vague and sometimes multiple origins, the word *biesan* was also believed to have another root, in pidgin English: *begsir* (beg sir). It was perhaps derived from Shanghai beggars using these English words (which were intended to mean "I am begging you, sir") in chasing af-ter foreigners on the street, or from mocking panhandlers as "Mr. Beggar."[12]

There was yet another widely accepted interpretation of the term. Biesan can be a homophone of *bisan* in the Shanghai dialect, which means "three graduations" or "graduated three times." It ridicules beggars as hooligans who "graduated" from three decadent behaviors: drug addition, gambling, and whoring.[13] Whatever the case, the word clearly was related to the pres-ence of English-speaking foreigners and to the city's scandalous lifestyle.

Originating in Shanghai in the late nineteenth century, *biesan* as a syn-onym for "beggar" was soon known nationwide. Mao Zedong once (in 1942) used this term as a figure of speech to criticize stereotyped party writ-ing (or *dang ba gu*, the "party eight-legged essay") that was in fashion among Communist cadres in Yan'an, the heartland of the revolution during the war. Mao remarked that the drab writing "reminds one of a *biesan*. Like our stereotyped Party writing, the creatures known in Shanghai as 'little *biesan*' are wizened and ugly. If an article or a speech merely rings the changes on a few terms in a classroom tone without a shred of vigour or spirit, is it not rather like a *biesan*, drab of speech and repulsive in appearance?"[14] Mao should have had some firsthand knowledge about Shanghai's beggars, for he had visited and lived in Shanghai six times before 1927.[15] His satiric tone reflected the power of a popular image: the stereotype of the urban poor in the mindset of this paramount revolutionary was virtually no different from that held by the public.

Although epithets for beggars can be diverse and to some extent can reflect various images of the street poor in the public's mind, beggars in China, as elsewhere in the world, were generally regarded as utterly destitute. An old saying in China pairs death with mendicancy: "There is no catastrophe except death; one cannot be poorer than a beggar."[16] Becoming a street beggar was seen as an obvious failure in life. It was common for Chinese parents to use beggars as a frightening example of failure in life to urge children to work hard in school, and one of the worst curses, often being thrown out as a Parthian shot, was something like "Your children and grandchildren will be beggars!"[17]

Despite the contempt, mendicancy has a long history as a profession in China, especially in cities. Few people would have happily chosen such a calling, nevertheless it was a *job* option for thousands of rural refugees and the urban poor seeking to eke out a living in late imperial and modern China.

Although mendicancy was primarily an urban vocation, we should note that vagrants and the like were not rare sights in Chinese villages. However, rural vagrants were more often engaged in banditry than beggary. The historian Kung-ch'uan Hsiao has quite convincingly demonstrated that many of the so-called beggars in rural China in the eighteenth and nineteenth centuries were but lawless marauders and bands who robbed rather than begged. Such "wicked beggars" could be found occasionally in towns and cities, but they were active mostly in rural areas, and indeed evidence of such rural bandit-beggars existed virtually all over the country.[18] Philip Kuhn has found that even in "the prosperous age" of the mid–eighteenth century, gangs of "beggar-bandits" (*gai fei*), who roamed essentially rural areas "taking what they wanted by force," sometimes become part of the documentary record of the Qing court.[19] Such documents, in fact, were not just confined to government officials or archival cabinets but were displayed in public as a warning or a countermeasure. The Qing stone tablets that were placed in various countries in Fujian province, for instance, bearing inscriptions of official documents indicate that "evil beggars" were frequently a knotty problem of the local yamen. Several scores of such beggars formed gangs that, during the day, demanded payments from villagers under all kinds of pretexts, and at night simply robbed and stole. These ruffians were called by various names, such as "ruffian beggars" (*gun gai*), "floating beggars" (*liu gai*), or simply "bandits" (*fei gun*), all of which suggested they were in fact brigands rather than beggars.[20]

Thus there can be little doubt that the "beggars" who haunted the countryside were mostly not "regular" beggars who roamed the streets for alms but bandits who took beggary as a tactic for seasonal robbery and extortion. As a Chinese proverb put it, "When people are starving, the weak among them become beggars, the strong become bandits."[21] To be sure, there were also truly impoverished and desperate people who wandered in villages for alms. But mendicancy as a calling was primarily an urban phenomenon. It is not difficult to imagine that villages, in any given period, were always much less favorable places for mendicancy than towns and cities. To give the most obvious reason, the distance between villages in a usual Chinese landscape was an insurmountable disadvantage for vagrancy. According to G. William Skinner, in most of China's rural areas in recent centuries, villages were located at an average distance of 3.4 to 6.1 kilometers (approximately 2 to 4 miles) from the "standard market town," that is, a town with periodic markets. Skinner's model of the spatial structure of rural China shows villages separated from each other by roughly the same distance.[22] These estimations and the model, although by no means applicable everywhere in the country, provide at least a general picture of the community (or village) density in rural China. If three miles per hour is normal walking speed, then trudging from village to village to beg was clearly a difficult proposition. In addition, what might be called the "work environment" of street beggars includes not merely the walking distance between likely spots for begging, but also the population density, the wealth of the residents, the level of commercialization, the receptivity to the plea for alms, and so on. In all these respects, clearly the city was a much more hospitable environment than the countryside.[23]

Chinese beggars were associated with or referred to as *liumin* ("floating people") or *youmin* ("wandering people"), terms that came into use no later than the Han dynasty (206 B.C.–A.D. 220).[24] In casual use, these words overlapped with each other to mean "vagrants" or "vagabonds." Most of the people so described had been peasants driven by catastrophes such as natural disasters and wars in their native places to leave home in search of a livelihood in safer or richer areas. But there were subtle distinctions between the two. Liumin refers to vagrants, but implies a tide of refugees that arises suddenly and on a large scale, and to people who have no choice but to flee their homes. As quickly as a liumin tide arose, when the trouble subsided, the tide receded and most of those who had fled returned to their homes. For various reasons, part of the liumin chose or was forced to choose vagrancy as a way of life and became so-called wandering people (youmin). Thus, when serious liumin problems evaporated, the youmin phenomenon lingered.[25]

Beggars were generally regarded as belonging to the youmin category, but they were a special group of the "wandering people." In his research on the rural economy of the lower Yangzi region in the late Qing, David Faure has noted the difference between youmin and beggars. He points out that youmin was a "perpetual phenomenon in 19th century China," and that the term itself implied the people so described "did not have a steady position" and "did not belong to the city." The last distinction, Faure emphasizes, "is not only terminological," because according to Qing administrative concepts, beggars were a part of the city population while youmin were not. "Beggars, like all professions, could be banded into *pao-chia* [baojia] under a beggar chief."[26] Quoting Faure's finding, William Rowe brings in the case Hankou (Hankow) as a comparison: "It may seem incongruous that such a distinction should apply as much in Hankow—the immigrant city *par excellence*—as in ancient patrician cities such as Soochow [Suzhou], but it clearly did."[27] In short, by the nineteenth century, Chinese beggars, despite their rural background, had long been regarded as part of urban society.

Mendicancy as an Occupation

RUNNING AWAY FROM HOME

The Chinese peasantry was often described as being earthbound and very reluctant to leave their land unless forced by circumstances to do so. "There is no other peasantry in the world which gives such an impression of absolute genuineness and of belonging so much to the soil," a European observer once melodramatically proclaimed.

> Here the whole of life and the whole of death takes place on the inherited ground. Man belongs to the soil, not the soil to man; it will never let its children go. However much they may increase in number, they remain upon it, wringing from Nature her scanty gifts by ever more assiduous labour; and when they are dead, they return in childlike confidence to what is to them the real womb of their mother.[28]

This home-loving sentiment has been well summarized in an old Chinese saying that exhorts people "to rest content with one's homeland and leave it with great trepidation" (*an tu zhong qian*).

However, a home-loving sentiment could not always be sustained in the face of the harsh reality of life. In contrast to the stereotypical image of the Chinese people as earthbound tillers, throughout history the Chinese in fact frequently left their homes in search of a better livelihood or sheer survival. Migration has been a familiar part of Chinese life since ancient times. As the historian Wang Gungwu has pointed out, "Chinese had been going out of China in small numbers since the tenth century, in larger numbers since the late sixteenth century, and in a veritable flood well beyond the region since the nineteenth."[29] Chinese domestic migrations were much more imposing and on a much larger scale than overseas migrations. Major migrations from the Yellow River valley to the south started as early as the early fourth century. The Chinese ethnic group in the south known as the "guest people" (*kejia*, or more commonly known in English by its Cantonese pronunciation, *Hakka*) has left living traces of large-scale domestic migration throughout history.[30] But the Hakkas are also an example of how migrants may be disliked and how assimilation to a new land can be extremely difficult. Migrating from northcentral China to the south and having settled there for centuries, these "guest people," estimated to number more than ten million in the southern provinces of Guangdong and Fujian in the early twentieth century, remained "strangers" and "shack people" (*pengmin*) there and were referred to by some southerners as "a barbarous, degraded set of people, little better than bandits."[31]

Hence the image of a conservative Chinese peasantry did hold some truth. Unless there was no alternative, few farmers—who were of course the great majority of the Chinese—left home or looked for another way of life. The harsh reality, however, was that Chinese peasants were frequently forced to leave home. In China, as elsewhere, migration and mendicancy were commonly allied. In eighteenth-century France, for instance, beggars who had lived all their lives in town frequently declared a rural birthplace, and French towns were described as "full of country folk, some of them recent arrivals, others domiciled over the years, few of them safely removed from mendicity."[32] In crisis-ridden modern China, the flood of rural immigrants to the city (and their difficult life there as beggars) was certainly much more pronounced.

The primary factor that drove people into an uncertain life outside their villages was the myriad famines caused by natural disasters, of which China has an unusually long history. From 1766 B.C. to A.D. 1937, there were 5,258 recorded natural disasters—mostly floods, droughts, plagues of locusts, and hail storms—giving an average of one recorded natural disaster every eight months.[33] Perhaps because in recent centuries official records on natural disasters were kept more accurately, or because the human abuse of the environment accelerated in recent centuries, or both, natural disasters—especially floods and droughts—were more frequent in the Ming-Qing period

(1368–1911). Droughts increased from 43 in the century of 620–719 to 170 in the century of 1520–1619.[34] Large-scale floods, defined as affecting an area of up to thirty counties, occurred 424 times in the Ming-Qing period, giving an average of three major floods every four years. Extra-large floods, defined as affecting an area of more than thirty counties, occurred 190 times, on average once every three years.[35] In North China, where rainfall was irregular and waterways were scarce, floods were no less uncommon. In the city of Tianjin alone, for example, major catastrophic floods occurred twenty-eight times during the Qing (1644–1911) and three times in the Republican period (1912–49).[36]

Famines and natural disasters caused enormous refugee problems. Government relief programs and social charity were always far from sufficient, and in China's modern history innumerable wars, revolutions, and rebellions left the authorities most of the time preoccupied with life-and-death politics and impotent to cope with the consequences of natural disasters and famines. Hunger was, of course, the foremost factor that drove people from home. For instance, in 1942, a severe drought struck Henan Province and thousands upon thousands of people were forced to eat bark, grasses, and weeds. When all the flora were eaten up, cotton quilts, ropes, and birds' droppings found their way into people's stomachs. Needless to say, under such circumstances whenever possible people fled. According to an official investigation conducted in Qishui, a rural county in Henan on the southern bank of the Yellow River, in June 1942 the county had a population of 95,371; by the spring of 1943, 29,648 people, or 31 percent of the population, had left home to beg outside the county. These people were relatively lucky compared to 3,446 people who did not leave and died of starvation and sickness, many of them poisoned to death by eating inedible "food."[37]

This was just a drop in China's sea of famine in recent history. For another example, during the great drought of North China in 1920–21, a house-to-house canvass revealed the following bill of fare:

k'ang [chaff], mixed with wheat blades, flour made of ground leaves, fuller's earth, flower seed, poplar buds, corncobs, hung ching tsai (steamed balls of some wild herb), sawdust, thistles, leaf dust, poisonous tree bean, kaoliang [Chinese sorghum] husks, cotton seed, elm bark, bean cakes (very unpalatable), peanut hulls, sweet potato vines ground (considered a great delicacy), roots, stone ground up into flour to piece out the ground leaves.[38]

With little or no official relief available, fleeing from one's home village to relatively wealthy and safe areas, especially to cities, was the most common and often the only way to survive. Millions of people lost their homes and contacts in the village and had to eke out an existence in the city; for many, mendicancy was often a solution, sometimes the only solution, to their desperate situation. Thus in China's recent history, famine and begging were always paired. To give just one typical case, the 1931 Yangzi River flood drove 40 percent of the people who lived in five provinces along the middle and lower Yangzi valley to seek refuge. For these people there were virtually only two alternatives to making a living outside their hometowns or villages: manual labor and beggary. On average more than 20 percent of the refugees in all the counties in these provinces adopted mendicancy as a way of making a living. In certain provinces, such as Hunan, well over half of the refugees became beggars (see Table 1.1).

Famines only highlighted the general and everyday poverty in rural China, where millet or sweet potatoes were the staple throughout the year. The city, even in famine-free years, was an attraction for the peasants. The writer Lao She (1889–1966) once personified this gloomy reality through his renowned protagonist, "Camel" Xiangzi, a farmer lured by opportunity to Beijing in the 1920s, where he made a living as a rickshaw puller: "The city gave him everything. Even starving he would prefer it to the village. . . . Even if you begged in the city you could get meat or fish soup. In the village all one could hope for was cornmeal."[39] This was certainly no fiction, as Japanese investigators found in 1937. Here are the details of the "cornmeal" menu in a village they investigated, only about twenty miles northeast of Beijing:

> In the spring, gruel for breakfast, "dry" boiled millet for lunch, and gruel with vegetable for supper; in the summer, "watered" boiled millet for breakfast, "dry" boiled millet and bean-noodles in soup for lunch, and boiled millet and a vegetable for supper; in the fall, gruel for breakfast, "dry" boiled millet and bean-noodles in soup for lunch, and "watered" boiled millet for supper.[40]

Such a diet was not uncommon for the common peasants in China, and a better diet along with job opportunities was always the primary reason why farmers left the villages for the city. For the peasants of rural Subei (northern Jiangsu province), the best thing about cities in the southern part of the Yangzi delta (Jiangnan) such as Wuxi and Shanghai was rice and money, as revealed in fieldwork conducted by Emily Honig:

> It mattered little that by Jiangnan or Shanghai standards the conditions under which they lived and labored may have appeared intolerable. A man who left Yancheng [a Subei county] in the early 1940s to work on the Wuxi docks explained that "life in Wuxi was completely different from life in Subei. My own opinion is that life in Subei was very tough. We ate turnips and sweet potatoes. Actually sweet potatoes were considered really good food in Subei. But when I came to Jiangnan I ate rice. Rice was one of the best things about Jiangnan!" When asked whether having to work as a coolie lessened the desirability of liv-

TABLE I.I

Vagrants in the 1931 Yangzi River Flood

(by percentage)

Province or area	Adult Males (number)	OCCUPATIONAL STATUS OF ALL VAGRANTS			
		Working	Mendicancy	Jobless	Unknown
Hunan	51	12	56	2	30
Hubei	62	41	28	10	21
Jiangxi	58	21	30	38	11
South Anhui	61	41	6	14	39
South Jiangsu	66	80	6	1	13
North Anhui	73	43	32	4	21
North Jiangsu	62	36	5	43	16
Average by province	62	39	23	16	22
Average by county	60	35	21	16	28

SOURCE: Adapted from Chi Zihua, *Zhongguo jindai liumin*, 111–12.

ing in Wuxi, he emphatically replied, "Of course Wuxi was still better—I was eating rice there!" Even when he moved to Shanghai, where he worked as a night soil collector and lived in one of the shack settlements, he remained certain that he was better off than in Subei. "At least we could earn some money in the shack settlements," he explained. "In the countryside we couldn't earn a cent."[41]

Small wonder, then, rural refugees from famine poured into the cities, where even if they exhausted all opportunities or totally ran out of luck, at least one option seemed always open: begging.

THE LAST STRAW

Although according to conventional wisdom becoming a street beggar signaled an obvious failure in life, mendicancy was nevertheless a *job* option for hundreds of thousands of the urban poor. Whether the cause of beggary was a famine or other catastrophe, mendicancy was an alternative to working as a laborer. Chinese beggars were not necessarily, as was commonly presumed, homeless people or people who had lost all family ties.[42] It was observed that Chinese beggars did not resent being called "poor people" (*qiongren*), but one had to be "very careful" not to use the word "beggar" to address them, because "many of them resent very much being called 'beggar' for they claim that they are not beggars, but that they are only poor people, using this means of getting a little of something to enable them . . . to live." This resentment was caused by the general assumption that "the beggar had no home and no family ties . . . whereas the poor man had some place to call home and some family ties."[43]

In fact the distinction was never clear. In a culture where the family and family values were the foremost foundation of society, most beggars, even if they took mendicancy as a profession or as livelihood for a length of time, kept some family ties back in the villages and maintained some kind of shack in an urban shanty area as home. Begging could also be a "family business," that is, an entire family could be beggars.[44] But first of all seasonal beggars from the countryside were mostly "family men." These people had their homes, and some had their lands, in villages, but regularly, almost as if on schedule, poured into cities to beg. The most prominent seasonal beggars were those from Fengyang, a rural county in Anhui Province on the southern banks of the Huai River, where there was a tenacious tradition since the seventeenth century of farmers leaving home in winter to beg in rich Jiangnan cities and returning to their villages before spring. This tradition lasted well into the twentieth century and, as a mark of its prominence in the mendicant culture, made the folk flower-drum songs, sung by Fengyang peasants during their seasonal adventure, the best-known begging songs in the nation.[45]

But the Fengyang custom, notorious as it was, was just one of many instances in China's impoverished rural areas of seasonal begging. Peasants from the poor countryside along the banks of the turbulent Huai River in northern Jiangsu begging in towns and cities was an officially acknowledged phenomenon. In the slack seasons, usually from late autumn to early spring, peasants left their home villages in groups and headed to towns, county seats, and cities in nearby provinces to beg. They held an official passport issued by their home county yamen with which they asked for aid when they arrived in a town. They also requested the local yamen to stamp an official seal in the passport to attest to their bona fides as they followed their way to their next destination. Sometimes such a group could be as big as several hundred people, forming an enormous "beggars' delegation." It is unclear when this practice started, but by the late nineteenth century it had become institutionalized, as the Shanghai-based *North China Herald* reported in 1856:

> They have come from the northern part of this province, where the country has been devastated by locusts, and are traveling with a passport, given to them by the chief magistrate of the place from which they have come—specifying the reasons for their traveling, and testifying to their good character, declaring that they are good, but *distressed* people.
>
> In times of scarcity of provisions—occasioned by inundation, drought, locusts, and the like, when the government is unable to supply the means of sustenance—such licensed bands of beggars are by no means uncommon to China. As the food cannot be brought to them—there being neither the money to purchase it, nor the ways and means of transporting it if bought—necessity requires that the distressed people should go to the food.
>
> In this land begging is moreover not a very dishonourable profession, and when, as in this case, a passport is given to the beggars, they go in high spirits and

are very bold; yet they rob nobody, take no denials, grow stout, and when the calamity is passed they usually return quietly to their native places—having travelled perhaps over half the length of the empire.[46]

This kind of seasonal begging was particularly common in the early years of the Guangxu period (1875–1908), apparently not just because of natural disasters but also because of the general rural deterioration in the area in the wake of the Taiping Rebellion (1850–64), which had heavily ravaged Jiangsu and Anhui provinces.[47] But seasonal beggars were a phenomenon not limited to this region, nor unique to the late nineteenth century. In ordinary years during the early twentieth century, in some counties of Henan Province at least 10 or 20 percent of village households left during the winter slack season to go begging on the roads. In 1934, residents of one village in Henan recalled that 90 percent of the population had had to leave at some point in their lives to beg or to work as coolies elsewhere.[48] In Beijing in the Republican period, every winter residents found there were more out-of-town beggars on the streets than usual. These beggars wore cotton padded jackets and trousers, typical winter attire in North China, which suggested they came from areas not too far from Beijing. According to some veteran vagrants in Beijing, these people were not homeless at all: "Every single one of them has a house and land in their home villages. But every year after the autumn harvests they left home, always as a group, and headed to Beijing, where they would wander the streets begging until the next spring when they went back to the farm."[49]

Beggars who permanently resided in urban areas often lived in shantytowns. For such people, begging on the streets was a regular way to supplement family income. Beggars were found among family members of a rickshaw puller, a dock coolie, an unskilled laborer, a street peddler, and others. A rickshaw puller, for instance, could send his children to beg on the streets; a begging woman on the street may have had a husband working as a coolie; and the adult males (the usual household heads) themselves could become street beggars. The background of Chinese beggars therefore could be extremely varied. The dynamic of this diversity of the origins of beggars was that mendicancy was frequently taken as a job option or a way out of destitution.

Shanghai was Republican China's largest and most prosperous city and, as an author who studied the problem of beggary at the time pointed out, it was precisely because Shanghai was "a center of commerce, richness and attractions" that it became "a center of beggars."[50] In that regard, it is also revealing to look at the background of beggars in the city. According to a 1933 survey of the previous occupations and incomes of 700 beggars (see

Table 1.2), the great majority (more than 77 percent) had an occupation prior to becoming beggars. In the process of losing or giving up their previous occupations to become a beggar, there was no "grace period" (such as being unemployed). Of the previous occupations of the 700 beggars, farmers were by far the largest group (27 percent), followed by petty traders (11 percent), pullers of rickshaws or other vehicles (7 percent), mill workers (6 percent), and factory and retail store apprentices (5 percent).[51]

Not surprisingly, well over a quarter of the beggars came directly from the peasantry; many of the other occupations listed were also rural based.

TABLE I.2

Shanghai Beggars' Previous Occupations and Incomes

(Samples from a survey of 700 street beggars conducted in 1933)

| | Number of Persons | | | Average Monthly Income (in silver dollars) | |
Occupation	Male	Female	Percentage of Beggars	Male	Female
Farmer	123	67	27.15	3.16	2.50
Unemployed	72	51	17.58		
Peddler	62	15	11.00		
Rickshaw or cart puller	45	5	7.15	12.37	9.16
Apprentice	38	0	5.43	0.00	
Factory worker	21	22	6.15	9.83	6.78
Unskilled laborer	20	2	3.14	7.19	12.50
Gleaning trash	19	10	4.14	5.19	4.50
Artisan	15	1	2.29	11.66	2.50
Soldier	15	0	2.14	6.39	
Shopkeeper	9	0	1.30	39.50	
Newspaper seller	8	0	1.14	10.35	
Boat attendant	6	1	1.00	16.25	32.50
Servant	4	4	1.14	10.83	2.50
Tailor or seamstress	4	4	1.14	7.50	7.50
Village teacher	3	0	0.43	10.83	
Student	3	0	0.43	0.00	
Barber	3	0	0.43	7.50	
Merchant	2	0	0.28	unknown	
Horse-drawn carriage driver	2	0	0.28	unknown	
Vehicle repairer	1	0	0.14	2.50	
Street cleaner	1	0	0.14	17.50	
Doctor	1	0	0.14	unknown	
Monk	1	0	0.14	unknown	
Cotton cloth merchant	1	0	0.14	32.50	
Private adviser (*shiye*)	1	0	0.14	17.50	
Shop assistant	1	0	0.14	unknown	
Singer	1	0	0.14	12.50	
Unclear	20	16	15.14		

SOURCE: Jiang Siyi and Wu Yuanshu, *Shanghai qibai ge qigai*, 150–54.

However, the beggars of Shanghai could not be described as just a bunch of former peasants. One is struck by the great variety of the beggars' previous callings in this survey: coolies, garbage collectors, artisans (including carpenters, coppersmiths, blacksmiths, lacquerware makers, bambooware makers, cobblers), soldiers, shopkeepers (for vehicle shops, snack shops, mat shops, rice stores, wedding ware stores, and groceries), shop assistants, newspaper peddlers, boat workers, servants, tailors, teachers, students, barbers, merchants, grooms, mechanics, street cleaners (scavengers), medical doctors (Chinese style), Buddhist monks, and singers. Because of the low income of some of these occupations, the investigators explained, these people "had been almost as poor as beggars, and once there was an incident in their lives they simply became beggars."[52] But one may also note that not only poor peasants and unskilled laborers became beggars. What might be described as elite occupations, such as doctors, school teachers, private advisors (*shiye*), and shopkeepers were also on the list.

In China's chaotic modern period, skilled workers sometimes became street beggars. For instance, during the Sino-Japanese War (1937–45), when the Japanese occupied Shanghai's Jiangnan Shipyard, many skilled workers left the factory, partly because they were forced out and partly out of patriotism. These workers made their living in the city by various means; the most common jobs were street peddlers, garbage gleaners (sifting trash for something to sell), rickshaw pullers, and so on; a number of them simply earned a living by begging.[53] But there was mobility in the other direction also. Some thrifty and shrewd beggars were able to save enough capital to open their own mini-businesses such as a sesame-cake store or a barbershop, or to become street peddlers selling small commodities such as freshly baked sweet potatoes or fried dough sticks. Some beggars managed to spin yarn or make toys at home to sell. When business was bad, they returned to begging. For many, becoming a beggar was, as the Chinese adage put it, the last "lifesaving straw" one could grasp before drowning.[54]

The 1933 survey echoed the findings of another survey of Shanghai beggars, conducted in 1927, which also highlighted the complexity of beggars insofar as their background is concerned. Of the 122 beggars surveyed, eleven had been unskilled workers, ten had been farmers, and ten had been cart or rickshaw pullers. The remainder ranged from personal servants, bricklayers, and snake hunters, to policemen and petty traders and merchants of all sorts.[55]

In spite of the various backgrounds and experiences of the beggars, most of them had been poor before slipping into beggary. As a missionary observed, in modern China "the line between extreme poverty and beggary is frequently so narrow that the passage from one to the other is an exceedingly easy one."[56] According to the 1933 survey, before becoming beggars, the average monthly income of those surveyed had been $9.68 ($10.28 for men, and $7.40 women). By comparison, the survey found that the average monthly income from begging was about $4.[57] This figure may not necessarily indicate a decrease in real income, because the food, clothing, and other daily necessities of beggars came entirely from alms—on top of the $4 in cash. In addition, although a beggar's previous occupation was a one-person job, begging as we have noted was frequently an entire family's undertaking, which means that family members who were begging could multiply the $4 income. Indeed, women and children were found to earn more alms than adult males, because of the general sympathy toward female and child beggars.[58] Under these circumstances, being a beggar represented no significant slip in income for the urban poor. As we shall see in Chapter 4, in some cases beggars earned much more than four silver dollars a month and for a few panhandlers mendicancy could be remarkably profitable.

Mendicancy as an Eccentricity

No doubt most people who turned to begging as a livelihood did so for sheer survival. In most cases only the desperate would take this devastating step. However, mendicancy, with its often-perceived nomadic pleasures and carefree lifestyle, seems to have had a certain appeal and attraction to people of all times. The Chinese had long been skeptical about the absolute misery of beggars. In his study of Chinese children, Isaac Taylor Headland (1859–1942), an American missionary and sinologist who taught at Methodist Peking University, found that beggars were the subject of toys for Chinese children and beggar figurines were "among the best clay work we have seen in China."[59] (See Figure 2.) A popular saying known everywhere in China, with a few slightly different local versions, states that "after three years of being a beggar one would decline an offer to be an official." To be an official was the pinnacle of success in Chinese life, the goal of millions of candidates who took the arduous civil examinations in the one and a half millennia before 1905. Thus to say one would not trade the life of a beggar for that of an official, as dramatic as it is, reveals that an unmistakable value was attached to mendicancy and vagrancy.[60] Chinese knight-errant (*wuxia*) novels, which were among the most popular readings of all time, often have as their theme righteous beggars or beggar gangs as part of the saga of the world of the "rivers and lakes."[61] Although in the West begging and vagrancy could be legal offences, a fascination about mendicancy and the wandering life, from medieval European Gypsies to modern-day American tramps, was also a familiar sentiment. Beggars in Louis XI's France in the fifteenth century, for

FIGURE 2. Beggar figurines as children's toys. The sinologist Isaac Taylor Headland described some toy figurines of beggars he saw in China, which were commonly available at the stalls of roadside peddlers, in the following words: "Two were fighting, one [was] about to smash his clay pot over the other's head: another had his pot on his head for a lark, a third was eating from his, while others were carrying theirs in their hand. One had a sore leg to which he called attention with open mouth and pain expressed in every feature." SOURCE: Isaac Taylor Headland, *The Chinese Boy and Girl* (1901).

example, received a most sympathetic depiction in Victor Hugo's *Notre-Dame de Paris*. The story of Thomas Platter (1499–1582), who rose from a beggar to a Renaissance man, has captured the imagination of recent scholarship.[62]

But any outsider's account of the bright side of mendicancy always runs the risk of romanticizing a sad life. A better way to comprehend the "advantages" of a begging life—if there were any—is to hear beggars' own voices. In the 1930s, a woman in Beijing named Ning Lao T'ai-T'ai (Mrs. Ning, born in 1867) candidly recalled her experience as a beggar, a calling she took up at age twenty-two:

> The life of the beggar is not the hardest one. There is freedom. Today perhaps there is not enough to eat, but tomorrow there will be more. There is no face to keep up. Each day is eaten what has been begged that day. The sights of the city are free for the beggars. The temple fairs with their merrymaking crowds, the candy sticks with fluttering pennants, the whirligigs spreading noise and the colour of the rainbow in the air, women dressed in gay colours, the incense burning before the shrines and piling up in the iron pots, the flames leaping high, are harvest time for the beggars. There is drama on the open-air stage. No lady can get as close to the stage as a beggar. The ladies have their dignity to maintain and must sit in a closed cart or on the edge of the throng in tea booths. No woman but a beggar woman could see the magistrate in his embroidered ceremonial robes ride to the temples to offer sacrifice at the alters of the city in the times of festival.
>
> At noon the beggars come to the gruel kitchen where all the other beggars have gathered, and find human companionship. There is warm food, pleasantry,

and the close feel of people around. There is no future but there is no worry. An old proverb says, "Two years of begging and one will not change places with the district magistrate." All this if the beggar is not sick.[63]

Interviews of Shanghai beggars found similar sentiments. Some outspoken beggars cited "freedom," "no rules," and "not having to work" for why they did not enter government-sponsored shelters and workshops that were available in some parts of the city in the 1930s.[64] More roguish beggars simply claimed dissoluteness as the greatest merit of mendicancy: "What freedom! The freedom to eat, to gamble, to take the 'old white' [drugs], and to hang out with the 'old widows' [prostitutes]."[65] A missionary report on beggars in Chengdu, Sichuan Province cited the cases of "voluntary beggars" as part of the difficulty of coping with the problem of mendicancy: "[Beggar] boys just starting on this life have been rescued; they have been washed and clothed and properly cared for for a few months or perhaps a year, but as soon as they got a chance they turned back to their old life of freedom and begging, evidently preferring this to the restraints of civilization."[66]

No doubt the majority in the army of beggars would not have fallen into this life if they had a choice. The investigation of beggars in Shanghai in 1933 mentioned above found that when asked if they had willingly become beggars, 417 of the 700 respondents replied "No." According to the investigators, the number could have been inflated, for part of the survey was conducted in government-sponsored shelters or detention centers where the inmates may not have dared speak their true feelings. Still, 247 of the beggars surveyed were ambiguous about their motivations, and thirty-six (twenty-three men and thirteen women) plainly declared their preference for begging.[67]

The minority of mendicants who were for some reason content with a beggar's life should not be taken as evidence to romanticize what was overall a miserable existence. What is really reflected in the fact that some beggars expressed satisfaction with their calling was the complexity and diversity of a subaltern group that was usually lumped together under a single term, "beggars." The tolerance of mainstream society for mendicancy also contributed to voluntary begging. In any case, eccentric beggars only occasionally entered the records of the writing elite, although they were probably more numerous than the records indicate. A few portraits can illuminate the unconventional and less noticeable behavior of Chinese beggars. Juliet Bredon (d. 1937), a British writer who lived in Beijing and studied the city for many years in the late nineteenth and early twentieth centuries, observed a beggar in Beijing nicknamed Tanglefoot (the sobriquet came from his habit of wrapping old sacking around his nether extremities). According to Bredon:

He comes from a good family who were suddenly stricken by poverty before there was time for him to learn a trade. Now mendicancy is a recognized institution in China, and included in the regular list of profitable professions open to a poor young man entering life. Therefore he said: "Mother, I know there is but one thing now to do. Let me become a beggar." The mother wept silently. Thus he began his career, lucky in his ill-luck.[68]

Tanglefoot apparently had a good rapport with Bredon and her fellow Europeans during many years of patronage before and after the turn of the century. Bredon described him as "a philosopher under his rags." And she gushed: "You would find Tanglefoot a very intelligent person and well worth talking to. He can tell, when he pleases, the most remarkable stories, true stories of human nature. Some are very terrible, some would make you laugh, and some would make you think. Between himself and the other beggars there is a difference of gentle blood."[69] It was a bit extraordinary for a beggar to make the acquaintance of someone like Bredon, whose family was virtually nobility in Beijing for much of the last four decades of the Qing dynasty—with both her father, Robert Bredon (1846–1918), and, in particular, her uncle, Sir Robert Hart (1835–1911), serving in the Chinese government in the post of the inspector-general of the Imperial Maritime Customs.[70] But men like Tanglefoot were not entirely extraordinary in Chinese society. The Chinese described people of this type as "down-and-out princes" (*luobo gongzi*), in other words, spoiled young men from once-wealthy but suddenly impoverished families. These "princes" typically did not possess any practical skills of value for making a living in the real world. Their financial situation might not been so dire as to drive them onto the street, yet many of them nevertheless had chosen wandering about in the world of "rivers and lakes."

There was yet another type of "voluntary beggar" who chose the calling not entirely out of any circumstantial reasons but because of a personal obsession with mendicancy. Such beggars were seen as cranks and at times some writers, who were often lifetime local residents, recorded their eccentric behavior as intriguing episodes of life in the town. For instance, an eighteenth-century anecdote has it that in Nanxiang, Jiangsu (now a suburb of Shanghai) there was a well-off man who one day declared he wanted to be a beggar. His family was shocked by the idea and desperately tried to dissuade him. One of his cousins was so earnest that he even offered to give him part of his farmland, the vital substance in an agrarian society, if he would give up the outlandish idea of becoming a beggar. But the stubborn man declined the offer, saying "there is nothing in the world that is more enjoyable than being a beggar," and went off to live on the largesse of the town.[71] In another case, the well-known writer and translator Lin Shu (1852–1924) reported that in the Guangxu period (1875–1908), a petty official in Lin's hometown, Fuzhou, resigned from his position in order to become a panhandler. As he always appeared in the streets carrying a bottle gourd, he gained the nickname "the Bottle Gourd Beggar." The man was a good calligrapher and occasionally, as he pleased, he would help local people by writing letters, greeting notes, scrolls, antithetical couplets, and so on. Every time he wrote he followed a little ritual: he would kowtow to the north, the direction of the capital, where the emperor resided, and at the end of each piece of writing he would sign his name as the Mendicant Subject of His Majesty Emperor Guangxu. When asked what made him, a poor moocher, so grateful to the emperor, the man replied: "I don't contribute to the country in the least but get food and drink everyday from hundreds of households, and the officials do not blame me for what I am doing. All this is because of the grace of our emperor." Whenever he got enough alms for a drink, he would go a local bar, fill up his bottle gourd with wine, and get drunk on the street. He then would toss his remaining coins on the sidewalk and for his enjoyment watch children snatch them up.[72]

Men such as these, eccentric as they were, may have had a cynical philosophy of life not unlike contemporary tramps and hoboes in the industrialized world who choose vagrancy as a release from personal frustration and confining conventionality. There was, however, another type of unconventional social parasite who straddled the world of mendicancy and the elite, obtaining alms while enjoying a psychological satisfaction of sorts (the latter seemed more important to them). Some failed men of letters and members of the gentry known as "kowtow rice eaters" in Nantong, a port city near the mouth of the Yangzi River, are illustrative of this kind of mendicant. These men were virtually beggars, although they had at least modestly comfortable homes and did not roam the streets. Instead, they cadged any family that was having a life-course event, such as a wedding, a funeral, a birth, a birthday, an anniversary, and so on. On such occasions, invited guests, mostly friends and relatives, were always served a repast, often a sumptuous one. But by custom if an uninvited person showed up to congratulate or condole the family, such a person would always be received and offered a seat at the dining table. The kowtow rice eaters were those who took advantage of this by going to every occasion in town year around. Upon arriving, they would politely perform the usual ritual kowtow to the main figure of the event—the deceased at a funeral, the newlyweds at a wedding, the parents or grandparents at the celebration of a birth, and so on—then proceed to the table and start eating. Customarily, after the meal, a cash gift, wrapped in a piece of red paper or put in an envelope, would be placed in their hands before they left. Many of these kowtow rice eaters were Confucian scholars who had failed the provincial-level civil examination for the degree that would qualify them for a position in officialdom before the system ended in 1905.[73] After the Qing dynasty collapsed in 1912 these men lost their last hope for climbing up the social ladder by studying the Confucian classics. But even in the cul-de-sac of their career, so to speak, they still maintained an air of a scholar. Being an uninvited guest, they would bring a cheap but highbrow gift to the host: a piece of calligraphy, a greeting note, or an oblong sheet of fabric with an appropriate message on it.

One of these men, by the name of Qian Mian, was quite innovative in bringing Confucian teaching to these occasions. Qian had taken the civil service examinations and obtained the Flowering Talent (*xiucai*) degree, the entry-level, licentiate title that put the degree-holder in the literati-gentry class and qualified him to take the higher-level test, but nothing else.[74] Qian had nevertheless put his knowledge of the Confucian classics to good use — as a kowtow rice eater. His trademark equipment was a cloth bag he carried all the time, which had four characters written on it, *ren qing wei tian*, meaning, "human sympathy is equivalent to farmland," a quotation from the Confucian classic, *The Book of Rites* (*Liji*). "Farmland" in a traditional agrarian society was, of course, the substance of life. The quotation indicates that one's good will toward other people can bring one rewards as profitable as farmland. One may say that in carrying this classic quotation on the street, Qian was advertising the Confucian notion of human harmony as much as giving a self-description of the kowtow rice eaters, who apparently had turned human sympathy into "farmland" for themselves. Another notorious kowtow rice eater was known as Grandpa You, who was an authentic member of the local gentry. Not only did he own a stocking shop in Nantong but also his son, You Fuhai, was a prestigious Elevated Man (*juren*) degree holder. The old man was so obsessed with kowtow eating that he did not hesitate, always against the will of his son who evidently thought his father's behavior disgraceful, to attend every possible occasion in town — only for the purpose of indulging in the food, talking, and being part of the scene at bustling social occasions.[75]

This sort of deviance and eccentricity was in part the effect of a social milieu that was more or less liberal and accepting of mendicancy. But this tolerance and receptiveness were not necessarily derived from a social sense of benevolence or mercifulness. Rather, what contributed to deviance was a society that was bewildered by mendicancy and conflicted about how to gauge it, as we shall see in the next chapter.

CHAPTER 2

Sympathy Versus Antipathy

FEW CALLINGS IN CHINA, and perhaps elsewhere in the world as well, relied on the goodwill of the public for their existence more than did mendicancy. Likewise, few callings in China were more contradictory and para-
doxical in the public's eye. While contempt for or dislike of beggars was
universal, the common human sympathy for beggars manifested itself on the
streets in almsgiving, which made mendicancy a feasible means of livelihood
and, in some cases, a profitable business. At the same time, the public sympathy for beggars seemed always entangled with the disturbing idea that the
army of street people was constituted in part of "bad elements," whose misfortune was largely caused by their own laziness or self-destructive behavior,
such as drug addiction and gambling, and many of whom were cunning parasites on the industrious part of the population. Furthermore, the controversy over mendicancy generated a certain amount of cynicism. This cynicism rejected conventionalities, seeing beggars not as inferior but ordinary
and begging as analogous to all other walks of life. These paradoxes preyed
on the public's mind, affected the relations between mendicants and the society they daily relied on, and reflected a subaltern spectrum of China's urban culture.

Sympathy and Sympathizers

Visitors to China in the late nineteenth and early twentieth centuries witnessed the country's ubiquitous poverty and misery but saw little corre-
sponding charity either from the state or society. This, perhaps not surprisingly, led some Westerners to conclude that the Chinese in general lacked
compassion. The sinologist Arthur Henderson Smith (1845–1932), for example, claimed that "absence of sympathy" was a distinguishing "Chinese

characteristic." His comment swayed many people, including the Chinese themselves.[1] Any generalization about "national characteristics" runs the risk of stereotyping and prejudging a people; this one is no exception, although it may be as well founded as any. In fact, China's three major cultural establishments—Confucianism, Buddhism, and Taoism—all took compassion as the foundation of their teaching. For centuries, the Confucian maxim, "The feeling of commiseration belongs to all men" (*ceyin zhixin, renjie youzhi*), has been not just a classic aphorism but an everyday proverb. Sympathy was not just regarded as basic to human nature, but as the foundation of Confucian teaching: that "the feeling of commiseration implies the principle of benevolence" was a touchstone of Confucianism.[2] To some extent, commiseration and its importance to "benevolence" (*ren*) as the core value of Confucianism has contributed to the widespread notion that Confucianism is a religion. Buddhism, like all other major religions of the world, preaches love and compassion as the way to salvation and elevates the merit of compassion to the position of the supreme virtue. "Compassion in Buddhism," as a contemporary Buddhist researcher has pointed out, "has been treated parallel to Godhood."[3] This is evident, to give just one small example, in the reverence for China's most popularly worshipped goddess, Guanyin, who is considered an embodiment of "Great Mercy and Great Compassion" (*daci dabei*). Finally, metaphysical Taoism is no less ardent in its humanitarianism. While the Taoists claim that the world is no more than the "dream of a butterfly" and that the best human action is inaction, the popular Taoist traditions of mysterious deities who descend to the earthly world to test human conscience have demonstrated, with a certain irony, an unmistakable zeal for human compassion.

Thus despite the usual sentiment of contempt for or fear of street people, the most common feeling toward them among the general public was compassion and pity. Every penny dropped into the beggar's bowl was a token of human sympathy. The accumulation of alms made mendicancy a means of living for paupers most of the time. Indeed, aside from poverty itself, it was the compassion of myriad almsgivers that made mendicancy an established vocation in China.

Public sympathy for beggars was reflected in the works of the so-called vernacular storywriters of late imperial China. These writers were arguably the most acute observers of the lives of the common people. Most of them were well trained in China's magnificent traditions of history and literature, and some no doubt belonged to the literary elite. Like most educated men of the time, they took the Confucian-based civil examinations for various academic degrees necessary for ascending to the ruling literati-officialdom, which was often a painstaking and sometimes lifelong process. However, at a certain point in life, either out of choice or an inability to go on with the pursuit of degrees, these writers diverged from the mainstream path of social mobility. Instead, they devoted themselves to collecting folklore, writing and preserving oral history, and recording stories and anecdotes that were typically circulated in public venues, such as teahouses, or told by itinerant storytellers. Some, once they had accumulated enough source materials, wrote stories of their own. These were China's great writers, who brought the vivid, raw, and not-so-respectable voice of the common folk to the genteel belles-lettres, much like Mark Twain (1835–1910), Herman Melville (1819–91), and others did in American literature in the late nineteenth century. Moreover, the profound tradition of integrating history with literature in China made these storywriters amateur historians. Thankfully, they have left us valuable records of ordinary people's lives that were generally ignored by the official standard histories (*zhengshi*). The stories they collected and wrote provide, often graphically and in detail, the social milieu, public opinions, conventional wisdom, common feelings, and local customs of an age.[4] In particular, these men lived in a time when vigorous commercialization had engendered in much of China a boom of urban culture, of which street people were a marginal but conspicuous part. Vagrants and mendicants thus could not escape the attentive observation of these storywriters. One of them, Li Yu (1610–80), who was among the best-known and most influential figures of this group, commented on alms-begging:

> Although begging is unworthy, it nevertheless is the avenue of escape for heroes who have taken a wrong step in their lives and the backdoor through which retreat brave men in dire straits. Begging is different from the world's other disgraces. If we count all walks of life from the bottom, begging is number three. The lowest type of people consists of robbers and bandits; the second lowest are prostitutes, actors, yamen runners, and lackeys; and then come beggars. These people did not want to be robbers and they disdained becoming prostitutes, actors, yamen runners, and lackeys. Thus they chose this calling.[5]

To place lawbreakers—robbers and bandits—at the bottom of the social ladder is perhaps understandable in any culture, but to put prostitutes, actors (entertainers), yamen runners, and lackeys as the "second lowest" seems arbitrary. But here Li Yu is not inventing new categories of social groups but following the conventional reference to the four "low and mean" callings in China, an age-old categorization that can be traced back to at least the early Han dynasty.[6] These four groups, although not necessarily designated by administrative regulations or legal codes as social outcasts, customarily represented the lowest callings in China. Beggars, however, were not included in this category. In late imperial times there were some officially designated "mean people" (*jianmin*), which included hereditary beggars. These people suffered legal disabilities and were banned from officially sponsored schools and the civil service examinations. But most of the "mean" categories were created as a political punishment and, moreover, they were essentially a regional phenomenon. These class restrictions were gradually lifted between 1723 and 1731.[7] Although for periods of time in certain areas (such as Shaoxing, Zhejiang Province) beggars and the like were officially categorized as "mean people," mendicancy in general remained an occupation above the popularly perceived "lowest four."[8] Earlier, another distinguished storywriter, Feng Menglong (1574–1646), had made a distinction among social classes regarding beggars that is virtually the same as Li's:

> Distinguishing the worthy from the base, we count among the latter only prostitutes, actors, yamen runners, and lackeys: we certainly do not include beggars. For what is wrong with beggars is not that they are covered in sores, but simply that they have no money. There have been men like the minister Wu Zixu, of the Spring and Autumn times, who as a fugitive from oppression played his pipes and begged for his food in the marketplace of Wu [Suzhou]; or Zheng Yuanhe of Tang times, who sang the beggar's "Lotus" ballad, but later rose to wealth and eminence and covered his bed with brocade. These were great men, though beggars: clearly, we may hold beggars in contempt, but we should not compare them with prostitutes and actors, runners and lackeys.[9]

As it is made clear in these statements, there was a consistent moral or social judgment about the status of beggars that placed them above certain occupations that were generally regarded as low and disgraceful. The excerpts from the writings of Li and Feng were used as the prologues of popular stories told to audiences at public places such as teahouses, temple squares, roadside pavilions, and market bazaars. This type of prologue—sometimes they can be quite lengthy—which usually carries worldly-wise advice and admonishments, served as an introduction to the theme of the story that followed. These comments were not only the writer's personal feelings but also reflections of the manners and the morals of the time, as these stories were aimed to reach out to and appeal to the common people. The historical names mentioned in Feng's comments have been the heroes of some of the best-known "rags to riches" stories associated with beggars in China for centuries, as we shall discuss in Chapter 3. To see mendicancy as morally superior to prostitution provided the ethical ground for a criticism of what was regarded as a shameful bit of snobbery, summarized in the popular saying "Ridiculing the poor but not ridiculing prostitutes" (*xiaopin bu xiaochang*). If it is beggary rather than selling sex that is to be scorned in a society, the saying suggests, the probity of such a society has definitely degenerated.

Having asserted that beggars were not the lowest people, Li Yu moved on to advise "All well-to-do people in the world": "You should show compassion and consideration toward beggars when you meet them." And he elaborated the reasons with gentle yet thoughtful suasion:

> If one sees gentle beggars, one should compare them with the second lowest group and think this way: "If these people had been willing to be prostitutes, actors, yamen runners, or lackeys, they could have made a living anywhere—why should they take up this type of difficult livelihood? A person who refuses to do certain things in order to make a living must also be a person who will do something in life. Who knows whether among the beggars there might be another Prime Minister Wu Zixu, who once begged on the street while playing a flute, or another Zheng Yuanhe, who was in dire straits? So it does not matter how many alms one can offer, just help out a bit. It is important that one should never treat these poor creatures high-handedly, scolding or humiliating them.
>
> If one sees fierce beggars, one should compare them with the first of the lowest type. Think of this: If these beggars had become robbers and had broken into your home at midnight, they could have taken all your possessions at will, not to say your life. This would be something that would cost you far more than one or two copper coins or one bowl or half a bowl of rice. So, why should we not give these people alms, but force them to become robbers?[10]

Clearly, Li incorporated a sense of benevolence in his rationale for charity. As has been pointed out, suasion of this sort should not be read as just the author's own thoughts but, like most of the scripts of colloquial stories, as a mirror reflecting the social morals of the time. Feng's and Li's pieces remained popular for centuries, suggesting the social acceptance of their thoughts and sentiments. The sympathetic view of beggars expressed in ancient colloquial storytelling lingered into modern times, as can be seen in a 1872 commentary in *Shenbao*, China's earliest modern newspaper. In terms of mirroring public opinion, or affecting it, modern newspaper commentaries may have played a role akin to the prologues of the vernacular stories in the late imperial period. In this case, the wording, manner, and rationale of the commentary on beggars are almost identical to those articulated in the writings of Feng and Li some two and half centuries earlier:

> Who are beggars? They are just poor people. They do not behave abominably nor commit criminal offenses; unlike prostitutes, actors, yamen runners, and lackeys, they are not despicable; they are not thieves and robbers. They beg for food because they have no choice, and this is their only glimmer of hope in their impasse. If one day they were to become financially secure, they would be considered upstanding citizens.[11]

Up to the early twentieth century, mainstream society still held the notion that beggars were just pitiable people and mendicancy, although unfortunate, was essentially not an offense against society. Much of the notion that begging is a social disease that ought to be eliminated was introduced in the

Republican era as part of the urban administrative reform at the time.[12] Before then not only newspaper commentators but also powerful politicians felt that beggars were somehow higher in social status and had a better reputation than, say, prostitutes. An anecdote during Yuan Shikai's Hundred Day Restoration may illustrate this point. Yuan Shikai (1859–1916), the first president of the Republic of China, once employed beggars as part of a major "public opinion poll" to support his notorious restoration campaign in the wake of the 1911 revolution that overthrew China's last monarchy.

One day in 1915, Yang Du (1874–1931), one of Yuan's most trusted political advisors, overheard two beggars arguing on a curbside in downtown Beijing. An elderly beggar shouted at his pal: "Where are the imperial laws of the land nowadays? This is all because of the Republic. If the emperor were in charge, you people would not be allowed to be so aggressive and lawless." Yang was at the time the head of the Society for Peace (Chouanhui), a group of conservative politicians who were launching a campaign to restore the monarchy and install Yuan as the emperor of a new dynasty.[13] It immediately occurred to him that the street people of Beijing could be useful for that purpose.

The restoration campaign involved an important stage of mobilizing people of all circles to sign petitions to Yuan to "persuade" him to assume the throne. This was of course a political show maneuvered by Yuan himself. While Yuan was the behind-the-scenes impresario, in public he repeatedly dismissed the idea of restoration in order to show the nation that he was not a careerist and he would not betray the revolution that had put him into the presidency just four years earlier. Yuan thus desperately needed what were called "persuading petitions" from all walks of life to project the image of popular support for the restoration. Once such public opinion was whipped up, as Yuan planned, he himself could play the role of an upright president of the Republic who has been reluctantly pushed onto the throne by popular demand.

The beggars' quarrel suddenly inspired Yang. He quickly ordered his steward to summon Beijing's beggar heads to his office and offered them a deal: If in three days the beggar heads could mobilize their fellows to sign the restoration petition at the rate of one silver dollar per signature, each of the beggar heads would be rewarded with 100 dollars. All the funds would be supplied by the Society for Peace. Sure enough, no mobilization was really needed. All the beggar heads needed to do was to spread the news, which, given the networks among the beggars in the city, was not a hard task at all.[14] Once the news was released, thousands of beggars swarmed in to sign the petition. Many beggars were utterly illiterate and unable even to sign their own names, but they always found a volunteer to sign for them.

In a matter of a few hours, not three days, a total of about 10,000 signatures were collected, which represented about half of the city's estimated population of beggars. This created a record since the beggars' petition had more signatures than any of the other petitions presented to Yuan during the restoration campaign.

Yuan was so pleased with the outcome that he recorded in person the first ten names on the petition in a confidential notebook, which he kept in a cabinet in his private room, for the purpose of rewarding those who had contributed to the restoration once he ascended to the throne. Although there were petitions signed by some other "unconventional" groups, including prostitutes, Yuan took the beggars' petition most seriously. After Yuan came to the throne on New Year's Day of 1916, Yang Du explained to a few confidants why Yuan was enthusiastic about the beggars' petition: "The emperor believes that prostitutes are people who insincerely flatter others, and so it is kind of indecent to employ them in politics. Beggars are different: they are only a bit poor but they are citizens as much as anyone else. Also, the beggars' petition earned the emperor a good reputation for caring for the poor and the disadvantaged." [15]

It is unclear if the ten beggars were really rewarded after the restoration. Yuan probably did not have time to hand out rewards to everyone on the list, and even if he did, the benefactions would not have lasted long, for the monarchy itself lasted merely about three months—hence it was notoriously known as the Hundred Day Restoration—and Yuan himself died in humiliation in June 1916.

Indeed the Yuan Shikai episode is not the sole case in Chinese history of vagrants being involved in politics at the very highest level. Although of a very different nature, the Qing sorcery scare of 1768, masterfully recaptured by historian Philip Kuhn, was another instance in which beggars and vagrants became the focal point of the throne, and on a much larger scale than in the Yuan case. The event initially involved some vagrants and beggars allegedly practicing "soul stealing" (a kind of witchcraft) in a few lower Yangzi towns in the late spring of that year. These originally seemed to be obscure and isolated local incidents, but they soon caused panic and terror that spread to much of the country. This alarmed Emperor Qianlong (reigned 1736–96), and as urgent confidential messages and memorials to the throne piled up his desk, there soon followed persecutions at the local and central levels of the bureaucracy. In the entire event, which intensively evolved for more than three months, the protagonists on one side were the emperor and his bureaucracy, and on the other side, beggars and vagrants. [16]

Although beggars' involvement in the Yuan restoration and the Qing sorcery scare were dissimilar in nature, the two shared one thing in common, that is, in both events beggars were passively involved in politics and, un-wittingly, were used by others to promote a political agenda. There was, however, at least one case in which street people, out of political conscious-ness, voluntarily participated in politics. During the peak of the May Fourth movement of 1919 when Shanghai was on strike in protest against the terms of the Treaty of Versailles, which transferred the German concessions in China's Shandong Province to Japan without consulting the Chinese au-thorities, beggars were rarely seen on the street for about a week. This was extraordinary, for Shanghai, like Beijing at the time, had more than 20,000 beggars who regularly roamed the streets. "No one, save a few being pro-tected by body guards probably, is free from being bothered by them," said one contemporary social worker. "They stop motor cars if one is rich enough to ride in such; follow rickshas [rickshaws] whenever they get a chance, create embarrassing situations when the stores are just having busi-ness; step on one's toes if he happens to walk." [17] What happened to these people during that week? It was reported that the unusual disappearance of mendicants from Shanghai was due to the beggar ringleaders who, together with pickpocket chieftains, in order to show their patriotism, had issued a notice banning begging and pilfering. Meanwhile, as a concrete measure to help with this strike, during the week the ringleaders distributed food among the beggars as compensation for not begging in the streets, an in-stance of the effectiveness of Shanghai's beggar organizations during the Re-publican period. [18]

Cynicism

When the Confucian sage Mencius asserted that the feeling of commisera-tion belongs to all people, he also listed three basic human sensibilities that parallel it: a feeling of shame and dislike, an awareness of reverence and re-spect, and a sense of approving and disapproving. [19] From a sympathizer's viewpoint, beggars are people who sacrifice basic human integrity, over-come their sense of shame, and constantly endure the dislike and disapproval of fellow human beings—people who suffer and weather all of these ordeals simply for the sake of sheer physical survival. Perhaps only desperate people would surrender virtually all human sensibilities to the basic instinct for sur-vival. From this sympathetic view springs a twisted variation of it: a cynical attitude toward the conventional contempt for mendicancy.

This cynicism can be traced far back into ancient history. The Tang dy-nasty Confucian scholar-official Yuan Jie (719–72) once wrote an essay en-titled "On Beggars" (*Gailun*), which in due time became a classic piece of cynicism. Yuan begins the essay by saying that in 748 (the seventh year of the

Taibao reign), in the Mid-Year Festival (Zhongyuan, the fifteenth day of the seventh lunar month), he toured the capital city, Chang'an, and made friends with a street beggar. As he was questioned why a person of his status (Yuan held the imperial Presented Scholar degree and served as a prefectural magistrate) would lower himself to make a friend among street people, Yuan replied:

> In ancient times, if there was no gentleman [*junzi* or "upright person"] in the village, then people made friends with mountains and clouds. If there was no gentleman in the neighborhood, then people made friends with pine trees and cypresses [symbols of integrity]. If there was no gentleman nearby, a man would make friends with wine and musical instruments. As one travels one would make friends with anyone who is a gentleman. My beggar friend is the only gentleman of the day. I am only anxious that I may not be able or qualified to have a friend like him!

Yuan then went on, under the guise of the words of his vagrant friend, to ridicule people who sought something in much the same fashion as beggars asked for alms. It is all too common, Yuan asserts in the essay, that people humble or even humiliate themselves for the sake of personal benefit and vanity—to establish lineage relations with upper-class families, to marry the rich and powerful, to garner honor and status, and to win favors of all kinds. In comparison with this sort of behavior, begging for food and clothing out of poverty is nothing to be ashamed of.[20]

Obviously, Yuan Jie wielded beggary as a weapon to criticize the social phenomenon of currying favor with the rich and powerful. Whether or not he truly had a vagrant friend, Yuan's essay satirized snobs and fawning behavior, rather than beggars per se. Yet using an almsman as a device to lead off his essay suggests that mendicancy was a subject that the Chinese literati, who professed to have refined taste, would not dodge. Yuan's essay has remained a classic and, more importantly, the sentiment it expressed lingered on into modern times. For generations the Chinese had a cynical attitude toward the usual hustle and bustle that few could avoid—a job, duties, obligations, striving for a better life—and related them to begging. The locution *tao shenghuo* (literally, "beg for a living") has been used to refer to finding an occupation, a livelihood, or, in a more spiritual way, the meaning of life. In a sense, tao shenghuo is comparable to the American idiom "to sell oneself," as when seeking employment or promoting an idea. If the latter locution is a manifestation of the bone-deep commercialism of modern capitalist society, then the former is a popular way of expressing the Confucian cynicism rooted in literati works such as Yuan Jie's classic.

This kind cynicism has been echoed by many people in China, especially intellectuals, and just as the sympathy expressed in the vernacular stories of late imperial China has its modern versions, a very similar kind of argument could be found in the twentieth century. In the discussion of the social role of literature and writers' moral responsibility to society and the nation, which was the subject of a heated debate among Chinese intellectuals in the wake of the New Cultural movement (1915–20), an author who claimed his family name was Wen (literally, literature) declared he wanted to adopt the given name of Gai (literally, beggar), so his full name would mean "literature beggar."[21] He went on to give himself an alternative or style name, Taofan (literally, "begging for rice," a common term for beggars). The author proudly took the name as a way to respond to the criticism from left-wing writers that some freelance authors were like "literature beggars" who beg for readership and royalties but show little concern for literature as a tocsin to wake up the Chinese people to the need for national salvation. The author, apparently a member of the conservative camp who disagreed with the viewpoint that literature should serve politics, declared:

> Except for those who could bring solid food from their mother's belly to eat all their lives, everyone is a beggar of sorts. In order to live in this world, probably everyone must depend on others to earn food and clothing; therefore our lives all are in the nature of mendicancy. Even if a person has a fortune of millions at home and from his mother's belly to the grave never had to work, still, his ancestor who got the fortune must have once been some sort of beggar. In this regard, there is not a single person in this world who is not a beggar.[22]

This seems a lame argument. But the real intention of the author, like that of Yuan Jie, was to counterattack what he regarded as hypocritical criticism from the left. The author ends his satire by saying that a mendicant has no less integrity than someone who "has assumed the position of the editor-in-chief of a literary magazine, used an alias to submit translated novels, claimed them as submissions from Beijing, and asked for a royalty of five silver dollars per thousand words." Here the specific target was Mao Dun (1896–1981), a prominent writer who was at the time one of the leading figures of the left-wing camp in Chinese literature.

Despite the hidden, or not so hidden, agenda that these individuals pursued with their comments on beggars, the sentiment lingered on and has found sympathizers even today. In a recent interview, Lu Hui, an artist from the northwest frontier city of Lanzhou, Gansu Province, expounded upon beggars in a fashion much like his predecessors: "Why should we laugh at beggars? What they ask for from others is small—just a bit of compassion and pity, plus a bit of help. Compared to rich people who would do anything to exploit others and steal what others have, beggars are far more decent and honorable." Lu Hui, a gifted artist who started painting at the age of five, had tramped for seven years in the 1990s from the Tibetan highlands via the Silk Road to Beijing seeking artistic inspiration. Since he refused to sell his art works below prices he thought to be fair, he could not make a living by painting. In Beijing, Lu lived much like a beggar, roaming the streets clad in a T-shirt bearing a plea for help written in both Chinese and English. Yet he considered this a more honorable way of life than selling his work underpriced, which he regarded as an insult to the arts. The itinerant painter dreamed of being the best artist in the world and took Van Gogh as a model of perseverance in the face of hardship. He contested the conventional contempt for almsmen: "In the final analysis, who in this world is not a beggar? As long as one lives one must beg: beg for clear air and water, beg for sufficient food and clothing, beg for love and compassion, beg for forgiveness and understanding. So, to be a beggar is just returning to the basic instinct of human beings; this is nothing about which one should feel uneasy or ashamed." [23]

Wen Gai's and Lu Hui's comments and sentiments were so much akin to Yuan Jie's that even the wording and the tone—note they lived more than a millennium apart—were strikingly similar. In this regard it would not be hard to find many comrades of Yuan Jie in modern and contemporary China. Such cynicism may have an agenda or it may take beggars as a way to give vent to personal discontent. But, as has been mentioned, the popular use of the idiom "begging for a living" conveys a similar sentiment and provides a supporting footnote to the public's empathy with the cynicism.

To the popular mind, the boundary between *begging for a living* and *earning a living* was quite vague in the first place. Just as people do not clearly distinguish begging for alms from asking for contributions by providing some kind of service (as discussed in Chapter 5), cynicism about mendicancy can be an exaggeration of common sense and sometimes it can be feigned. Time after time people may detest the way they make a living and bitterly describe it as a beggar-like vocation, and they can even go further and satirize all walks of life as a sort of mendicancy. The fact remains, however, that in the public mind such an analogy was more applicable to mendicancy than to other social disgraces, such as thievery and prostitution. Although to have a self-imposed image as a beggar was regarded as cynical or even somewhat philosophical, to relate a person's character or morals to those of a thief or prostitute would certainly be considered an insult. The difference reveals a subtle social status of the subaltern population that, as we have seen, both socially attentive storytellers of late imperial times and politically sensitive commentators of the modern era had noted.

Parasites on Society

In contradicting its sympathetic views, the public also always perceived some beggars as cunning and brassy people who did not want to work for a living but took advantage of human compassion to make a living, or sometimes even to make a fortune. No doubt most people saw street people as unfortunate and utterly destitute, but more often than not contrary stories circulated among the public. The institutionalization of professional beggars under a ringleader taking mendicancy as a means of life was common knowledge to many people in the cities, which raised mendicancy to the level of a trade while decreasing public sympathy for it. Urban residents throughout the country frequently caught sight of vagrants' roadside parties, which indicated that beggars may not have been as miserable as people generally thought. That beggars were well off was occasionally recorded in personal notes of men of letters or other educated individuals and more frequently in the twentieth century was reported in newspaper articles and social surveys. The sentiment against mendicancy was particularly common in large cities, where beggars were an everyday part of the street scene.

Early in the twentieth century, the prosperity of Shanghai and its full-to-the-brim mendicancy made this sentiment stronger and more widespread there than in most other cities of China. This feeling was found prior to Shanghai being opened as a treaty port in 1843 and continued in the Republican era, when it had become the largest metropolis of the country. Meanwhile, what one might find in Shanghai regarding the "comfortable circumstances" of beggars and public antipathy toward them was frequently replicated in cities of smaller size and less prosperity, indicating the commonality of the phenomenon.

In the summer of 1842, right after the Opium War, during which Shanghai, then a walled county seat, was occupied by invading British troops for five days (June 19–23), a scholar, Lin Yuancun, observed the life of a group of beggars who lived in a temple near his home inside the city. Lin noted that all the beggars he saw dressed in silk and wore boots. A pavilion attached to the temple was used by beggars as a place for gambling, and rice, woodchips, coal, silk, clothes, and bedding were "piled up there like hills." While adult beggars were gambling, "child beggars attended wine jars and three big cooking pots, from which wafted a delicious aroma from hams, dog meat, edible seaweed, chickens, and ducks." At the same time, another Shanghai resident, Zhu Ye, observed a group of beggars who lived in Dongjiadu, a ferry crossing south of the walled city. The living conditions of the beggars that Zhu noted were akin to those observed by Lin, except that the beggars in Zhu's account had all types of fine tables and chairs, and had a mechanical clock, which was surely a luxury at that time.[24]

Given the time of these records, the comfortable circumstances of the beggars could have been a result of the war; that is, these beggars might have taken advantage of the chaos created by the foreign invasion (say, to steal or to rob) and, perhaps temporarily, become better off than usual. But observations of this kind of beggars' roadside gatherings were not uncommon elsewhere in the country. W. A. P. Martin (1827–1916), an American Presbyterian missionary who lived in China for more than sixty years from the age of twenty-three and served for twenty-five years as the president of China's Imperial Tongwen College, observed: "There were a great many professional beggars, who during the day plied their calling as blind, halt, or dumb, and in the evening met together to spend their gleanings, suddenly recovering from their infirmities, as in Victor Hugo's '*Cour des Miracles.*'" According to Martin, in the late nineteenth century one Mr. Russell of the English Church Mission once encountered a group of beggars in Ningbo: "Walking on the wall one evening, [he] noticed a comfortable-looking party seated at table. Saluting them in passing, they politely invited him to take a cup of tea. To their surprise he accepted the offer, and by way of opening a usual conversation, inquired, 'What is your nobles' profession?' 'We are beggars,' they replied, to his surprise."[25]

Ningbo, like Shanghai, was a prosperous county town in the mid-nineteenth century and, also like Shanghai, was one of the five "treaty ports" open to the West in the wake of the Opium War. But after that Shanghai quickly emerged as the leading treaty port and by the end of the nineteenth century Ningbo, and indeed all other cities in China, lagged behind Shanghai in development. One of the major episodes that stimulated Shanghai's growth was the Taiping Rebellion (1850–64), China's largest peasant uprising, during which hundreds of thousands of refugees poured into Shanghai seeking protection in the city's foreign concessions. Gradually, after the war, Shanghai came to be viewed as a land of opportunity and was often metaphorically described as a place where one could pick up gold off the ground. Beggars, precisely because of their common image as being utterly poor and pitiful, were used as an example to illustrate "rags to riches" transformations. A late nineteenth-century poem entitled "Oh, Shanghai Is Good" described thirty different aspects of life in Shanghai, of which one reads that a person would "worry about being rich but not being poor," because in the city "great savings and fortunes can be lost suddenly while a street beggar may become a new person beyond recognition."[26]

Needless to say, such dramatic social mobility was rare and largely poetic. But beggars' easy circumstances, including curbside parties, were a frequently observed reality in the city. Xu Ke, a Shanghai-based scholar and journalist, commented on beggars early in the second decade of the twentieth century: "It is common that beggars are unable to get enough to eat after they have dried and exhausted their mouths by begging on the streets. But this cannot apply to the beggars of Shanghai. . . . The daily income of the canny beggars of Shanghai was more than double that of ordinary coolies." Xu also observed some street scenes in Shanghai that were similar to what Lin Yuancun had described: A group of beggars sat on curb, smoking cigarettes and drinking wine, with a stove and cooking utensils by their side and fresh cooked foods—chicken, ham, bean curd—in front of them. Such a picnic-like vignette led Xu to comment that Shanghai's beggars were poor only in housing and clothing, but their daily fare might be better than that enjoyed by an average Shanghai family.[27]

Observances and comments made by Xu's contemporaries echoed his sentiments. An article solicited by *Shanghai zhoubao* (Shanghai weekly) in 1933 on the topic of various aspects of winter in Shanghai drew a picture of the life of beggars akin to that presented by Lin and Xu. The article is titled "Beggars in Winter Shanghai" and is subtitled "Don't Scorn These Poor People, They Have Their Own Joys!" The author described the city's mendicant population in different begging spots and indicated that the beggars (whom she banteringly called "grandpa *biesan*") who roamed the area of the Temple of the City God (Chenghuangmiao) inside the old Chinese city were the "most joyful of Shanghai's beggars." On most days, the candles brought by pilgrims gave them a regular income (that is, they collected the candles for resale) and there was plenty of sacrificial food available in the temple and nearby. On festival days and in the winter, the old city was a center for shopping and entertainment, such as listening to Suzhou storytellers in teahouses (a popular pastime), or eating winter specialties in numerous tiny but popular restaurants near the temple. More candles and food were brought in than usual on those days. Some beggars took advantage of the festivities and milled in the crowd picking pockets. Most notably, this was largely the same spot where Lin Yuancun observed beggars in 1842; nearly a century had passed, but the scene remained strikingly similar: "When evening is approaching, these grandpas biesan gather in a broken-down house behind the Temple of the City God where they sit circled around a bonfire made of straw, drinking wine and eating pork. After the meal, they sing songs . . . then they break up into groups—three to five persons in each group—to play cards until midnight."[28] Again, this kind of street party was not necessarily exclusive to Shanghai's beggars. Similar scenes could be found elsewhere in the country. In the hinterland city of Chengdu, some 1,200 miles west of Shanghai, pedestrians could always see beggars gathered for dinner near the four gates of the walled city. In particular, the area near the East Gate Bridge was favored by beggars for such gatherings for a few decades prior to the 1950s. At the riverside under the bridge abutments, beggars put an earthenware pot on three stones and made a fire in the triangular space beneath the pot. A number of these bonfires were set on the river banks to cook for the more than one hundred beggars who daily gathered there. This cooking method had become so standard that it came to be known as "three rocks holding a wok" (*sanshi ding yiguo*). These vagrants' "happy hour" often attracted a number of idle bystanders who leaned over the bridge to watch the evening gathering. According to one of these eyewitnesses,

> The smell sent forth from underneath the bridge was quite inviting. . . . Because in the evening beggars do not go out begging, they were always in a good mood at dinnertime. They sat in groups and treated each other in a friendly and polite manner. As a rule, the sick who could not go out begging during the day had the right to join their fellows at mealtime, which makes the dinner scene livelier and more harmonious.[29]

Most of the food the beggars ate was leftovers from restaurants and banquets. The food may have been short on meat, as one can tell from the various names the beggars gave to their dishes. "Lantern Chicken" implied that so little meat was left on the bones that the chicken resembled the framework of a Chinese red lantern. "Comb Fish" was also named by analogy: the skeleton of a fish is much like a comb, with the bones resembling the teeth and the tail, the handle. "Moon Pork" described a bit of meat attached to a piece of pork skin that was as thin as the crescent moon. "Star Wine" conveyed an image of wine that was collected from what had been left in the glasses after a banquet: the wine glistened with tiny drops of oil on the surface, like sparking stars in the sky.[30] These names were creative and imaginative, reflecting the street people's sense of humor.

Since the early twentieth century, Chengdu had been the home of the famous Sichuan cuisine and its people were known for food-loving and a tradition of frequently eating out. In the 1930s, Chengdu, with about half a million residents, boasted thousands of restaurants and more than six hundred teahouses.[31] The East Gate area was one of Chengdu's busy commercial districts, described by one American traveler in 1917 as a place full of "noise and shouting and confusion."[32] It was dotted with all kinds of eating places, which in part made it possible for the beggars there to take leftovers as the main source of their daily food.

But for beggars in other areas, leftovers could be too scarce in quantity and too inferior in quality, and time and again the search for food led to thievery. In Wuhu, a port city on the lower Yangzi River, beggars usually bought vegetables on their own and found a way to capture (or rather, steal) live animals, especially domestic fowl, for meat. According to an insider, "Beggars are shabbily dressed, but they are careful about the food they eat. This is critical to them, because they need to keep a strong body to tough out their life of vagrancy."[33] These beggars ate a variety of meats, including dogs, tortoises, turtles, fish, snakes, rats, birds, and chickens, which they were very creative in getting, either by stealing or hunting. It was most common for Chinese households, both rural and urban, to raise a few domestic fowl at home and let them look for food near the premises during the day. And in Wuhu, like in most other Chinese cities, farm fields and open country—places where one could hunt small animals—abutted built-up areas. Many beggars were skilled hunters and thieves. They could kill a barking dog instantly with just one fatal strike on its nose, and tame a fierce snake by swiftly removing its poison glands, and they were particularly ingenious at capturing the most common target—chickens.

One way to lure a chicken close was to hold a mouthful of rice in one's mouth and blow it onto the ground in a straight line. When the chicken pecked close enough, the beggar would snatch it from behind in an instant. The trick was to grab the bird firmly and quickly in the right place, the belly, so that it would not be able to make a noise. A skilled beggar was able to hide seven or eight dead chickens inside his ragged jacket. Another way was to make a tiny, springy bamboo nail that was sharp on both ends and squeeze the device into a grain of wheat to be scattered with other wheat on the ground. Once a chicken pecked the bait, the hidden bamboo nail would spring out and fatally block the throat: the poor creature would not even be able to squawk before being captured. There was yet another way to snare a chicken: feed it a handful of rice that had been soaked in 60-degree white spirits; watch the chicken for a couple of minutes until it passed out from ingesting the alcohol-soaked rice; and then take the drunken prey with ease.[34]

Stealing chickens could also be a group activity, depending on how many chickens were available in a household. The usual tactic was go out in pairs, one to steal, and the other to be the lookout. In Wenzhou, a city in southeastern Zhejiang Province, group chicken theft was so common that beggars had developed some secret jargon to be used on the spot. If a housewife came out from the targeted home, the lookout would warn his fellow beggar: "The Sound Observer is out." The counter measure to her presence was "Set the Bottle Gourd on fire." The "Sound Observer" (Guanyin), as we have mentioned, was the most popular goddess in the Mahayana Buddhist tradition; the name refers to the belief that this goddess constantly hears prayers and observes the world with her boundless mercy (hence she was also known as the "goddess of mercy"). In the beggars' cant, it refers to the housewife. The "Bottle Gourd" was a metaphor for the male privates, and "set fire" was lingo that was to be decoded by its antonym, "release water." Hence "Set the Bottle Gourd on fire" means to urinate in front of the woman. As was anticipated, at the moment the man lowered his pants to pass water, the reaction of the woman was to get back into the house. She would think she was escaping from an unpleasant rascal, quite unaware of the hidden trick behind the indecency.[35]

Here, as it was common for beggars to do things in addition to begging, the beggars were petty thieves. But they had a bit of "professional ethics" that prevented them from causing too much bitterness or too strong resentment among the public because of their thievery. This can be seen as quite prudent, in a way reflecting the maturity of the "trade." Beggars always rotated the areas where they stole chickens or killed dogs so that no particular neighborhood would be a constant victim, obviously to minimize the damage to their public image as poor beggars not wicked thieves. They followed the wisdom summarized in an old saying, "The rabbit will not eat the grass near its lair," that is, they would not steal in the immediate vicinity of their "home."[36] Also, in general they did not steal roosters, for as late as in the middle of the twentieth century many households still could not afford a mechanical clock and relied on a rooster for the morning wake-up call.[37]

If most of the stories of beggars' roadside dinners were told by outside observers, the following account is valuable because it was given by a participant. Hu Xiang, an elementary school teacher in Wuhu who had known many local beggars ever since he was a child, recalled that in the late 1940s he was a frequent visitor to the beggars' den adjacent to the Hall of the Circling Dragon (Huilongdian) in suburban Wuhu near the elementary school where he taught. Life was precarious for a schoolteacher at a time when China suffered from astronomical inflation, with wholesale prices often increasing tenfold in a single month.[38] Hu's pay for teaching an entire school term in 1948 was only sufficient to buy a pair of tennis shoes. Hu cited a Chinese metaphorical adage, "Those who have the same illness sympathize with each other," in recounting that poverty had made him feel close to the street people. He often mingled with the beggars and joined them in their evening gatherings at the den.

> The beggars picked up firewood on the way back from their daily begging, and they started to cook and then have dinner. The air was heavy with the aroma of dog meat over the bonfire. Wine was put in rough bowls, and they ate while chatting. After the meal, some beggars smoked pipes and others hummed ditties. Then they would recline on a dog skin chatting about what they had seen and

heard that day. At that time I, having brought a set of mahjong tiles and cigarettes, often sat in the midst of the group listening as they told of interesting episodes and fantastic stories from all over the country.[39]

Although beggars' eating well seemed not uncommon in many parts of the country, in terms of receiving cash alms, Shanghai beggars still stood out from their counterparts elsewhere, and this had made the public antipathy to beggars more apparent in that city. A beggar told a reporter in 1926 that from Chinese New Year's Day to the Lantern Festival (the fifteenth day of the first lunar month), and on the first and fifteenth days of each lunar month (which were traditional dates for pilgrimages), he could get at least three silver dollars a day by begging in the temple area of Shanghai's old Chinese city. Other days during the year, his daily income from begging was over one silver dollar.[40] These figures were consistent with Xu Ke's estimate that the daily income of a Shanghai beggar was about one silver dollar.[41] By comparison, the average monthly wage for a worker in the textile mills, which was the largest industry of Shanghai, at that time was about 10–15 silver dollars, barely half of a beggar's monthly income.[42]

Little wonder some people bore a grudge against beggars. A Cantonese published an article in 1920 in a weekly journal of a Cantonese native place association in Shanghai, attacking his fellow men who begged on Shanghai's streets for making "a living without working."

> Beggars are poor creatures of the world and we ought to have sympathy for them. If we don't have compassion for them, we should still not have the heart to attack them. But I was astonished to know that the facts are quite the opposite of what we may think. Based on what I have heard and seen, these people dress in rags and look extremely poor and sad, but their daily expenses for "white rice" [food] and "black rice" [opium] are no less than a silver dollar or so, which is in fact [equivalent to] the household expenses of an average middle-class family.[43]

On the one hand, stories such as these may not be representative of average beggars in Shanghai. The Cantonese mendicants begged mainly in North Sichuan Road and Wuchang Road in the Hongkou area, where the city's largest Cantonese community was located, and in general the Cantonese residents of Shanghai were relatively well-off. The downtown of the old Chinese city, the area around the Temple of the City God, was, as we have mentioned, a destination for Buddhist and Taoist pilgrims and consequently a favorite place for begging. Most of the beggars there, known as "big beggars," were well connected; that is, they were organized professional mendicants, not occasional panhandlers.[44]

On the other hand, these stories cannot be dismissed as just an expression of the bias of the more fortunate against the disadvantaged. According to a variety of sources on the amount of alms a Shanghai beggar could garner, in the 1920s and 1930s (before the outbreak of war in 1937), on average, a street beggar's daily income in cash varied from 500 – 600 *wen* (this applied mostly to new beggars) to 2,000 wen. The latter was equivalent to about two-thirds of a silver dollar and exceeded the monthly income of an average factory worker.[45] And this income was in cash and did not include food and other alms. Some beggars were able to save their money and use the savings to become usurers. An aged beggar who died in 1936 left almost 800 silver dollars underneath his dirty pillow. Since he did not have an immediate family, he left the money to his brothers' sons, who then had a nasty dispute over how to divide the legacy.[46] This story echoed a similar phenomenon in nineteenth-century England, where cases of aged beggars having contrived to amass considerable sums of money by the time of their death were frequently reported.[47] But Shanghai beggars seemed more this-worldly, that is, they tended to use the money while alive. Tales of thrifty beggars saving money and eventually getting a "modestly comfortable home" (*xiaokang zhi jia*) were not sensational news in Shanghai, and cases of beggars becoming usurers, owning a private rickshaw, hiring servants, or having concubines were not unheard of.[48]

Stories like these naturally reduced people's sympathy for street people. When Lin observed the wealth of his beggar neighbors in the wake of the Opium War he could not help remarking with a rhetorical sigh that "[the life of] people of my kind is not as good as that of beggars."[49] Over the decades since then, this kind of sentiment has endured, as can be sensed in a popular portrait that aimed to illustrate "mendicancy as a profession." A series of New Year's Pictures (*nianhua*, a form of folk art) entitled "360 Professions" was printed in Shanghai in the 1920s in which each picture is an image of a profession or a job. The anonymous artists tried to draw hundreds of such pictures to illustrate the "360 walks of life," meaning "every walk of life" or "all professions." Begging, as one of the professions, was presented as a gentry-like old man attired in a long gown with decorations on the front, wearing a skullcap and cloth shoes; there was not a single patch on his apparel. The portrait contradicts the usual image of beggars as clothed in rags. One may think that this is because of the nature of New Year's pictures, in which an artist may idealize a subject to meet people's concern about an auspicious start for the new year. But the whole series was plainly drawn, more for the purpose of collecting than putting on a wall as decorations. Moreover, a number of characters in the series, such as the pear seller and the gold-leaf maker, appeared in patched clothes and looked poorer than the beggar.[50]

The "well being" of beggars was also a topic that popular magazines such as *Shanghai Life* (*Shanghai shenghuo*) did not miss. One article on mendicancy spoke of an "Emperor Beggar," a popular epithet that revealed the grudge the many people bore.[51] Another article used a similar metaphor but stated the grievance more straightforwardly. It called a particular beggar a "genuine and true veteran Great General of Stretching Out the Hands [that is, asking for help] (*shenshou dajiangjun*)" who levies taxes on the city's residents without any sanction whatsoever. The article depicted an image that probably would have aroused much sympathy—not for beggars but pedestrians—among Shanghainese. The General patrolled the Nanking Road area, the city's busiest commercial district, where he exercised the right to levy a variety of taxes: a "wealth tax" on well-dressed people who were shopping, a "property tax" on relaxed pedestrians who were taking a stroll, and a "mandarin ducks tax" on couples who were dating and absorbed in sweet conversation (mandarin ducks are a symbol of love and courtship). Such taxes, the author satirized, did not need to be passed in the parliament or provincial legislature, but nevertheless they were more effectively imposed on the people than those that had been duly approved.[52] The nickname "General of Stretching Out the Hands" apparently was commonly used to describe beggars. For instance, the *Popular Pictorial* (*Tongsu huabao*), a magazine published in Chengdu from 1909 to 1912, used it to satirize that beggars had long arms in order to snatch pancakes from snack shops, or more generally, to imply that beggars were pilferers.[53]

"Sympathy versus antipathy" in regard to the street people of China involved the classic question, debated in many societies in modern times, of whether the poor are "deserving or undeserving" of public assistance. However, the image of beggars in the public's mind in urban China, for better or for worse, was not fractured into a binary construction of poor paupers and cunning parasites. Drawing from the rich mine of Chinese literary and folk tradition, the public perception of beggars could diverge dramatically from the image of a mere vagabond. The beggar was frequently perceived as someone who was directly related to personages who, according to common sense, could not have been more remote from the destitute: deities, sages, ministers, kings, emperors, and so on. If the controversies over beggars discussed in this chapter were due to public images that were pressed on the beggars, then, as we shall see in the following chapters, beggars actively and sometimes ingeniously created a public image in their favor. But they did not achieve this alone. China's religious beliefs, secular folkways, and elite literature all helped with framing some remarkably creative images of beggars, indicating an intermingling of mainstream culture and subaltern culture.

CHAPTER 3

Legend Has It

THE MYSTERIOUS REALM of *jianghu* ("rivers and lakes") was long thought of as a world apart from mainstream society, one where able men and unusual characters were cast down but might well spring back to fight another day. Jianghu, the home of these "crouching tigers and hidden dragons" (*canglong wohu*), was thus a place for talented men in eclipse. Another metaphor is also sympathetic to superior men facing adverse or hostile circumstances: "A tiger on flat land will be bullied by a dog; a dragon swimming in shallow water will be tricked by a shrimp."[1] The implication is that men of character may be wronged but they will eventually overcome adversity, like a tiger returning to the mountains or a dragon to the sea. This notion carried over to vagrants, who were often seen as temporarily thwarted figures. Heroes and worthy men rising from the ranks of vagrants are among the best-known themes of centuries-old Chinese sagas. Few peoples in the world have drawn from history and legends such rich and vibrant images of beggars as have the Chinese. Kings and ministers, generals and literati, priests and philosophers, all were invited to see their reflections in the ranks of mendicants.

Rising from Mendicancy

Until modern times, nearly all established trades, professions, or callings in China recognized a forefather (*zushiye*), that is, a man (or sometimes a woman) who was regarded as the founder of the trade and worshiped as its "patron saint" (*hangye shen*). Among the best-known trade forefathers are Lu Ban (active ca. seventh century B.C.) in carpentry, Cai Lun (d. 121) in paper-making, Zhao Gongming (active third century B.C.) in finance and banking, Lu Yu (733–804) in the tea industry, Huang Daopo (active the late thirteenth century) in cotton spinning and weaving, and Luozu (Luo Yin,

d. 909) in barbering, to name just a few. A recent study of Chinese trade forefathers and deities found that in traditional times at least 160 trades and professions worshiped a patron saint.[2] Although some forefathers or patron saints were legendary or mythological figures, most were true historical personages who made or were believed to have made great contributions to the trade. Often—sometimes hundreds of years—after their death, they were reincarnated as deities with the power to protect the calling's followers. In most cases the establishment of a trade or a profession was not the achievement of just one particular individual but involved generations of collective work. A patron saint or forefather, nevertheless, provided the people in the trade with a sense of unity and shared identity, faith, and what might be called psychological protection. This is evident in any guild house anywhere across the nation, where the image of the trade forefather was placed at the center of the meeting hall. In ritual ceremonies, these images were the most important icons for worshipping.

Like all well-established professions, mendicancy had its forefathers. Indeed, it had a long list of progenitors. In China, many trades, including mendicancy, were "polytheist" in regard to creators and trade deities: Chinese mendicants had at least half a dozen commonly worshiped procreators (Figure 3). The exact forefather a particular group of beggars chose to worship may have differed from place to place, but without exception beggars' patron saints were all heroic figures and included prominent and powerful personages who seemed least likely to be associated with a subaltern calling such as mendicancy.

For instance, both Confucius (551–479 B.C.), the single most influential sage in East Asia, and Sakyamuni (ca. 565–486 B.C.), the founder of Buddhism, were worshiped by some beggars as the forebears of their calling. Like most stories about beggar forefathers, to connect Confucius or Sakyamuni with mendicancy was farfetched, but it was not totally without basis. Confucius once was invited to visit the state of Chu, but on his way he and his followers were obstructed by the states of Chen and Cai, both rivals of Chu. In the border area between the two states the travelers were isolated and without food for seven days. Confucius, who was described as like "a lost dog" (*sang jia zhi quan*), was so starved that his "face looked like a green vegetable" (*mian you cai se*).[3] Legend has it that Sakyamuni, a prince of a northern Indian kingdom (in the Himalayan foothills of what is now southern Nepal) left home at age twenty-nine to seek enlightenment and eternal salvation. After six years of wandering the subcontinent, one day while sitting and meditating under a bodhi tree Sakyamuni suddenly achieved enlightenment. He was thereafter known as the Buddha, or the "enlightened one," and his teachings eventually evolved into a world religion. In later days,

FIGURE 3.   In an open-air opera show in the town of Zhujing near Shanghai, a group of almsmen got into a street fight with the opera actors and were defeated. As they fled to their den—an ancient temple next to the opera stage—their foes ran after them. In desperation, the beggars hung out the image of their "patron saint" and prayed for his protection. SOURCE: *Dianshizhai huabao* (The Dianshi Study pictorial).

wandering monks seeking alms—a long tradition that continued into modern times—were thought to be following in his footsteps.[4]

Not only did almsmen claim the most sacred sages as the founders of their trade, but also, more frequently, they associated mendicancy and street life with great secular leaders in history. It is quite ironic, although understandable, that the poorest and most vulnerable members of society, beggars, proclaimed the richest and the most powerful, the monarch, as their "forefather." Among such forefathers were the King of Jin, known as Double Ears (Chonger, 697–628 B.C.). When he was the prince of Jin, he was driven out in a court coup d'état in 655 B.C. and forced into exile. He wandered in North China for nineteen years before he was able to claim the throne in 636 B.C. Later, he led Jin to hegemony over rival kingdoms.[5] The nineteen-year exile and hardship that Double Ears endured and his ultimate success made him a heroic figure in Chinese history and, in the minds of Chinese beggars, a forebear of their calling. The Song emperor Taizu (Zhao Kuangyin, 927–76) was also among the monarchs beggars claimed as their forefathers.[6]

Three historical figures from the pantheon of Chinese paladins were by far best known for their experiences as vagrant and therefore widely worshiped by beggars across the country: Wu Zixu, a royal advisor and political strategist in the fifth century B.C., whose protracted yet valiant search for revenge makes Edmond Dantes in Dumas's *The Count of Monte Cristo* look like a mere nineteenth-century imitation; Han Xin, the foremost military general of the Han dynasty; and Zhu Yuanzhang, the mighty emperor who founded the Ming dynasty (1368–1644).

EVER SINCE EMPEROR ZHU

The story of Zhu Yuanzhang (1328–98), who rose from obscurity—indeed he had been a beggar as a boy—to found one of China's greatest dynasties, is a remarkable saga and one that inspired some prominent political figures in recent history, including Mao Zedong (1893–1976).[7] The youngest son of a poor peasant family in Fengyang, Anhui, Zhu Yuanzhang, in the year 1344, at the age of sixteen, fled from his home village due to a terrible drought that was followed by a plague of locusts. For over three years Zhu wandered about eking out a living by begging in seven counties in the provinces of Anhui and Henan. In desperation he joined a rebellious throng against the ruling Mongol dynasty in his hometown in 1352 (at age twenty-four), which later proved to be a decisive move in his life. For the next sixteen years he fought numerous bloody battles, rose from a mere foot soldier to regiment head and then to general, defeated his formidable rivals among the rebels, and eventually, at the age of forty, declared himself emperor. After becoming emperor, Zhu never attempted to cover up his humble past. Instead, he referred to the hardship of his youth as a spur to his great achievements (Figure 4).[8]

Zhu's hometown, however, did not benefit from producing an emperor. Fengyang, a county located on the southern banks of the frequently flooded Huai River, remained a famine-ridden place during the succeeding Qing dynasty, and in popular culture Zhu was blamed for the misfortune of his hometown. Mixing Chinese geomancy, known as *fengshui* (literally, "wind and water"), and Fengyang folklore, local people believed that because one single person had such great fortune as to rise from beggar to emperor, all good fengshui (that is, good luck) had been taken by him, leaving Fengyang impoverished.[9] By the early twentieth century, beggary had become an infamous Fengyang custom. Among all of modern China's beggar rhymes and ditties, the Fengyang flower-drum song, typically sung by the beggars in the

FIGURE 4.   The first emperor of the Ming dynasty wanted to be remembered as a regal figure, as depicted in an official portrait on the right, executed by a court painter, but the caricature on the left, by an unidentified painter of his time, is probably a more faithful rendition of his appearance. The scars on his face left by smallpox are an unmistakable mark of his miserable childhood as a homeless vagrant. SOURCE: The National Palace Museum, Taipei. Reproduced from Charles O. Hucker, *China's Imperial Past* (Stanford, 1975).

Huai River area, was the best known of its kind (see Appendix). The song, which became popular in the late seventeenth century and which to this day many Chinese can hum, blamed Emperor Zhu for the misfortune of Fengyang:

> Speaking of Fengyang, talking about Fengyang:
> Fengyang had been a fine place until it brought forth Emperor Zhu.
> Since then
> Nine out of ten years there were famines.
> [This is followed by a coda in which the singer imitates the rhythm of
>   drum beating.]
> *Long ge long dong qiang!*
> *Long ge long dong qiang!*
> *Long ge long dong qiang dong qiang lai qiang!*
>
> The rich families sold their lands,
> The poor families sold their children.

I have no children to sell,
All I can do is to carry a flower drum on my back
and wander about the world.
Long ge long dong qiang!
Long ge long dong qiang!
Long ge long dong qiang dong qiang lai qiang![10]

Needless to say it is unjustifiable to blame one individual, even if the person was an emperor, for the famines of Fengyang. The Fengyang custom of begging was the direct result of an ecological disaster. Beginning in the late twelfth century, when the Song dynasty and its northern nomadic neighbors were frequently at war in the central Yellow River valley, the Yellow River flooded and invaded the Huai River. By the sixteenth century, the tremendous amount of mud brought by the Yellow River flooding eventually silted up the mouth of the Huai River and caused more frequent floods in the Huai River valley.[11] As a county on the banks of the Huai River, Fengyang was bankrupted by the Republican era, especially after a horrendous flood in 1930.[12]

But the full explanation for Fengyang's impoverishment goes beyond purely ecological or economic factors. According to an anecdote, after Zhu Yuanzhang established the Ming dynasty, he ordered 140,000 wealthy households from the Jiangnan region to resettle in Fengyang in the hope of enriching his hometown, where after the war much farmland remained deserted. Anyone who dared to flee was severely punished. However, these people did not make Fengyang a better-off place. They missed Jiangnan, where their family tombs were left unattended. For a nation where ancestor worship was virtually a religion, this was obviously going to be a source of discontent. Every year these forced migrants disguised themselves as beggars and went back to their hometowns to "sweep the graves," that is, to clean the family graveyard, offer sacrifices, and pay their respects to the ancestors.[13]

Official records verify that in its effort to build a "central capital" (Zhongdu) in Fengyang as the second capital to the primary capital, Nanjing, the Ming government ordered 140,000 people to migrate from Jiangnan and stationed 72,600 soldiers in the projected capital. The work of constructing the huge capital started in 1369 and continued for six years before it came to a sudden halt. The emperor personally ordered the suspension, apparently because the enormous cost exceeded what the Ming government could reasonably afford. It is unclear if the migration plan was fully implemented.[14] The tale, however, can be taken as another case in which society, if not beggars themselves, gave a sympathetic explanation for mendicancy. Here beggars were portrayed as formerly well-to-do families who had fallen victim to the notorious Ming autocracy. The Fengyang flower-drum song obviously blames the emperor: note that the famines suffered in nine years out of ten came after Fengyang had brought forth Emperor Zhu!

PURGATORY AND REVENGE

Among the most frequently worshipped mendicant forebears was Han Xin (d. 196 B.C.), the military commander and strategist who helped found the Han dynasty (202 B.C.–A.D. 220), which was a contemporary of the Roman empire and matched if not surpassed its greatness. Han Xin's valiant military exploits, brilliant strategies, and subtle relations with the emperor were favorite topics of Chinese literature, drama, and various types of local performances. But two often-told stories about Han Xin's humble youth were particularly inspiring for they depict his character and provide a striking contrast to his success in later years (Figure 5). Both stories were recorded by Sima Qian, China's most renowned historian, in the first century B.C. The first story has been taken as a classic moral that a man who has prodigious ambitions should tolerate temporary disgrace or humiliation in order to accomplish great deeds in the future:

> Han was a vagabond in his youth and constantly dependent on others for his meals. Thus many people in his hometown of Huaiyin [in the north of what is today Jiangsu Province] considered him a pitiful nuisance. Although he was a vagrant, he seemed more like a sluggard than a street thug and was sometimes bullied by the hooligans of the town. Among the butchers of the town was a young man who once jeered at Han Xin, "You're big and tall and love to carry a sword, but at heart you're nothing but a coward!" In front of a crowd of people in an open market he insulted Han Xin, and then said, "If you feel like dying, come on and attack me! If not, then crawl between my legs!" Han Xin looked him over carefully, and then bent down and crawled between the man's legs. The spectators in the market place all roared with laughter at Han Xin's cowardice.[15]

The other story tells that Han Xin once was desperately hungry and went fishing in the Huai River at the foot of the wall surrounding the city of Huaiyin, hoping to catch something to fill his empty stomach:

> On the riverside there were some old women who were washing raw silk to bleach it. One of the old women noticed that Han Xin was nearly starved and she fed him, and continued to do so for the twenty or thirty days until the bleaching was finished. Han Xin was very grateful and said to the old woman: "Some day without fail I will pay you back handsomely!" But the old woman was offended and replied, "I could tell you had no way of getting food for yourself, young man, and so I felt sorry for you and gave you something to eat. What makes you think I was looking for any reward?"[16]

The term "bleaching mother" (*piaomu*), referring to the old woman who fed Han Xin, entered the Chinese lexicon as a synonym for "benefactor" or

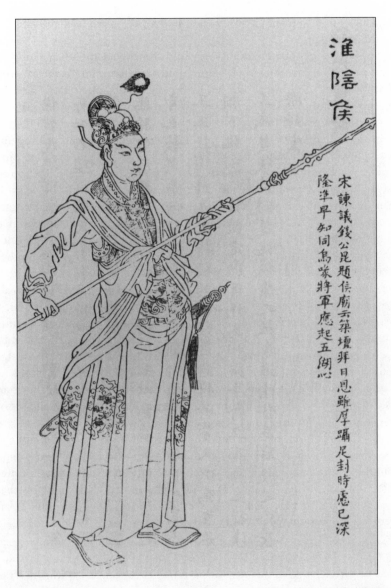

淮陰侯

宋諫議錢公題侯廟云築壇拜日恩雖厚躡足封時慮已深

隆準早知同鳥喙將軍應起五湖心

FIGURE 5. A traditional portrait of Han Xin. After helping found the Han dynasty, Han Xin was given the title of the Marquis of Huaiyin, Huaiyin being his hometown, where he spent his youth as a humble vagrant. SOURCE: *Wanxiao tang huazhuan* (1743).

"philanthropist"—particularly a person who offers much needed help to a youthful stranger.

The stories of Han Xin's humble youth captivated the imagination of Chinese beggars, and numerous beggar guilds designated him as their patron saint. By doing so they apparently were hoping to encounter many "bleaching mothers" in their daily ventures. To take Han Xin as the forefather of mendicancy was also to imply that there were "crouching tigers and hidden dragons" in the ranks of street people and therefore they deserved the public's sympathy and charity. In the eyes of the street people, the bleaching mother apparently had the right human compassion and even the vision to extend a helping hand to a roadside stranger who turned out to be a great man. If a man like Han Xin could once have been frustrated by circumstances and have fallen into the life of a vagabond, why not assume that among the mendicants there was no lack of worthy men and thus why not offer them help? China has a long tradition of seeing "failure as the mother of success" (hence the proverb) and frustration as a gift bestowed by the gods to temper one's abilities, leading to ultimate success in life. For centuries almost all educated people in China could quote the saying from *Mencius*, a text by the philosopher (of the same name) whose importance to Confucianism was next only to that of Confucius: "Heaven, when it is about to place a great burden on a man, always first tests his resolution, exhausts his frame and makes him suffer starvation and hardship, frustrates his efforts so as to shake him from his mental lassitude, toughen his nature and make good his deficiencies." [17] This quotation had become an inspiration to millions of people in China for thousands of years. Indeed the Chinese were able to cite many cases in history to support Mencius's comforting words. One of the best-known stories of tolerating humiliation and later enjoying revenge concerned Wu Zixu (d. 484 B.C.), who lived in Spring and Autumn times (770–476 B.C.), when China was divided into several rival kingdoms that were frequently at war, each seeking to establish its hegemony. Sima Qian recorded in his monumental work, *Shiji*:

> Wu's father, Wu She, was the imperial tutor of the crown prince of the Kingdom of Chu. He had been trusted by King Ping of Chu (r. 528–516 B.C.) until in 521 B.C. when a minister named Fei Wuji convinced the King that the crown prince was plotting a coup against him. Fei was formerly a tutor of the crown prince but felt no loyalty to the prince. When King Ping assigned Fei the job of finding a bride for the prince in the state of Qin, Fei found an extraordinary beauty there. Instead of bringing the woman to the prince, however, Fei persuaded the King to take his prospective daughter-in-law for himself. Soon the Qin woman bore King Ping a son and became the King's most favorite concubine. Now, Fei had ingratiated himself with King Ping and gained a firm stand-

ing in the court, but he feared that once the crown prince came to the throne, the latter would kill him. Hence he filled the King's ears with the prince's short-comings and eventually slandered him by spreading the rumour of a revolt. When the King issued a warrant for the prince's arrest, the prince escaped to a neighbouring country. Wu She tried to defend the prince as innocent, which only infuriated the King, who put Wu in jail and intended to execute him.

King Ping knew that Wu She had two sons, Wu Shang and Wu Yun (Zixu), both worthy men, and was afraid that they would one day seek to avenge their father's disgrace. Following Fei's advice, the King took Wu as a hostage and sum-moned his two sons to court, saying that if they came he would spare their fa-ther. The Wu brothers both knew that this was only a pretense to lure them to the court in order to execute them. But, as their father had anticipated, they re-acted quite differently. The elder bother, Wu Shang, wanted to obey the sum-mons out of filial duty. He said to his younger brother: "I know that even if I go I can never hope to save my father's life. It is just that I would hate to think that he called me to save his life and I failed to obey." Wu Zixu replied that if the whole family was destroyed, nothing could be done. The best way to wipe out their father's disgrace, Wu Zixu believed, was to flee to a rival state of Chu, en-list outside help, and seek revenge on the ruler of Chu later on.

The brothers therefore decided to honor their father in different ways. Wu Shang submitted himself to the court and, as he had foreseen it, only to die with his father under the executioner's sword in 522 B.C. Wu Zixu refused to go and narrowly escaped arrest.[18]

Wu Zixu fled from Chu (which was in the middle Yangzi River valley area, roughly what is today Hunan and Hubei provinces) and headed eastward for the state of Wu (in the lower Yangzi River valley; roughly southern Jiangsu Province today). A sympathetic fisherman ferried him across the Yangzi River. But the state of Wu was still hundreds of miles away and Wu Zixu fell sick on the road. Even after he entered the state of Wu, he had no means of supporting himself except to wander on the streets begging. The hardship he endured following this journey was what later associated him with beg-gars. According to Fan Ju, Wu's contemporary and a political advisor to the King of Qin:

> Wu Zixu hid himself in a sack and so escaped through the Zhao Pass, travelling by night, hiding by day, till he reached the Ling River, when he had not a morsel to put in his mouth. He crawled on his knees, inched over the ground, bowed his head, bared his arms, drummed on his stomach, and blew a flute, begging in the marketplace of Wu, yet in the end he raised Wu to greatness and made its ruler, King Helü, a hegemon.[19]

Here Fan Ju was using Wu Zixu's example to persuade his king to seek he-gemony over the rival kingdoms of the time. In 511 B.C., Wu finally reached the destination in his long journey for revenge. The Wu army defeated Chu and occupied Ying, the Chu capital. Because King Ping had died a few years earlier, Wu Zixu searched for his successor, King Chao, in order to exact revenge. Failing to find him, he proceeded to dig up the grave of King Ping, expose the corpse, and inflict three hundred lashes upon it. Although this was criticized at the time as too extreme and inhuman, it nevertheless went down in history as an example of thorough reprisal.

Wu's story was recorded in a number of sources, but Sima Qian's account has been regarded as the most detailed and authoritative. The grand historian had no intention of concealing his admiration of Wu Zixu's spirit, as he ended the story with a passionate comment:

> If Wu Zixu had joined his father, She, and died with him, he would have been of no more significance than a mere ant. But he set aside a small righteousness in order to wipe out a great shame, and his name has been handed down to later ages. How moving! At that time Wu Zixu suffered hardship by the riverside and begged for his food along the road, but in his determination he did not for a moment forget Ying. He bore all secretly and silently, and in the end achieved merit and fame. Who but a man of burning intention could have accomplished such a deed?[20]

Sima Qian had good reason to empathize with Wu Zixu, and in the commentary he was speaking of himself as much as of Wu. In defending Li Ling, a betrayed general, in 99 B.C., Sima Qian offended Emperor Wu (posthumous title, the "Marshal Emperor," reigned 141–87 B.C.) and was sentenced to castration, a punishment next only to execution. Instead of committing suicide to save his dignity, which in his time was a common practice of a person of his status, Sima Qian endured the humiliation in order to complete his then ongoing work, *Shiji* (Historical Records), a project he inherited from his late father, who was also a grand historian in the imperial court. In 91 B.C., in mortification and oblivion, he finally completed one of China's greatest magnum opuses, a masterwork that has made him immortal.

In a sympathetic way, *Shiji*, with its paramount influence in Chinese history and literature, preserved Wu Zixu's story, but the saga went beyond *Shiji* and other historical writings and was integrated into popular literature and various types of local dramas and folk plays, such as teahouse storytelling and roadside puppet shows. In Chinese popular culture, Wu was a hero who personified righteousness and just revenge. Often, when people quoted the saying, "Ten years' time is not too long for an upright person to seek revenge," they cited Wu Zixu's story as a case in point.[21] In particular, the image of a persecuted gentleman begging on the street is so compelling that the saying "Wu Zixu blowing a bamboo flute on the streets of Suzhou" became a synonym for a man enduring dark days in the course of fighting for justice.

In the minds of the ordinary people of Suzhou, Wu Zixu was also the kind of person who knows gratitude and seeks ways to return the kindness of others. A legend surviving to this day tells how he cleverly managed, even after his death, to save the people of Suzhou from a catastrophic famine. King Helü, once he established his hegemony, became arrogant and imperious. Wu Zixu was often at odds with the king over various issues and their relations deteriorated. When the king ordered a wall to be built around the city of Suzhou, Wu Zixu thought the project was unnecessary, but he was unable to persuade the king. After the wall was completed, Wu secretly told his trusted subordinates: "Should there be a famine after my death, you should dig out the foundation of the wall and the people of Suzhou may survive." Eventually, Wu Zixu offended the king and ended his life by committing suicide. Soon the neighboring state of Yue invaded Wu and destroyed the kingdom. As if this was not enough of a disaster for the people of Wu, the following year a severe famine struck. In desperation, Wu Zixu's followers recalled his exhortation. They tore down the wall, dug three feet down into the ground, and to their great joy found that the bricks that formed the foundation of the wall were actually made not of the usual clay, but of sticky, glutinous rice. These rice bricks saved the people of Suzhou. It was believed that, because Wu Zixu once begged in Suzhou, this was his way of showing his gratitude to the people of Suzhou who had generously fed him (Figure 6).[22]

The stories of Han Xin and Wu Zixu personalize Mencius's words about tempering the strength and willpower of those who were chosen to play a great role in the world. The sufferings of these individuals in their early lives were seen as a transit through purgatory and a test: those who endured were made stronger. This may sound too romantic for an average beggar, but if the "rags to power" scenario was largely a fantasy, it was a fantasy beggars needed. Moreover, most of the forefathers beggars chose to worship were true historical figures who were widely known across the country, and beggars were wisely using them, as much as they could, to boost the image of beggars and justify mendicancy. For this, Chinese beggars were in a favorable environment, for society was not only receptive to the idea of social mobility, it provided moral support to those who stumbled along the road. When true human stories were scarce, myths were created. If there were not enough Emperor Zhus and General Wus in history to fill the dreams of beggars, gods and deities would be conjured up.

Poverty Blessed

Mixing together history, oral traditions, myths, fables, and folklore, Chinese society produced numerous legends about mendicancy, many of which con-

FIGURE 6.   A traditional portrait of Wu Zixu collected in the Suzhou area where Wu begged on the streets and later rose to prominence. Although Wu was not born in the area, the people of Suzhou proudly regarded him as a local sage. The caption reads "A portrait of Premier Wu." SOURCE: *Wujun mingxian tuzhuan zan* (1829).

tinued to be popular in modern times. To some extent these legends and the folk beliefs attached to Chinese beggars have raised an urban underclass to a level unimaginable in the West.[23]

DEITY INCARNATIONS

A frequent subject of Chinese legends is mendicants as mysterious figures who disguise themselves as the destitute to test the conscience and compassion of mankind. For nearly two millennia since the late Han dynasty (23–220), Chinese literature has been rich in stories of deities incarnated as beggars, the aged, the disabled, or otherwise poor creatures who seek help in human society. Those who gave alms to the poor received salvation or were unexpectedly rewarded, or as a popular Buddhist concept had it, "giving in public, rewarded in private" (*mingqu anlai*),[24] and those who were indifferent to the poor were punished, often in mysterious ways. *Biographies of Immortals* (*Liexian zhuan*), a third-century anthology of Chinese legends, contains the following story about a beggar named Yin Sheng of Chang'an, once the capital of the Han empire:

> Yin Sheng was a beggar boy who lived under a bridge spanning the river Wei at Ch'ang-an [Chang'an]. He used to take up his stand in the marketplace and beg from those who did business there. On one occasion, disgusted by his importunity, they bespattered him with filth. Yet, when he appeared in his place again, his clothes were in their normal condition and showed no trace of dirt. The authorities, getting wind of the affair, had him arrested and thrown into chains; and yet he continued to beg in the marketplace. Being again arrested, and threatened with the death penalty, he left the city. But the houses of all those who had bespattered him collapsed in ruins, killing some dozen people. Hence the jingle which is current in Ch'ang-an:
>
> > "If you meet a beggar boy, give him a drink,
> > Or your house will fall down before you can wink."[25]

The implication here is of course that the beggar boy was a deity incarnated who wandered the capital to assay the citizen's compassion for the poor, and in this particular story both the earthly state and society seem to have failed the test.

Fables of this sort in later years, especially after the Southern Song period (1127–1271), were associated with the famous Eight Immortals (*baxian*), who in Chinese folk religion were symbols of good luck, longevity, and miracles. Each of the Eight Immortals has distinguishing characteristics, and they all carried with them at all times their individual trademark accoutrements, such as a palm-leaf fan, a bamboo flute, a straw hat, a rattan basket, and a bottle gourd.[26] They usually appear in folk art as a group of deities who descend to the earthly world to bring people good luck and long life (Figure 7). Individually, these deities and others often appeared as eccentric vagrants.[27] One of the tales relates how a beggar-deity punished a wicked rich couple while rewarding their kind-hearted slave girl:

> Long time ago there was a rich couple living alone without children. They bought a maid servant but treated her brutally. This was no surprise because the couple had a heart of stone and never gave away a farthing in charity. They considered poor people despicable and always cursed and drove beggars away with a stick. The Immortals heard about the cruelty of the couple and wanted to find out the truth. One of them turned into a barefooted, scurvy-headed beggar, and went the couple's house, clad only in a few tattered rags and called out at the door, pleading for food in a desperate manner. It happened that the old couple had gone out and only the maid was at home, heating the stove. She used rice straw as fuel, and occasionally there were grains left in the ears. She had been collecting them for some time and now she had a bag full of over two thousand grains. So sorry was she for the miserable beggar that she gave the beggar the bag and urged him to leave immediately: "If my masters see you there will be trouble, although the rice I am giving you I collected myself."
>
> When the Immortal saw that she had such a kind heart he did not leave but gave her a handkerchief. "You must wash your face with this," he said, "but be careful not to let other people use it." Just at this moment the couple returned. They were furious seeing the girl talking with a beggar. They tried to beat the beggar, who ran away, but the poor girl received another dreadful whipping, for the old couple suspected she had given alms to the beggar. From then on the girl used the handkerchief to wash her face and she became prettier everyday. Her masters were very surprised and questioned her closely. Knowing she could not keep the secret, the girl told the truth. Needless to say, the couple immediately took the treasure away from her. Next morning the wicked couple both washed their faces with the handkerchief, hoping to become as beautiful as their slave girl. But as soon as they had used it, their faces and whole appearance changed, and eventually hair grew all over their bodies and they turned into monkeys. They ran off into the mountains and were never seen again.[28]

The moral of stories such as this, summarized by a Chinese proverb as "punishing the evil and rewarding the kind-hearted" (*cheng'e yangshan*), was virtually universal in all cultures. But the Chinese seemed particularly to like to portray miserable beggars as messengers of the gods. This particular tale had at least fourteen close variants in Japan, indicative of its broad influence and popularity in East Asia.[29] Another Chinese tale about a dissatisfied benefactor bears the same moral on greed as does the famous fable "the fisherman and the golden fish," but it takes beggars, instead of golden fish, as the protagonists.[30] The story goes that a wealthy man did a great many good and charitable deeds and his fame spread far and wide. Eventually, the Immortals in heaven heard about it and wanted to test him. Two of them descended on a cold winter's day disguised as shoeless, half-naked beggars and started

FIGURE 7. A late nineteenth-century depiction of the Eight Immortals, who in Chinese folklore often appear as street beggars to test human compassion. Iron Crutch Li, the dark-skinned man sitting at the front of the boat with his left hand holding an iron crutch and his right hand resting on a bottle gourd, is said to have reincarnated himself in a deceased, lame beggar's body. SOURCE: The author's collection.

to quarrel and indeed fight near the rich man's home. The man came out to mediate and then provided food and lodging for the beggars. Despite their disgusting manner and ungrateful attitude, the man showed unfailing kindness to them. After they left, the rich man found, as he had jokingly wished, the water in the well of his backyard had turned into wine. He then wished water in his bucket to turn into spirits, which also happened. But as he continued to wish more, the beggars reappeared. "You are too grasping," they said to the man, who soon found the spirits in the bucket had turned back into water again and the well water had ceased to be wine.[31]

FOOD INNOVATIONS

The popularity of these beggar-related tales sometimes gained commercial value. This is particularly true in the food business. Chinese food traditions often associate fine cuisine with refined tales and anecdotes and make eating more a cultural experience than a mere treat for the taste buds. Beggars, despite their ragged and filthy appearance, have frequently entered what could be called the cultural ingredients of Chinese cuisine. Famous dishes that have a mendicant-related tale to tell might have originated in an authentic beggar food. But the tales could also be inventions of the Chinese literati class, whose imaginations seemed to have been particularly stimulated by a full banquet table. Or, the beggar nexus of a dish could be the result of commercial marketing, as in the case of the legend about the venerable Tieguai Li and his association with the well-known Lu Gaojian stewed pork.

Tieguai Li (also known as Li Tieguai), one of the Eight Immortals, generated numerous folktales in which he almost always appeared as a barefoot, lame beggar with an iron crutch, hence the name Tieguai Li (literally, "Li with the iron crutch").[32] According to one story, the owner of a small delicatessen, Lu Rongtang, in Suzhou once treated an aged and sick beggar kindly, providing him with free room and board for two weeks in a totally unpatronizing way. When the beggar was fully recovered, he departed one morning without saying good-bye, leaving Lu only the straw mattress on which he had slept. The next year, a shortage of firewood in the area led Lu to use the mattress one day as fuel to stew some pork. A wondrous thing happened when the mattress was put into the oven: the pork suddenly sent forth a delicate aroma that made everybody's mouth water, and from then on pork stewed in Lu's delicatessen was always better than that prepared elsewhere. Stewed pork therefore became a specialty of the delicatessen, and Lu renamed the delicatessen "Lu Gaojian" (Lu's Straw Mattress), in memory of the beggar who was believed to be an incarnation of Tieguai Li.[33]

By the late nineteenth century, Lu Gaojian had become a famous chain of delicatessens and the fairy tale had been commonly known for about two centuries albeit, like most such tales, it remained essentially an oral tradition and few people knew its origin. But as late as in the 1960s some old Suzhou residents could still pinpoint what was believed to be the original site of the Lu delicatessen, near the Congzhenggong Bridge. There the tale had been taken seriously. A stone tablet was erected in front of the restaurant soon after the allegorical Tieguai Li event, which was dated "early in the fourth lunar month of the second year of Kangxi [1663]." The tablet was about four feet high and inscribed in the formal or standard style (*zhengkai*) of Chinese calligraphy. It provides details of the encounter with the deity consistent with the popular oral tradition that spread in later centuries. The Lu delicatessen was in operation on the site until about 1895, when it closed because the family had no heir to continue the business. The tablet, however, remained at the side of the bridge until the early years of the second decade of the twentieth century.[34]

Inscribed stone tablets to commemorate an event or memorialize an individual are not unique to China, but compared to elsewhere they have a particularly long history in China, which has valued them for thousands of years. Stone tablets of all ages are among the nation's most treasured cultural relics and can be seen everywhere. Inscriptions on stone tablets were considered solemn and more credible than paper documents (not to say oral traditions). More often than not, erecting a stone tablet was an event sanctioned by local officials or even directly approved by an imperial decree. In the case of the Lu tablet, it was not official but was intended to record an unusual event. The assumption was that a tablet of durable material such as stone could provide hard evidence of the encounter with a deity.

Still, paper can overpower stone to reveal that the encounter with a deity was indeed a fabricated myth. Jing Wanxiang, a history and literature teacher in Suzhou and the author of an unpublished anthology on Suzhou's local history, found in the early twentieth century in his family genealogy some clue as to the true origin of the Lu Gaojian story. According to Jing's narrative based on his family history, the real chef who made the delicacy was Lu's wife, Mijie, who had been a maid in the Jing family before she married Lu Rongtang, a butcher who owned a small delicatessen by the Congzhenggong Bridge. Because the shop was not located in a busy commercial area, business was slow despite Mijie's excellent stewed pork. But the store did attract some loyal customers. Among them there was a Taoist priest who resided in a nearby temple. The priest frequently patronized Lu's store, not only because he loved the food but also because he felt it a pity that such a delicacy had not attracted more customers. Finally, his sympathy grew to the point that he volunteered to invent the deity story for Lu; erecting a stone tablet in front of the store was also his idea. Mijie's old master, Mr. Jing, was invited to write the script for the tablet. The store sign "Lu Gaojian" was also the calligraphic work of Jing. These machinations proved to be a masterful business tactic. Since the Eight Immortals reincarnating as miserable beggars to test human compassion was an enduring common folk belief, the priest's fable just added one more bit of evidence. And Mijie's stewed pork was exceptionally good—to combine the two made a perfect myth.[35]

What was not a myth was that the Lu delicatessen boomed ever since. It is unknown how Lu rewarded the priest for his ingenuity. Mijie, during Chinese New Year and on other festive occasions, as a token of gratitude to her old master for the calligraphy, always offered stewed pork she made to the Jing family. But Lu's benefit from the myth was indeed minor, no more than good business for his little local store. The commercial value the myth generated went much beyond the expectations and imagination of anyone who was involved. Since Lu Gaojian stewed pork had earned a phenomenal reputation and since at the time there was virtually no such concept as patent rights for store names, the name "Lu Gaojian" was liberally used by delicatessens and butcher's shops in Suzhou and elsewhere.[36] By the early twentieth century, Lu Gaojian had become a ubiquitous name for delicatessens. Competition over use of the name led to store signs in many cities that read "True Lu Gaojian," "Original Lu Gaojian," "Old Lu Gaojian," "Senior Lu Gaojian," "Pioneering Lu Gaojian," and so on, each seeking to assure customers that it was not an imitation. In fact, because of the great popularity of these stores, the name "Lu Gaojian" was itself almost equated with "delicatessen" or "butcher's shop." For instance, a standard Shanghai guidebook of 1919 listed twenty-eight delicatessens; among them, twenty-four bore the name "Lu Gaojian."[37] The name was so closely associated with pork that, instead of cursing a person by calling him a "swine," a slang expression was often wielded: "The guy sure is the stuff in Lu Gaojian!"[38] For better or worse, the story about the mysterious beggar who came to test human compassion spread with the fame of the store.

The real attraction of the delicatessen, of course, was not the myth but the food itself. The stew was made of carefully selected pork, flavored with delicate seasonings, and simmered just the right length of time and at just the right temperature. The result was that the pork was sweet and savory, rich but not greasy, and delicious. For a sophisticated gourmet or for an average customer, the Tieguai Li story provided an intriguing "cultural flavor" to the fine dish.[39] Nevertheless, the fact that the story of the sick almsman was not dismissed from the cultivated tradition of Chinese cuisine suggests that mendicancy had a comfortable niche in Chinese culture. Indeed, Lu Gaojian stewed pork is not the only Chinese food that has a beggar-related story to tell. There are a few other famous Chinese dishes that also have "patents" belonging to beggars. All are inventions that stemmed from a particular circumstance that in effect only vagabonds would encounter.

For instance, "bamboo rice" (*zhutong fan*, rice steamed inside a freshly cut length of bamboo), was regarded as a typical "beggar food," although it was actually served in restaurants. Since beggars often lacked cooking utensils, they sometimes put uncooked rice and water inside a fresh bamboo joint, which was easy to get for free in most parts of China, and tossed the bamboo container on a bonfire. Once cooked, the steamed rice has the delicate natural fragrance of fresh bamboo. Another Chinese dish, "fish in a green bamboo tube" (*qingtongyu*), was cooked in the same manner, just that the rice was replaced with a whole fish. This dish, however, requires more delicate timing and adjustment of the fire to assure that the fish is baked just right: ideally, the fish skin turns to light golden brown while the flesh remains tender and white. A fish so prepared is creamy, juicy, and smells like it has been cooked with fresh bamboo sprouts, a favorite ingredient of Chinese cuisine. Qingtongyu, after much elaboration, was said to be on the menu of the Qing imperial court and it was a chef d'oeuvre of an emperor's cook. As the case may be, it certainly survived the Qing dynasty. One piece of evidence was that, by the middle of the twentieth century, Huang Jinglin, a well-known chef in Sichuan, had turned fish in a green bamboo tube into the house special at Auntie's Banquet (Gugu yan), an upscale restaurant in Chengdu.[40]

The famous Fujian dish with a bewildering name, "Buddha jumps over the wall" (*Fotiaoqiang*), is associated with a number of legends as far as its origin is concerned, but it was best known as a dish created by beggars. Legend has it that once upon a time outside a Buddhist monastery in Fuzhou, the capital of Fujian Province, a few beggars sat on the ground, leaning against the monastery wall and having their supper in the twilight. They put all the food they had obtained for the day in an earthenware pot and boiled it on a bonfire, much like making hobo soup in a backyard. They had had good luck that day: most of the food they got consisted of different kinds of meats and they had a half bottle of rice wine, which they poured into the pot. The food sent a delicious and inviting aroma over the wall to the temple hall where a group of monks were having their daily evening meditation. The aroma was so tempting that the monks could no longer immerse themselves in spirituality. In fact they were so desperately eager for the food that they "jumped over the wall" to share the dish with the vagabonds. That the monks would not hesitate to break the rigid Buddhist commandment of vegetarianism to taste the beggars' meal that was made mostly of meat demonstrates how wonderful the dish was, hence the name. "Buddha jumps over the wall" is, of course, much more than just hobo soup. It requires an enormous amount of effort to cook, which sometimes involves a couple of days, and contains as many as thirty main ingredients and a dozen condiments. In addition to chicken, duck, and pork as the essential elements, the ingredients include such things shark's fin, fish lips, sea cucumber, fish stomach, pork tendon, pork stomach, duck gizzard, and so on.[41] The dish remains one of the "flagship dishes" of Fujian cuisine (one of the major branches of Chinese cuisine) and, as a vestige of its vagrant origin, authentic Buddha jumps over the wall must be served in an earthenware crock.[42]

But the best-known Chinese delicacy associated with mendicancy is simply called "Beggar's chicken" (*jiaohua ji*), originally a local specialty of Changsu, Jiangsu Province, but now it is on the menu of some of the best restaurants nationwide. The name comes from a story of a beggar who was wandering about in a little town at the foot of Mount Yu in Changsu on the eve of the Chinese New Year. Every household in the town was preparing for the holiday, while the beggar, walking from under the eaves of a local temple where he had taken shelter, only starved. No one cared about him and he knew he was a nuisance in the bustle of the preparations for the New Year's festivities. He then saw a woman carrying a slaughtered chicken and walking with a little girl toward a stream. In this foothill town, nature had bestowed a ready water supply in the form of streams running down Mount Yu. Apparently, the woman was going to wash the chicken while babysitting the girl. The child, probably excited by being out of the house, suddenly dashed for the stream. The woman was panic-stricken that the little girl might fall into the water so she dropped the chicken on a roadside flagstone and ran after her. The beggar, seeing this as an opportunity from heaven, swiftly made off with the chicken. He was in such a hurry that he tripped down on a muddy hollow and lost one of his worn-out shoes, but he kept running until he felt safe with his prey. However, when he finally reached the temple, he looked at the plump chicken and realized that he now faced an obvious dilemma: he could not eat a raw chicken but he had absolutely nothing to cook it in; he did not even have a way to remove the feathers. Looking at his muddy feet, the beggar suddenly had an idea. He quickly wrapped the chicken in a thick layer of mud and went back to the temple where the incense burner still had some embers, with which he managed to start a bonfire in the backyard of the temple. He then placed the muddy ball—the chicken—on the fire. About two hours later the miry stuff had turned to a rough piece of earthenware. The hungry man could no longer wait and he simple dropped the earthenware ball heavily on the ground. As the clay smashed open it pulled the feathers from the bird. To the beggar's delight, the chicken had cooked to glorious tenderness, basting in its own juices.[43]

The historical part of the tale, like many beggar-related stories in China, elaborately connects mendicancy with aristocracy. Weng Tonghe (1830–1904), the Grand Imperial Tutor for Emperor Guangxu (reigned 1875–1908) and one of the leading reformers of late nineteenth-century China, was banished from Beijing to his hometown, Changsu, in June 1898. Three months later, on September 21, a court coup led by Empress Dowager Cixi (1835–1908) put the emperor under house arrest and ended the so-called Hundred Days Reform, of which Weng was a principal supporter. As Weng was now ordered to remain in his hometown under the "strict supervision" of local officials, he lived much like a retired gentleman. On that New Year's eve, Weng happened to take a stroll near the Buddhist monastery. He was lured to the temple backyard by the sudden, delicious smell as the beggar had just smashed open the casing. The pauper, thrilled with the delicacy, delightedly offered a piece of his precious food to Weng, quite unaware that the uninvited guest was the famous grand tutor of the emperor. Weng amiably tasted the piece and was amazed by the effect of such a creative cooking method. An experienced gourmet himself, Weng introduced the cooking technique to the nearby Wang Number Four's Restaurant (founded in 1887), of which he was a frequent patron. Among other delicacies on the menu, he particularly liked the restaurant's homemade sweet-scented osmanthus flower wine.[44]

The chicken made at the Wang Number Four's Restaurant under the direction of the grand tutor was, needless to say, much more elaborate than the beggar's rude dish. The cooking was in some way like roasting a turkey in the Western tradition, but more intricate. The process starts with choosing a plump chicken and removing all the viscera. Stuff the chicken with a variety of ingredients, such as fresh pork, shrimp, Cantonese sausage, dried mushrooms, and lilacs and also twelve condiments, including green onions, ginger, salt, cassia bark, cloves, star anise, and soy sauce. Coat the chicken with a thin layer of lard before wrapping it up with fresh lotus leaves. Then coat the wrapped chicken with a thick layer of yellow mud (preferably mud that has been used to seal a jar of the famous Shaoxing rice wine, so that the scent of wine in the mud gradually permeates the chicken). Bake the whole chicken on a pile of slow burning charcoal for about four to six hours. Once it is done, use a hammer to break the mud coating, and serve.[45]

Such a meticulous way of cooking was not unusual in the tradition of Chinese cuisine, but it certainly went beyond what street people could afford. The quintessence of the invention, nevertheless, belongs to the beggar. Thus Grand Tutor Weng, who was a gifted calligrapher, wrote the characters "Beggar's Chicken" on a scroll as a gift for the owner of the restaurant, Wang Number Four, who had the scroll mounted on the wall of his restaurant. Later Wang Number Four's Restaurant moved to the more prosperous city of Suzhou, twenty miles south of Changsu, where it has remained open under the same name to the present day and still has the reputation of making the best beggar's chicken in the country.

Since the dish was usually offered in upscale restaurants, there were some efforts to use one or another alternative name on the menu, so as to avoid the not-so-pleasant word "beggar." There was recourse to "teaching and converting," a homonym of "beggar," and "rich and noble," an antonym, as well as others. But none of them worked well. As a historian and food critic has pointed out, "to name a chicken 'rich and noble' is rather vulgar and in poor taste. Beggars and the 'rich and noble' live in entirely different worlds, but their taste for delicacies is the same. It is nonsense to have another name."[46] No matter what the argument, in the end the original name, beggar's chicken, prevailed.

TURNING THE VULNERABLE INTO THE VALUABLE

Connecting beggars with cuisine reveals the general receptiveness of society to things mendicant. As we shall see, such receptivity went beyond the realm of cuisine. While beggar-related anecdotes provide a cultural flavor to some distinguished Chinese cookery, in a somewhat more critical area, health care, almsmen also played a role. There were a few folk medicines and treatments that were almost exclusively associated with mendicants and vagabonds. For instance, the use of herbs to treat the wounds and poisoning caused by snake bites was seen as a typical "beggar's calling."[47] Furthermore, not only were beggars trusted to treat some particular types of ailments, but they also, according to folk beliefs, possessed certain powers, of which they were unaware, to protect lives. In other words, as a part of the culture of mendicancy, arguably the most vulnerable group in society had been transformed into one of the valuable.

Chinese medicine has a type of herb plaster known as *gaoyao* that is used like a bandage for injuries such as fractures, contusions, and sprains. It may also be applied to certain areas of the body for internal lesions caused by overexertion. Legend has it that in the ancient town of Zhangzhou (Anyang), Henan, a herbalist named Wang, who owned a herb plaster store, one day treated for free a small skin ulcer on the leg of a lame beggar whom he met on the street.[48] However, the plaster did not work as usual and the beggar came back with the sore on his leg worsened, accusing the herbalist of practicing "quack medicine." Wang felt so ashamed and guilty that he let the beggar stay in his home and resolved to cure him at any cost. Strangely, his dog furiously barked at the beggar and would not let him in, and Wang, fearing for the safety of his patient, killed the dog. Wang then went out to pawn his precious belongings in order to purchase expensive herbs for the beggar. When he returned home with the medicines he saw the beggar was barbecuing the dog meat and enjoying a meal. The beggar put a handful of herbs on his sore and then covered it with a piece of hot dog skin. As he removed the dog skin, his ulcer was miraculously cured, leaving only a pinkish scar. A few seconds later, the beggar disappeared, and instantly Wang realized that the beggar was an incarnation of Tieguai Li, who had descended to earth to inspire him to make an excellent herb plaster. To this day, colloquially herb plasters are still called "dog-skin plasters," although no plasters have ever been made of dog skin; and it is said that because the beggar had accused Wang of quack medicine, in slang the phrase "dog-skin plaster" is also a synonym for "fake" or "quack."[49]

The more credible business history of a traditional pharmacy also points to a connection with beggars. The Yizheng Plaster brand of herb plasters from the Yizheng Pharmacy in Zhenjiang, Jiangsu, has been one of China's best known. The Yizheng Pharmacy, founded in 1622 and still open at its original site on Fifth Street, is probably the oldest surviving pharmacy in China. Its plasters had a reputation as a "miraculous panacea" and remain popular in China and in Southeast Asia to the present day.

The founder of the pharmacy, Tang Shouyi, was born into a poor family in Henan Province, on the banks of the Yellow River. When the river flooded around 1660, the family was forced to leave their home. They settled in Zhenjiang, then a prosperous town on the southern banks of the Yangzi River. The young Tang worked as an apprentice at the Mao Zhaosheng Cotton Cloth Store on Fifth Street. He could have remained an obscure shop assistant all his life had not an old beggar changed his life. According to the Tang family history, soon after Tang started working a beggar came to the store asking for alms and Tang, an apprentice with limited means himself, was the only person who gave him a few copper coins. Perhaps his childhood experience of having to flee the flooded Yellow River made him sympathetic to the poor. In any case, Tang never failed to give alms to the old man, as he came back quite often after Tang's first charity. One day, the old beggar came again and he pulled out a piece of paper from a packet inside his shirt and said: "This is a secret recipe for making herb plasters. I hand this to you and would like you to very carefully follow the instructions and make a medicine that will benefit people."

The almsman left without another word and never appeared again. The curious apprentice started to make plasters following the recipe. It was not an easy task, for the recipe listed more than eighty different types of herbs, vegetable oils (primarily sesame oil), and cinnabar. However, when the first bunch of plasters was made, they were put on the counter free for those who needed them as a gift from the store. These soon proved to be effective and the word spread in the town and its vicinity. Later, because there was a big demand, the cotton cloth store could not afford to give them away, but instead began to sell them at cost. Eventually, Tang decided to quit his job to run his own herb plaster business. Tang opened his store on Fifth Street, and later passed it down to his offspring. In 1723, both the pharmacy and the plaster were named "Yizheng," a coined word consisting of characters meaning "faithfulness and integrity." The mysterious beggar who gave the recipe, now kept as a family secret, became a legend.

The reputation of this local folk medicine began to spread to the national level early in the eighteenth century. This was related to the Qing government's project of dredging the Yellow River and its numerous tributaries that had become silted up. Hundreds of thousands of laborers and soldiers worked on the banks of the Yellow River and connecting waterways. Injuries and lesions were common, but numerous workers found a cure in the Yizheng plasters. The plaster consisted of a small square of thick blue cotton cloth with a dark brown pad containing medicine in the middle. Applying the plaster to the right acupuncture points (*xuewei*) also strengthened feeble bodies. The cures were often quite dramatic and complete. This of course greatly contributed to the labor-intensive waterway project. In 1711, Chen Pengnian, the director general of the Yellow River Administration, issued an award to the Yizheng Pharmacy, citing the third-century work *The Biographies of Immortals* to praise the Yizheng plasters as a deity-bestowed medicine.[50] Apparently, the mysterious beggar story had been reported to the director general.

Unlike Lu Gaojian, the Tang family never romanticized the beggar as a deity incarnation. But the director general's praise boosted the plasters and, like the Lu Gaojian delicatessen, imitation and counterfeiting followed. The Tang family, however, was tough on counterfeiters and fought against fakes for nearly two centuries. At least seven lawsuits over counterfeit Yizheng plasters were recorded during the period from 1715 to 1889. Probably because faking medicine was no laughing matter and the recipe of the Tang family was unique, which made it easy to identify counterfeit products, the authorities always sided with the Yizheng Pharmacy. In 1869, the county magistrate Wang Kunhuo, authorized by the imperial court in Beijing, granted the store a stone tablet to "permanently ban counterfeiting of Yizheng plasters." The tablet was erected in front of the store and remains at the site to the present day.

The store reached its peak during the Guangxu period (1874–1908) when Tang Elou, an eighth-generation descendant of Tang Shouyi, was in charge. To further combat counterfeiting, Tang Elou had his own portrait registered as a trademark with the Ministry of Industry and Commerce. Tang's portrait was printed on the plaster boxes and remained a prominent symbol of the medicine until it was removed in 1967. The best of the plasters, which were classified into a few types based on their quality, was such a treasure that, elegantly boxed, it was used as an article of tribute to the imperial court and aristocrats, as well as a favored wedding or birthday gift. By the Republican period, prior to 1937, when Zhenjiang was occupied by the Japanese, the pharmacy had developed into a virtual factory, employing about sixty pharmacists, who tended more than thirty huge woks that "slow cooked" (*ao*) the paste that was used to fill the plaster pad.

The beggar's legacy lived on. Although the Tang family did not claim the beggar to be a deity and the official history of the pharmacy quite cautiously referred to him as an "unusual person" (*yiren*), the image of the beggar was clearly associated with various myths similar to that of Lu Gaojian's stewed pork. In any case, the Tang family contributed to charities in memory of their ancestor, Tang Shouyi, and the family's benefactor, the nameless beggar. The pharmacy often placed a gigantic wooden bucket in front of the door full of free porridge for the poor, like a mini soup kitchen. The plasters at the beginning were all made of blue cotton cloth. From the middle of the eighteenth century, the pharmacy began to use red cotton cloth for their plasters, but still produced the blue plasters, which were now exclusively for charity.

When the Communists took over China in 1949, the store had passed on to the tenth generation. In 1956, in the Socialist Collectivilization campaign, which aimed to eliminate private ownership in business and commerce, the owners, the brothers Tang Jian and Tang Jun, submitted the age-old secret recipe of the plaster to the government and the pharmacy was integrated into the state-owned Zhenjiang Pharmacy. The Yizheng plasters survived the Cultural Revolution era and remain popular. Understandably, the nearly four centuries of continuous history of this pharmacy have made it into a tourist attraction.[51]

These successful businesses were all sparked by a mysterious beggar. Given the widespread assumption that able men hid themselves among vagrants—or unfortunately sank to that low rank—few people questioned the authenticity of the beggar stories. Even the obvious myths, such as those of Lu Gaojian's pork and the Zhangzhou dog plaster, were taken by many as credible. Of course, miracles have always captured the imagination and fascinated people. In this regard, mendicants seemed to have held a particular appeal for the common people of China. In his autobiography, the writer Xiao Qian (1910–99) tells how a beggar turned into a living god. As a child, Xiao lived in poverty: his father died a few months before he was born and his mother passed away when he was ten. Raised by his elder cousins in the Dongzhi Gate area in northeast Beijing, he became acquainted with witchdoctors and beggars in the neighborhood. When he was in elementary school there came a beggar who suddenly started ranting in a dilapidated temple just outside Dongzhi Gate and claimed that the temple's deity had been reborn into his body. The news spread far and wide. One of Xiao's cousins, Number Three, who was ten years his senior, was unemployed at the time and was desperate to worship any god who might get him reemployed. So he took Xiao with him and went to the temple to pay homage to the beggar-deity. Xiao vividly recalled the trip:

> The temple was tiny and previously had been quite off the beaten track. Now its gable ends were covered with red and yellow banners bearing solemn phrases like "If your belief in him is sincere, he will be efficacious," followed by the names of pious donors. We had to force our way through a huge crowd before we could reverently approach the great censer in the main entrance hall. Only after performing many deep kowtows were we fit to enter the throne room beyond, where the beggar was lazily reclining on a *kang* [brick bed]. I was certain that he'd never had a bath in his life, for his skin was earth-colored and greasy.
>
> My cousin gave me a nudge, making me kneel down with him as he presented the box of cakes he had brought as his humble offering. I admired the beggar for his calm effrontery. Hardly bothering to look up, he lifted his dirty hand, broke off a piece of the apple he was eating and bestowed it upon my cousin, who accepted it as if it were a great treasure. Then he implored the beggar to intercede for him with the Bodhisattvas, so that he might find work again. He waited. The beggar god gave us an enigmatic grunt. We stood up and departed. At least my cousin treasured that piece of apple stained with the beggar's saliva too much to allow me to share it with him, for which I was very grateful.[52]

This sort of satirical tone permeates Xiao's memoir. Growing up under the omnipresent influence of Chinese folk superstitions (as a little boy he used to sleep with his aunt who was a witchdoctor) and having received almost all his formal education in fundamentalist Christian missionary schools, Xiao turned out to be an atheist.[53] But this atheist's account of a spurious deity reveals just how popular beggar-gods were among the common people. And that people put their faith in a "divine" mendicant, which was by no mean uncommon in China, shows how beggars had stimulated the public's imagination.

Partly influenced by the Buddhist concept of reincarnation, Chinese folklore had it that in one's lifetime one had a limited amount of good fortune, the amount decided by one's fate or, in the Buddhist notion, one's karma. Abusing one's good fortune (*zuofu*) would deplete one's designated "storehouse of fortune" quickly and could lead to disaster. By the same token, through suffering one may accumulate some "fortune credits" and offset bad luck in the future. Furthermore, a person who has endured great suffering may have developed the kind of "hard fate" that can safeguard the fortune of other, average people. Beggars, being utterly destitute and unfortunate individuals, fit the bill perfectly. Therefore, being a beggar—in other words, surviving misfortune and enduring poverty—could gain some commercial value. In a way, poverty could become a commodity to sell.

There was a widespread folkway in China in which people voluntarily associated themselves with mendicancy and poverty, in the belief that this was a way to cure disease, protect life, or achieve longevity—even if it worked only psychologically. The following account draws evidence from the vast areas along the Yangzi River, the 3,500-mile-long waterway that stretches from the Tibetan highland to its outlet on the Pacific near Shanghai and has hundreds of millions of inhabitants in its valleys, to demonstrate that these folk customs held sway in many geographically and culturally diverse regions.

In Chongming, China's third largest island, at the mouth of the Yangzi River, a folk custom, practiced mostly among women, was put into play when someone saw a mouse slip and fall from a high place, say, a roof beam. This was a bad omen that presaged the death of a family member or another disaster. To avert this, one must go door-to-door begging rice from nearby farmers. Back home, the whole family would eat the begged "hundred households' rice" to offset the omen and prevent a disaster. Even a woman from a wealthy family would disguise herself as a vagrant and beg for rice if she happened to see a mouse fall.[54]

In Ji'an, a major county in central Jiangxi Province, following an old custom, when a bride rode a sedan chair to the groom's house for the wedding ceremony she had to wear a ragged and filthy coat borrowed from a beggar, who was usually hired as a trumpeter for the occasion. This must have been an unpleasant trip for the bride, for she was confined in an enclosed sedan chair; the air was stuffy enough already, and now she was compelled to breathe the foul odor of the beggar's coat. Moreover, she had to be careful about not contaminating her formal attire, the precious red garment with golden embroidery that she wore underneath the beggar's coat. Few people could explain the rationale behind the custom, but that did not stop them from following it.[55] Obviously, the beggar's coat was a symbol of protection for a woman entering a new stage in her life. From the believers' point of view, the short ordeal in the sedan chair was worth a lifetime of happiness for the bride.

The custom of having beggars as a "foster parents" was also derived from the notion that poverty may be protective. The average life expectancy in early twentieth-century China was around forty years.[56] Premature death, even among middle-class families, was common, and a couple who were able to raise all their children to adulthood could be considered lucky. A high rate of infant mortality and suffering throughout life contributed to the superstition that if a person with a "tough fate" adopts a child, it could protect the child.[57] Thus beggars were ideal adoptive parents: the fact that they suffered the misery of mendicancy but still survived made them ideal "protectors." Aged and experienced beggars were particularly valued in this regard. Thus it was popular to have a beggar, known as a *baobao* or "protector," as a nominal father or mother for a child.[58] For instance, a wealthy Cantonese who sojourned in Shanghai in the late nineteenth century had his first son in his late fifties. Worried about the future of his precious only son, the man picked up an old beggar on the street to be the boy's foster father (Figure 8). The explicit rationale for this "charity" was that the old beggar's "fate" was tough enough to endure many misfortunes and thus it could protect the child.[59] This old beggar was sure to feel fortunate for the encounter, but his luck was dwarfed by some aged almsmen who had not just one but a bunch of foster sons. In Shifang, Sichuan, a county seat about thirty miles north of the provincial capital of Chengdu, there was a beggar who, since his fiftieth birthday, had been a "protector" for numerous children. As he reached the age of eighty in the late 1940s, he had so many nominal children that they jointly hosted a lavish birthday party—the invited guests filled up several dozen banquet tables—in honor of the old man. As was customary, the beggar also received from the guests a handsome number of red envelopes, each containing cash.[60]

A similar case was found in the port city of Quanzhou, in the province of Fujian. By all accounts Blind Dan was a very unfortunate person, having lost his sight because of glaucoma and having legs so terribly crooked that he could not stand up. He walked by using his hands and scooting along on his bottom. Yet he seemed intelligent and eloquent, for he often sat in front of Tonghuaidi, a local Taoist temple, explaining the hidden messages in the poems people drew from the temple, a type of fortune-telling. Ironically, his misfortune brought him some good luck, that is, people in the town liked to have him as foster father for their small children. The rite of the adoption was simple. Blind Dan would bless the child by touching his head and the parents thereafter were supposed to send Blind Dan a gift on holidays and give him a treat on the child's birthday. By the late 1940s, Blind Dan managed to gain his independence from the local beggars' guild he had once belonged to, because by that time he had more than 300 foster sons in town on whom he could depend. He remembered the birthday of each and every foster son, and on that day he would hire a pedicab to go to the family to receive his treat. Blind Dan lived to the 1950s and died at the age of ninety.

FIGURE 8. An old beggar is invited into the home of a wealthy family to be the "godfather" of a newborn baby. Note that he is honored with abundant food and wine, while his begging paraphernalia, a bamboo basket and a stick, have been left on the doorstep. SOURCE: *Dianshizhai huabao* (The Dianshi Study pictorial).

He was nevertheless seen as a beggar to the very end, an identity in the minds of these families that was precisely his value. Once he died, gone was his power: none of his numerous foster sons showed up for his funeral.[61]

Compared to these apathetic "sons," the renowned Chinese writer Shen Congwen (1902–88) was affectionate to his vagrant foster father. Shen recalled that in his childhood he suffered malnutrition caused by digestive disturbances. His parents tried many folk medicines, but none worked well. According to a folk belief in his hometown in western Hunan Province in the middle Yangzi River valley, any illness that could not be cured by medicine was a matter of fate. To counteract fate, Shen's family found him a nominal father who had roamed the country most of his life. Although at the time the man was settled in town and indeed had a herb shop right on the bridge across the Xiang River, a branch of the Yangzi, he was regarded as a vagabond of sorts, hence, in the eyes of Shen's parents, he qualified for foster fatherhood. The illiterate man was a fortune-teller, folk herbalist, and martial arts practitioner, all of which were typically associated with vagrancy and mendicancy. Shen recollected, with wry amusement, that because of his nominal father, from the age of six, he took more then a hundred different sorts of herb medicines and for an entire two-year period he ate chicken livers as a treatment for his ailment.[62]

But foster parenthood and its like could be more casual than in the cases mentioned above. It was just a matter of psychological comfort for those who had few means of dealing with an uncertain and often disaster-ridden life, and there were plenty of such people in the chaotic society of modern China. In the early 1940s in the streets of Chengdu people often saw a middle-aged man pulling a rickshaw on which sat an old woman who took advantage of her advanced age to beg. As they rolled through a busy street, the man off and on stopped the rickshaw and introduced the old woman as his nominal mother. At the same time, the old woman murmured: "The year of Daoguang Dingwei, let me connect you gentlemen with longevity; I am 103 years old, let me connect you gentlemen with longevity." She had bound-feet, her hair was completely white, and so-called longevity freckles dotted her face. Judging from their accent, the pair were not local people. The year of Daoguang Dingwei by the Chinese dynastic calendar was 1847; if this was truly the year of her birth, she should have been ninety-three years old in 1940. Although the woman might have added a decade to her age in order to market her seniority, she did look like the "goddess of longevity" in Chinese folklore. Regardless, such an old beggar woman exactly fit the folk belief that aged and much experienced vagrants were protective of the vulnerable, especially children. Thus most of her benefactors (or rather, customers) were young mothers who gave some cash to the "goddess of longevity" in exchange for her blessing their children. Upon receiving the alms from a mother, the old woman would tie a red string on the child's wrist, which was believed to have the power to help drive away illness and bad luck. She also served as a pediatrician of sorts, treating some minor ailments by offering her incantations on the street.

"I myself and many other children were her patients," a local resident recalled. "But even we children were suspicious about her ability to effect cures, because all she did was to pinch us right under the nose with her long and dark fingers and murmur a few words that did not make any sense to us: 'pinch gold-gold, pinch gold-gold,' and that was it!" Nonsense it might be, but she had her market, for she continued to appear on Chengdu's streets well into the 1940s.[63]

Poverty Justified

Except for some cynics or eccentrics who may despise the conventional social value of financial well-being, few people in the world would be happy living in poverty, much less be proud of it. However, for beggars who lived with sheer indigence day and night, the reality of poverty was something they had to respond to with a certain level of equanimity and calm.

ADVERTISING POVERTY

On the one hand, in private most paupers understood that anxiety and anger over living in poverty would not do them any good. Many of them adopted an attitude like that exemplified in the saying, "If you have wine today, get drunk now" (*jinzhao youjiu jinzhao zui*). A beggar's ditty reflects this attitude:

> Carefree and without a job,
> Kowtowing to no deities but to the bamboo stick.
> Never worrying about being robbed,
> [Because we] have no money, only our stomach.[64]

On the other hand, in public beggars had to display their poverty and neediness as much as possible in order to arouse sympathy. As always, beggars were eager to demonstrate their penury and misery to potential almsgivers—to such an extent that they seemed proud of being poor. In fact, the ability to effectively advertise poverty was taken as an essential quality for leadership among beggars, as the following story that circulated in Sichuan about the succession of a beggar ringleader reveals. An aged beggar head was going to pass his "office" on to one of his three best disciples. He therefore called them to his presence and lectured them sententiously: "In eating our kind of bowl of rice [that is, in our calling], the keyword is 'poverty.' You folks each compose a poem on poverty, and I shall pass my power to the one who best describes the poor conditions in which we live." The most senior of the three stepped forward first and uttered some doggerel:

> All the food I have is inside my stomach,
> All the clothes I have are on my body,
> Living in a "bridge mansion" [that is, living under a bridge],
> Sleeping on an eight-legged bed [that is, sleeping on two benches].

The old headman frowned: "You have food and clothing, you have a home and a bed—you are not poor." So the senior fellow was out. The second disciple knew he had to make the life of beggars sound worse:

> My clothes are inside my stomach [meaning, he has sold his clothes for
>   food],

My food is on my body [meaning, he will sell his remaining clothes for
    food],
My clothes are my bed quilt,
My clothes are my bed sheet.

Again, the old beggar shook his head: "How come all these clothes? You can
almost open a tailor shop—this is not poverty." Now it was the turn of the
youngest disciple, a quick-witted fellow, who depicted a beggar's life in these
words:

I wear the "clothes of a thousand families,"
I eat the "grains of ten thousand households,"
I sleep on my backbone,
covered only by the skin of my belly.

It would be hard to outdo this description of a street pauper: How can a person be more impoverished than surviving entirely on food and clothing
begged from "thousands of families" and sleeping with no covering at all?
The youngest beggar succeeded to the chieftainship.[65]

This fable-like story quite faithfully reveals the beggars' strategy: the
poorer, the better; the more one can sell one's poverty to the public and
stimulate compassion, the better the chances for obtaining alms. But Chinese mendicants were more philosophical than this. Over the years they had
developed a moral logic that went beyond simple utilitarian strategies of
begging. They asked the fundamental question: How should we justify our
"right" to beg in public? Or, to put it in a more social–scientific way: Why
should society bear the obligation or even the responsibility of helping the
destitute? Behind this simple and plain question were the classic issues of
class, stratification, and social inequality. Chinese beggars as a group were
not among the educated, nor were they, even in modern times, actively mo-
tivated by social theories or Communist activists. Yet their answer to this
question bears some striking similarities to the Marxist notion of class and
class exploitation. This is reflected in an extremely widespread story, which
has a few slightly different versions, about Confucius borrowing food grain
from Fan Dan, also known as Fan Ran (112–85), a sage at the end of the
Eastern Han dynasty who was known for his unfailing integrity despite living in poverty.

COLLECTING ANCESTORS' DEBTS

Fan Dan lived in the seclusion of a straw hut surrounded by a fence of forty-
eight sorghum stalks. When Confucius and his disciples ran out of food in
the state of Chen, Confucius sent one of his foremost disciples, Zilu, to borrow some grain from Fan Dan. The sage received Zilu in his straw hut with

all due courtesy, and then said: "I have a couple of questions for you, and you must give the right answers before I can lend you any food. Here are the questions: In this world, what exists in abundance and what is scarce? What makes people happy and what annoys them?" Zilu halted and was unable to answer. As he returned home empty handed, Confucius asked his very best student, Yan Hui, to go and try. When Yan Hui stepped into Fan's hut, the recluse asked him the same questions. Being well prepared, Yan Hui answered with confidence: "In this world, human beings are abundant, but upright persons are scarce. Being able to get a loan makes people happy, being asked to return the loan makes people annoyed." Pleased with Yan Hui's response, Fan lent him rice and wheat and put the grain in two sacks made of goose feathers. Yan Hui brought the food to Confucius, and as he emptied the two bags, grain fell to the ground and magically soon two little hills of rice and wheat appeared where the grain had fallen, much more than what the sacks had contained. Confucius and his disciples thus had abundant food to tide them over the famine.

Obviously, Yan Hui's answer involved a cynical and witty criticism of human nature and the inconstancy of human relationships. The ideas it conveyed may be little more than conventional wisdom, but that the fable had Yan Hui, one of China's most prominent sages, vocalize these sentiments indicated that this was regarded, at least among beggars, as a sagely sizing up of human society. Indeed in a slightly different version of the story Yan Hui initially answered "a wedding makes people happy, a funeral makes people annoyed." It was Confucius who tutored Yan Hui on what to say, which further elevated the authority of the response.[66]

From here the story had two versions, both of which justified mendicancy. One version has it that, later, Confucius went in person to Fan Dan's hut to thank him for his generosity. When Confucius asked how he might return the favor, Fan Dan replied, in a rather patronizing manner: "Let my disciples in future generations go door-to-door to your disciples' homes to collect the debts." The other version relates that immediately after receiving the much-needed food, Confucius wrote a few words on a pair of bamboo slips and sent Yan Hui to give them to Fan Dan. On the bamboo slips Confucius wrote a poem:

> Fan Dan has lent us grain,
> It is Confucius's responsibility to pay back the debts in the future.
> Please wait in front of the households that have antithetical couplets;
> No single family should treat you with contempt.[67]

Antithetical couplets—written with a brush on a pair of red paper slips or wooden boards—are typical door decorations of the educated elite, and thus they were a symbol of, as in the story, the "disciples of Confucius." But the Confucian literary tradition was so widespread and deeply rooted in Chinese society that placing antithetical couplets on the door was a custom not only of the educated, but also of average households. For the latter, putting a new pair of antithetical couplets on the doorway was a must—almost like a ritual—during the Chinese New Year and other festival occasions (such as weddings). Thus in Confucius's poem, "households that have antithetical couplets" means countless ordinary homes.

This story has no historical foundation whatsoever, for Confucius and Fan Dan lived at least eight centuries apart. But, as in any culture, the importance of any fable lies not in whether it is based on fact but rather in the social mentality that created it and contributed to its circulation. In the tale here, we see a society clearly divided into two: the world of the subalterns and the world of "decent" society. Given the status of Confucius as China's "crowned saint" and Confucianism as the official orthodoxy that dominated the values and social norms of traditional China for two millennia, the Confucianists in this story represent not only the elite but also the normal society that beggars encountered daily. By the same token, Fan Dan represents the unorthodox, disadvantaged, and neglected who seek justice, vindication, and integrity in the Confucian-dominated world. By portraying the Confucianists as the beneficiaries, beggars have cleverly turned general society into debtors. Here mendicancy is no longer a humble act of begging but a justified request for the return of an overdue debt that society owed mendicants for generations. This rationale of "collecting ancestors' debts," simple and unadorned as it is, may presage the Marxist theory that the proletariat has the birthright to seek the return of the "surplus value" that has been expropriated by the modern capitalist class. Such a mentality may also be reflected in the thinking among some disadvantaged social groups in the contemporary world.

Fan Dan was a rather obscure figure, known only for living in poverty, but he kept his integrity. According to an official biography, during the reign of Emperor Huan (147–67), Fan Dan was appointed the magistrate of Laiwu, a county about sixty miles northeast of Confucius's hometown, Qufu. Fan Dan did not take the office since he was mourning for his deceased mother at the time. He served as a fortune-teller in marketplaces for a while, but this vocation was soon banned by the authorities. For more than a decade he wandered along with his wife and children, but no matter what adversity he faced, he never compromised his integrity.[68] Unlike Han Xin and Wu Zixu, who were heroes in numerous types of popular literature and dramas and therefore widely known among the common people for centuries, Fan Dan was the type of historical figure that only specialists would encounter in the course of research. As is true of virtually all folktales associated with mendicancy, the author of this fable is unknown, but it may well be that some members of the literati who were down and out, or possibly even became beggars themselves, fabricated the tale to air their grievances over social injustice. Or, perhaps some little-educated but creative vagrants invented the story, possibly inspired by an already existing oral tradition.

No matter who should be credited with the authorship, there is no doubt that the tale was immensely popular among Chinese beggars and was passed on generation after generation all over China. For the destitute, the idea that society owes them a debt was enormously appealing. The poem attributed to Confucius was the basis of a variety of songs that were sung by mendicants when they were begging in front of "households that have antithetical couplets."[69] The story also contains an allusion to two common practices in mendicancy. One was that as mendicants sang begging ditties they usually tapped a pair of bamboo slips to make a loud clapping sound to mark the rhythm of the song. The origin of these bamboo slips, it was said, lay in the ones on which Confucius wrote the poem for Fan Dan. The other was that, in a more elaborate version of the story, Fan Dan asked how his disciples could collect the debts from the "households that have antithetical couplets" since these residences usually had a watchdog guarding the door. Confucius, who was inwardly angered by the question, replied: "Bring a stick to beat the dog!"

Thus, as it has been interpreted, the typical beggar in China always had his trademark stick, known as a "dog beating rod" (*dagoubang*), in hand.[70]

CHAPTER 4

Coping with Mendicants

THE QING GOVERNMENT attempted to cope with street beggars in three ways. First, at the beginning of the dynasty, it established numerous county poorhouses and seasonal soup kitchens for the poor. Second, from the eighteenth century on, it planned to put beggars into the *baojia* neighborhood mutual responsibility system. The government issued detailed regulations to have all street beggars registered at the county yamen and placed under the supervision of beggar heads. But governmental charities were always insufficient and the baojia system was largely impractical. A third and much more effective measure was simply to endorse a grassroots institution that emerged over the centuries: beggars' self-regulated and guild-like organizations.

Regulating Beggars in the Baojia System?

The plan for putting street people into the baojia community mutual responsibility system was intended to control beggars and prevent potential social unrest caused by drifters. In 1777, the Ministry of Punishment discussed the issue of street beggars and made a plan that called for the "strict supervision" of young and able-bodied beggars by beggar heads who would be responsible for any wrongdoings of their inferiors.[1] To carry out the plan, the ministry designed a three-section registration booklet that was to be distributed among local beggar heads. The first section, the cover of the booklet, included three items: the name of the beggar head, the names of the neighborhoods (*fang*) under his supervision, and the total number of beggars in each of these neighborhoods. The second section, which constituted the bulk of the booklet, contained files on each neighborhood. Each file started with the total number of beggars in the neighborhood, and then provided information on each beggar in that area:

Name:
Age:
Native place:
Nature of beard (in three categories: no beard, has beard, and has a little beard):
With or without family:
Whether or not handicapped:
Current address or dwelling (give the name of the ancient temple or wayside pavilion where the beggar regularly resides):
Any criminal record:
Any recent involvement in banditry or robbery:

The third and concluding section provided the date of the file and recorded personnel changes in the beggar head's territory: the number of beggars under his supervision in the past, newly accepted beggars during the period (since the last update), and dismissed beggars, as well as the actual number of beggars now under his supervision.[2]

According to the regulations, every registered beggar was to be given a wooden or bamboo plaquette, known as a "waist plaquette" (*yaopai*), to be carried, as its name suggested, on the waist, not unlike the badges or plastic employee identification cards common in industry today (Figure 9). On the front side of the plaquette was an official order reading:

The county magistrate instructs local beggars:
Your type of people are easily mixed with wicked persons and bandits. Now I give each of you a waist plaquette to be carried at all times. If there are any beggars from other places, you should cross-examine them carefully. Report any suspicious person immediately to the beggar head. Do not violate this order. *Sealed.*

The back of the plaquette gave information about the beggar in the following order: name, neighborhood, age, physical features (description of beard and handicaps, if any), the date the plaquette was issued, and its ordinal number. Beggars were supposed to carry the waist plaquette day and night. If a beggar died or left the authorized area, it was the beggar head's responsibility to recover the plaquette.[3]

Little is known about the extent to which these regulations were carried out or, if they were, how successful they were. The Qing government frequently emphasized the importance of the baojia system and the emperor sometimes directly expressed his concern. Yet the system was too idealistic. During the Qing period, the baojia as a whole—not just the part dealing with mendicants—never worked as it was planned and remained largely an example of "Chinese Utopianism."[4] Even the ruling elite, who were re-

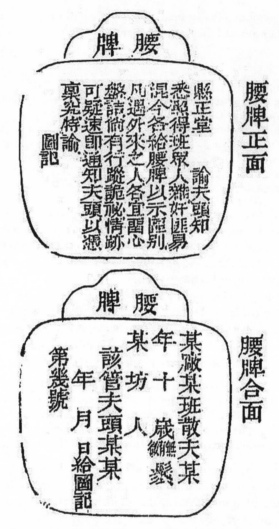

腰牌正面

腰牌

縣正堂　諭夫頭知
悉照得班眾人雜奸逃易
混令各給腰牌以示區別
凡遇外來之人各宜留心
盤詰倘有行蹤詭祕情跡
可疑速即通知夫頭以憑
稟究特諭　劇記

腰牌合面

腰牌

某廠某班散夫某
年　十　歲鬚無鬚
某坊人
該管夫頭某某
年　月　日給圖記
第幾號

FIGURE 9. A sample beggar's "waist plaquette," showing both the front (upper sketch) and back (lower sketch) sides. SOURCE: Xu Dong and Ding Richang, *Bao-jiashu jiyao* (The essence of the *Book of the Baojia System*) (1871).

sponsible for implementing the system, did not have full confidence in it.[5] The state intended the system to become a controlling mechanism for checking up on essentially the urban population. Street beggars were part of that target population, but they were perhaps the last group the state was actually able to reach. If most of the time the baojia remained merely a blueprint in settled and stable neighborhoods, it was doubtful it could have been made to work among vagrants, who by the nature of their livelihood and lifestyle were usually unstable, unrooted, and, therefore, unruly.

But the baojia regulations on beggars did reveal an intention to contain street people. As was patently clear in these regulations, the intent of the government was to prevent vagrants from other areas mixing with local professional beggars. As part of the baojia policy that had been reaffirmed on various occasions, the eighteenth-century regulations were included in a handbook providing guidelines on the baojia system compiled by two high-ranking officials in 1863. This booklet was an indication that, in theory at least, these regulations were still valid in the late Qing.

Although the baojia rules on beggars may not have been truly implemented, they were not issued entirely in vain. By the nineteenth and early twentieth centuries, it was common for professional beggars to be organized under a ringleader who had connections with the local government, a practice that reflected certain of the thinking behind the baojia system. The headman was either officially appointed by the county magistrate or his power over local beggars was a fait accompli that the officials had acknowledged. In either case, the beggar head was responsible to the local government for his group's good behavior, which included primarily not violating the rules of begging in designated areas and on designated dates. Punishment for minor offensives committed by beggars—such as stealing, fighting, and harassing—was also within his authority. In return, the beggar head received a certain amount of government funds to run the local poorhouse or soup kitchen. But the most substantial support from the authorities was their acquiescence to the beggar head collecting a lump sum of cash alms from the stores (and in some cases also residences) in town on certain dates, a system in due course that came to be known as "beggar taxes." The alms collected constituted the basic operating fund for the beggar head and his guild. One may see the shadow of the baojia in this system and in many cases the yamen backed this protection racket to some extent. However, essentially these practices arose not out of a government program, but were inventions of the beggars themselves.[6] By the late nineteenth and early twentieth centuries, such beggars' guilds were ubiquitous in China and had proven to be more successful than the baojia in coping with poverty and street crime.

Poorhouses

Beggar's guilds arose largely because government poorhouses were inadequate. In the eyes of the Chinese state, refugees that appeared suddenly and in large number were a problem that demanded immediate attention. Regular vagrants, however, received only marginal attention or simply did not appear on the official agenda. In a nation that believed it was best to rest content on one's native land, the state had long regarded vagrants as part of the so-called *you* people, or the "bad elements," who were like "bristle-grass in rice fields [that is, weeds]." As long as such people did not cause a major threat to public security, no serious measures were taken either to contain them or help them.[7] The Qing administrative regulations on beggars, including the baojia system and the state poorhouses, therefore, were more for the purpose of preventing refugees from becoming regular beggars than anything else.

In theory, all counties in the Qing had state-funded poorhouses—an institution inherited from previous dynasties—where a handful of vagabonds were sheltered and clothing and food were to be dispensed to the destitute during famines.[8] The variety of names applied to the poorhouses reflects their nature as charities: field of compassion, succoring home, universal granary, and so on. A late seventeenth-century manual for county magistrates states: "Today all the departments and [counties] have their poorhouses (*yang-chi yuan*), where rations of clothing and food are given out, so that the destitute may have proper shelter and nourishment. This is provided by the grace of the imperial court."[9] In reality these poorhouses were only semiofficial and often depended as much on private donations as government funds. Regular or standing shelters for beggars provided by local gentry or wealthy families were common in the Qing.[10] Donations to charities, especially for famine relief, were often employed by upstarts as a means of obtaining imperial degrees, as the practice of degree purchasing had become conventional in the late nineteenth century.[11] The semiofficial nature of the poorhouses allowed them to survive the collapse of the Qing regime and as an institution they continued to operate up to the Communist takeover in the late 1940s. Although almost right from the beginning poorhouses across the country revealed unmistakable signs of mismanagement, they had been operating for centuries by the time of the Communist takeover. The following is a summary constructed from the records of a few county poorhouses.

Ningjin, a county located on the northwestern plain of Shandong, about 200 miles south of Beijing, is proud of its reputation as the "hometown of acrobatics" for producing nationally acclaimed acrobats. But until very recently it was in fact so poor that parents used to send their children to become circus performers at a very young age. Itinerant entertainers, in the eyes of the public, were hardly better than street beggars. Ningjin's poorhouse was established early in the eighteenth century and was renovated in 1896–98. By that time it had three offices and more than twenty rooms where it housed its regular quota of sixty-seven inmates. There was a precise budget. The annual food allowance per person was 3.6 taels, which

works out to barely 0.01 tael per day.[12] This meager support was less a problem than the small number of available spots for the homeless. Ningjin had
a total population of about a quarter million, not counting the usual vagrants
in the area. A quota of sixty-seven could hardly begin to accommodate all
those in need of shelter. Also, while the population of Ningjin increased several fold over the years, the quota remained largely unchanged.[13]

The same problem can be observed in Pingquan, a prefecture in Hebei
about fifty miles north of the Great Wall and 183 miles northeast of Beijing.
The prefecture's main town, also called Pingquan, was developed early in the
eighteenth century as part of the transportation project associated with the
Qing summer palace in Chengde, the largest imperial resort in the country.
At the center of the town, a spring produced a pond several feet deep in
which fish flourished. The town hence earned the name Pingquan (literally,
"Ground Spring"); it became the official name of the town in 1778.

An imperial edict of 1744 allowed refugees from China proper to settle
in areas north of the Great Wall. After that poor peasants from Hebei and
Shandong provinces migrated in large numbers to escape the frequent natural disasters in North China, but a great many of them were still impoverished in the new land. The poorhouse, started in 1759, aimed to cope with
this problem. It was founded by Sima Jialu, the prefectural magistrate, upon
instructions from his superior. Fund-raising among local gentry and well-off
families resulted in 505 taels of silver, which was used as the first endow-
ment. Interest on the fund and other donations yielded an annual budget
of 145 taels for the poorhouse. Luckily, Pingquan was only sixty miles east of
Chengde, where the Qing government's "banner fields" (land reserved for
Manchu aristocrats) were located. Part of that land was set aside to subsidize
the poorhouse; namely, the banner fields provided rice for the poorhouse on
top of its regular budget. This institution therefore could provide relatively
generous support for the poor. Renovation of the poorhouse was undertaken
in 1763, 1801, and 1826. In the final renovation, in 1826, the poorhouse was
rebuilt in brick and stone. According to an official document dated 1826,
each adult inmate received daily 0.8 liters of rice, plus five copper coins in
pocket money; children were given half that amount. Herbal medicines
were provided for the sick and coffins for the dead. The poorhouse also provided a certain amount of traveling expenses for paupers passing through
town.[14] The poorhouse continued to operate until 1948 when Communists
took over Pingquan, at which time it had eight rooms and seventy-two inmates. In a county with a population of over 200,000 (236,619 in 1949) and
with widespread poverty, the poorhouse was obviously overwhelmed.[15]

The inadequate capacity of government poorhouses was a nationwide
problem. If we leave North China and look at the situation in the scenic

town of Guilin in the deep south, we encounter a similar situation. As the capital of Guangxi Province in the Qing period, Guilin had a number of government-sponsored poorhouses. The earliest in the Qing period was initiated by Huang Xingzhen, the lieutenant governor of Guangxi, in 1686. Its annual subsidy was 47.97 *dan* of "original rice," that is, unhusked rice. It was estimated that an average male adult in Qing China consumed about 3.6 dan of unhusked rice a year; thus the house could barely support fourteen persons.[16] In 1714, Governor Chen Yuanlong founded two poorhouses for the elderly. By the Jiaqing reign period (1796–1820), Guilin had four poorhouses, all of which continued to operate until 1949. These were located roughly in the four sections of the town, hence they were known respectively as the East House, the West House, the North House, and the South House. As late as in the 1980s the sites of these poorhouses were still recognizable.[17]

In Republican times, the monthly stipend for the inmates was thirty-two copper coins per person. This was far from enough even for a meager subsistence. The inmates therefore still needed to do something to supplement the stipend. Blind female beggars went out on the street to perform lotus ballad singing to earn a few coppers. More able-bodied inmates turned the poorhouses into small workshops. They picked up or sometimes purchased scrap and waste, such as hog bristles, animal bones, and chicken and duck feathers, with which to make petty items for sale. Hog bristles were used for making brushes, feathers for dusters, and bones were ground down to powder for fertilizer. The South House was relatively well off. It had a section used as a temporary shelter for vagrants and offered a comparatively high monthly stipend: 20 *jin* (22 pounds) of unhusked rice.[18] At any rate, as elsewhere in the country, the main problem with the city's poorhouses was not the meager level of support but that there were simply not enough of them to keep up with the population growth. In 1906, Guilin had about 80,000 residents. Six years later, the population dropped to 30,000 when the provincial capital was moved to Nanning, but the population rebounded rather quickly because of a tide of refugees caused by various wars in the region. By 1940 Guilin was already a city of nearly 200,000, of which more than 24,000 were categorized as "floating population," a term generally applied to vagrants and the like. A huge wave of refuges inundated the city in the early 1940s, expanding the population to more than half a million in 1944.[19] Only one more poorhouse was added to cope with the situation: in 1943 the city authorities added a poorhouse—with a capacity of sixty-three inmates in 1945—to an existing orphanage.[20]

As early as the seventeenth century, many government poorhouses were uninhabitable and the rations of clothing and food were misappropriated by the officials in charge. But this type of charity was in principle for emergencies only and was denied to regular beggars.[21] Government charities were, as has been pointed out, more for the purpose of preventing social unrest than for dealing with humanitarian concerns. A government bulletin stated this clearly. Since documents like this were typically posted at public venues, such as city gates and market places, it caught the eyes of the missionary John Henry Gray (1828–90):

> When at Shanghai, in the winter of 1875, I observed a notification issued by . . . [the] *toutai* [*daotai*, circuit intendant], setting forth that certain houses had been set apart for the reception of homeless wanderers. The vagrants frequenting these houses were, I found, provided with bundles of rice straw, on which they slept, and, twice daily, small quantities of boiled rice were doled out to each inmate. This refuge, I believe, owed its origin, not to any feeling of benevolence of the *toutai*, or of the government which he represented, but to a well-grounded fear that burglaries and other serious offenses might become rife, unless the numerous wanderers traversing the streets of Shanghai were provided with a home. The notification stated that those who did not avail themselves of the refuge would be regarded as bad characters, apprehended, and punished severely.[22]

In winter shelters in North China, the stuff used as "quilts" to keep the inmates warm was chicken feathers, hence these asylums were known as "chicken feather houses."[23] A more temporary and primitive kind of charity—primarily opened in populous cities and in the winter season—consisted of soup kitchens that provided, within limits, hot rice gruel and sometimes also clothing and cotton wool for street people and other urban poor. Like the poorhouses, soup kitchens were often officially endowed, but business communities and religious institutions were almost always on the donor list.[24]

Soup kitchens were perhaps best operated in Beijing, for the obvious reason that the city had been the national capital for more than five centuries until 1928 (Figure 10). In the late Qing, government soup kitchens operated for about seven months each year, from the first day of the tenth lunar month (late October to early November) to the fifth lunar month (late May to early June). In addition to food, each recipient also received a set of cotton padded clothes.[25] The relatively long charity season was less because of the harsh winters of North China than out of concern for Beijing as the place where the emperor resided. By the Republican period, twelve soup kitchens were still in operation in the city, but the charity season was shortened. The distribution of free food followed no definite schedule but began as soon as the weather turned genuinely cold and continued, if funds provided, until spring, with a minimum length of 100 days and a maximum of 120 days. For example, in 1918, the soup kitchens were run from Decem-

FIGURE 10.   Tattered, filthy, yet high-spirited, two boys in the line at a Beijing soup kitchen waiting their turn for a scoop or so of hot porridge. The soup kitchen was set up in a school. Note the list of students and their academic rankings on the wall, which provides a sad contrast to the beggar boys for whom food is all they could hope for from life; for them, an education would be an unimaginable luxury. Photo taken in 1924 or 1925. SOURCE: Courtesy of the Sidney D. Gamble Foundation for China Studies.

ber 1 to April 1, while in 1915 they did not open until January 2, and then ran until April 20.[26] In the mid-1920s, the soup kitchens did not begin operation until January.[27]

The food furnished consisted of a hot porridge of millet and rice, mixed in a proportion of seven parts millet to three parts rice. The allowance per person averaged from 3.5 to 4 ounces of grain.[28] Although thousands of meals were distributed every day in Beijing, the lines in front of the soup kitchens never seemed to end.[29] The crowds were fenced in to assure that nobody got a second serving. The writer Xiao Qian recalled that as a child he often had to wait hours before dawn in line at one of the soup kitchens. This was in an open space at the end of Shepherd's Lane in the Dongzhimen district in northeast Beijing. People brought their own bowls and queued up:

In the darkness we could hear the clinking of many bowls. . . . As the sky turned from black to gray, we kept looking back anxiously to see how far the line went. There was only so much porridge to distribute, so if the servers saw the line lengthen, they had to water it down. One morning the line was joined by a "big nose" [a white Russian]. . . . After he slunk into the line, I heard someone yell, "There's not enough for us Chinese. Get the big nose out of here." But some-one else said, "let the old man be. I'll put up with a little less."

The argument raged. Perhaps it was a way of staying warm.[30]

A few days after this, Xiao Qian saw the man die on the street. The police picked up the body and marked it as a "nameless corpse." It must have been a bit remarkable for a European to die on a Beijing street and hence it was embedded Xiao's memory. The fact was, however, that in the winter "nameless" Chinese corpses lying at the curbside were literally an everyday scene in major cities, not just Beijing. A Shanghai resident recalled that in the late 1940s "just a half a kilometer from my home, carts routinely col-lected at dawn the bodies of those who had died from illness and starvation during the night."[31] There were simply too few seasonal soup kitchens to cope with the rampant poverty in urban China.

Under these circumstances, beggars had to find a way to help themselves. Organized mendicancy was the most practical method of self-reliance. In the beginning, spontaneous beggars' guilds may not have been on the gov-ernment's checklist. But it did not require exceptionally sound judgment for a county magistrate to quickly figure out that this was indeed a ready-made institution that could help him in his ordeal of dealing with vagabonds. Beg-gars' secret societies often became entangled with the defunct official poor-houses and the baojia. Beggars' organizations to a large extent did not just dovetail with the state's goal of containing its vagrant population, they cost the government little. Thus this institution endured the great political up-heavals of late Qing and Republican China and survived until 1949. Let us take a closer look at these organizations in a few localities in various parts of the country.

"All Beggars Under Heaven Belong to One Family"

A small street named Yuhuating in the city of Hengyang in the central Chi-nese province of Hunan was in some ways charming—at least on the sur-face. It was a mountain trail on the eastern foothills of the scenic Wild Swan Ridge. Adjacent to the street was the Temple of Longevity (Shoufodian), a Buddhist monastery that regularly attracted crowds of pilgrims. Operas and local plays were periodically performed on an open-air stage in the temple courtyard. The street was named after a nearby pavilion with a poetic appellation, Yuhuating, meaning, the "pavilion for admiring blossoms on a drizzly day." However, this beguiling setting could not hide the bitter reality that this back street, about 200 meters long and 2 meters wide, was the beggar den of Hengyang. A stone tablet dated 1764 indicated that this was originally the site of the town's official poorhouse. Another stone tablet, dated 1884, recounted the status of this shanty area. By the Republican period, the street was home to about eighty households, two of which made incense for pilgrims—all the rest were panhandlers. In total, about 200 people, of which more than 160 were beggars, lived on the street. The beggars were under the control of three ringleaders, each of whom was in charge of a particular group: able-bodied local beggars, handicapped local beggars, and "temporary" and non-native beggars (that is, homeless wanderers from outside Hengyang).

Yuhuating had the quintessential elements for producing a beggars' den. The temple, the theater, and the mountain scenery attracted pilgrims, spectators, and tourists. The resultant crowds made Yuhuating a favorable spot for begging. Moreover, it was on the outskirts of the town, in an area less desirable for average townspeople, and therefore it was relatively easy for squatters to take over. As elsewhere in the country, once it had become a shantytown swarming with beggars, the local authorities "selected" it as the site for the municipal poorhouse. However, despite this official status and the fact that by the Republican period the city administration still subsidized the poorhouse based on the number of inmates officially on the roll, this place was more a guild run by beggars' own ringleaders than a governmental institution. It had its own rules and laws and charged a two-dollar membership fee, payable by begging if an applicant did not have cash.[32]

This guild was just one of countless beggars' organizations in China. Such organizations were too obscure to be formally affiliated with some of the better-known secret societies in China, although the beggar ringleaders usually had personal connections with one or more prominent gang bosses in town. The origins of these guilds are not entirely clear, but this in itself is revealing. It suggests beggars' organizations were formed spontaneously, clandestinely, and gradually, and in due course their origins had become murky.

A beggars' guild always had a physical base, which was either an officially designated poorhouse or a beggars' den that had gradually formed at a likely spot. In fact, the distinction between the two was vague. Official poorhouses were always located in the least desirable area of town. As we have noted, these houses were rarely run on the official budget alone. Instead, they mostly—if not sometimes entirely—relied on the alms given by the local business community—mainly, retail stores. An inadequate government budget and general mismanagement had rendered official poorhouses a decrepit institution by the beginning of the Qing, leaving them largely in the hands of the inmates themselves. Under these circumstances, if a charismatic leader emerged from the mass of beggars, as almost inevitably happened, the magistrate would be happy to endorse his authority by appointing him the beggar head and leaving the "dirty work" to him. Sometimes things evolved the other way around, that is, when there was originally no official poorhouse in town, little by little street people formed their own den, often in a place such as a rundown temple, a deserted graveyard, or a shanty-filled lot, and gradually from among them a ringleader emerged. The local authorities thereupon acknowledged his status or retroactively appointed him the official tramp-major of the town.

The raison d'être of the subaltern organization was the need for mutual help, the feeling of brotherhood, and the practical demand for control and stability. In other words, vagrants can be thought of as an interest group. A popular song widely known among beggars in the late Qing and the Republican period expressed the desire for unity and fraternity:

> People who have a family want to leave the family;
> People who do not have a family look for a family.
> Brothers and sisters, let's hug one another:
> All beggars under heaven belong to one family.[33]

Another folk ditty that served almost as the anthem of the Company of the Poor (*qiongjia hang*, a general name for beggars' guilds in North China) goes like this:

> Getting together, we call each other brothers;
> Dismissed, we head in all directions [to beg].
> Cripples, the blind, the old and the sick, we are all one family;
> Nothing can separate us—not even death.[34]

Simple and clear, these rhymes reveal the comradeship that drew these people together. Inadequate assistance from the state left beggars little choice but to organize themselves in order to exact the maximum from the society outside the beggars' world and to regulate themselves inside. Once a beggar gang had formed, like all secret societies, the key for self-protection was to keep information strictly confidential from outsiders.[35] The general public regarded beggars' organizations as a murky cabal at the very bottom of society. Few people outside knew what happened there, much less were in a position to record the goings on. As for beggars themselves, the great majority of them were illiterate; many had never once held a pen in hand and virtually none wrote a word about beggary and life inside the beggars' den.

Nonetheless, it has long been an open secret in China that the seemingly scattered and disorganized vagrants on the street were indeed organized in their own guild-like societies. An early record of a beggars' guild comes from Feng Menglong (1574–1646), a prominent Ming-dynasty writer who was best known for compiling and preserving folk tales and storytellers' scripts dating from the tenth century through his own time. One of the scripts Feng saved and edited was a story about a turbulent marriage of the only daughter of a twelfth-century beggar headman by the name of Jin Laoda (Chin Lao-ta). The prologue of this story gives us a glimpse of a beggars' guild at the time:

> It is told that in the Shaoxing reign-period [1131–62] of the Song dynasty, although Lin'an [Hangzhou] had been made the capital city and was a wealthy and prosperous district, still the great number of beggars had not diminished. Among them was one who acted as their head. He was called the 'tramp-major' (*tuan-tou*), and looked after all the beggars. Whenever they managed to beg something, the tramp-major would demand a fee for the day. Then when it was raining or snow lay on the ground, and there was nowhere to go to beg, the tramp-major would boil up a drop of thin gruel and feed the whole beggar-band. Their tattered robes and jackets were also in his care. The result was that the whole crowd of the beggars were careful to obey him, with bated breath like a lot of slaves, and none of them dared offend him.[36]

According to this story, the position of "tramp-major" was hereditary, along the lines of a lineage. Jin Laoda was the eighth generation tramp-major in his family, which means that by the twelfth century the institution of beggars' guilds was already a well-established tradition. Jin's story was often cited as evidence that beggars' guilds appeared no later than in the Song period.[37] It is perhaps safer to say that by the seventeenth century, when Feng Menglong collected or rewrote the story, beggars' guilds were already common.

The following account of a handicapped man rising to become a beggar head in a county seat in the seventeenth century reveals how common beggars' guilds had become by that time. The protagonist of the story was Mao Tanzi, or "Paralytic Mao," a native of Tianchang, a county in eastern Anhui near the border of Jiangsu.[38] Mao was born with a paralytic disease and could only move along by dragging himself on the ground. Being poor and handicapped, he grew up as a beggar. Having roamed about the streets of the county seat from childhood, he was a familiar sight to the people of Tianchang and was known as a man of upright character. The official gazetteer of Tianchang indicated that the county had an age-old reputation for being overrun with rascals and vagabonds, who sometimes were able to control the town's four marketplaces.[39] Mao stood out as a beggar who was aboveboard. But he would certainly have been a forgotten figure if a riot had not occurred in 1659 when the county was occupied by a rebel band headed by a salt merchant. In the chaos, the county magistrate fled from his yamen, but was unable to escape from the besieged town. He ended up by hanging himself at the doorway of a residence inside a back alley. No one seemed to notice that the magistrate's body was exposed in the alleyway unattended—until a few days later Paralytic Mao passed the alley and recognized the corpse. "Is this Our Master, the county magistrate?" Paralytic Mao exclaimed. Nobody was around to help. In tears, the handicapped man jeopardized his own safety and managed to dig a grave in the county drill ground and bury the magistrate there.

The rebels were soon suppressed and order restored. Paralytic Mao's good deed was reported to the new magistrate, who thought the heroic act deserved recognition. As a reward, the magistrate issued a bamboo slip bearing his signature, appointing Paralytic Mao the headman of the town's poorhouse. Mao became a respected and respectable figure in the town. One of his privileges as headman was to have a beggar serve as his means of conveyance. Every time Mao appeared in public he was straddling a beggar's shoulders, just like one rides a horse. He became, literally, a "man on top of men" (*ren shang ren*, a Chinese synonym for "upper class"). Paralytic Mao, of course, no longer had to beg, since he had regular support from both the county yamen and the "donations" from the stores (that is, the beggar taxes). He was able to build a three-bay thatched-roof home and, like a well-to-do man, he acquired a wife and a concubine. Since he was paralytic, there was no furniture in his house but mats: his wife's mat was placed in the central room and the concubine's in a wing. Every year on Paralytic Mao's birthday, his wives prepared a banquet in his honor and all beggars in the town came to congratulate him.[40]

Obviously, this saga has survived only because of the dramatic act of the hero. The rise of this particular beggar may have been exceptional, but what the story reveals is something ordinary: a county poorhouse, a beggar head appointed by the local magistrate, and the perceived qualifications for being a beggar headman (in this case, righteousness).

Not Strange to the Strangers

By the nineteenth century, Westerners who had lived in China for any length of time could not fail to note beggars' guilds. Even Commodore Matthew Perry, who paid two visits to China in his 1853–54 expedition to Japan, noted beggars' guilds and beggar taxes and recorded them in his journal in some detail.[41] Foreigners' observations on such an indigenous and esoteric subject may be doomed to superficiality, but one should bear in mind that with respect to beggars' society, almost all observers, be they Chinese or foreigners, were outsiders. An obvious merit of foreign witnesses was that they saw with fresh eyes phenomena that might have been familiar and unnoteworthy sights to natives. Some foreigners managed to visit beggars' guilds in person and glimpsed their physical setting and operation; many foreign observers had become quite familiar with various beggars' practices in China. Thus a few excerpts from foreigners' accounts of Chinese beggars are valuable supplements, especially considering that these reports came from virtually everywhere in the country over the span of nearly a century since the serious Western encroachment on China in the mid-nineteenth century.

John Gray observed in Canton (Guangzhou) a feast at one of the city's public halls, an event organized by the beggars' guild with financial support of wealthy shopkeepers in town:

> On the 3rd November, 1866, I had an opportunity afforded me of being present at a banquet of this nature. It took place at the Tchaong-Heng tavern in the Tsing-tsze-fong street of the western suburb. When I entered the first dining hall the beggars were called upon by one of their leaders to rise as a mark of respect. They continued standing until they were told to resume their seats. I was then escorted to an upper room in which were a few tables only. My companions at table were the elders of the guild or society of beggars, theirs being the privilege of sitting in the uppermost rooms at feasts.[42]

In its formality and civility, this orderly gathering of beggars was not unlike an assembly of any other professional group. Chester Holcombe (1844–1912), an American who went to China in 1869, first as a missionary and then from 1871 as a diplomat until his departure in 1885, noted that mendicancy "is reduced to a system in China." Because the government "makes no regular provision for the support of the pauper element among its people, it tacitly recognizes begging as a legitimate occupation." The comment was based on fifteen years of attentive observation of Beijing's beggars "of both sexes and all ages." Holcombe even got acquainted with a few beggars who for years had maintained their usual begging spots near the American legation.

"Peking [Beijing] beggars," Holcombe said, "have a regular guild or organization, presided over by a king and a queen. . . . The entire city is carefully divided into districts, and no beggar is allowed to intrude upon the territory of another."[43] Chinese sources indicate that this regular guild was called "the beggar factory" (*gaichang*). It was presided over by a chieftain, and underneath him were district ringleaders known as, depending on their status in the hierarchy, Senior Number One, Senior Number Two, Senior Number Three, and so on. All ordinary beggars were called "disciples" (*tudi*).[44] Holcombe never had a chance to meet the chieftain and he believed that this should be expected, because "the king is said never to be seen by profane eyes." He was, however, close enough to Beijing's beggars to have met and spoken with their "queen." Holcombe described her as "a respectable, well-dressed Chinese lady of sixty-five or seventy years of age."[45]

Two thousand and five hundred kilometers southwest of Beijing, in Chengdu, the missionary Joshua Vale gave a similar report on the beggars in that city at the turn of the twentieth century. Vale, a member of the British China Inland Mission, claimed that no place was more suitable than a provincial capital for studying Chinese social life, "for there you generally get everything to perfection—the pomp and show of the richer classes and the degradation and poverty of the poor." He closely studied "the conditions of the poorest class," that is, the beggars of Chengdu, and gave a report in 1907 based on what he believed to be "sufficient material" on the subject.

Vale found out that governmental charity for street people, which included the imperial grant of rice given out in the winter months and distribution of warm clothing purchased out of the provincial budget, was "a feeble attempt to mitigate the suffering of this class of people." Like their counterparts in Beijing, beggars in this provincial capital organized themselves. Vale noted that "a king, who is recognized by the local magistrates, ruled over the beggars and is responsible to the authorities for their good behavior." The beggar king, according to Vale, "can often be seen standing on a bridge outside the great east gate and levying a tax upon his followers as they go out of the city."[46] Chengdu at the time had, out of a total population of 350,000, an estimated 15,000 beggars who regularly roamed the streets. In fact, no single "king" ruled this army of mendicants. Instead, the city was divided into a number of begging turfs, each presided over by a ringleader. The man standing at the bridgehead was not the sole "king" who controlled the city's entire mendicant population, but a district beggar head.[47]

Beyond capital cities, in remote towns Westerners observed beggar organizations and their organizations that bore similarities to those in bigger cities. In 1927, Amelia O. Stott, a visitor to Pingyang, a county seat along the southern coast of Zhejiang Province, reported a fascinating encounter with the beggars' guild there. Stott's first sight of the local beggars was right at the moment she stepped into her hotel room. As she described the scene, she saw in a large courtyard below the window of her room: "Ragged beggars of all ages and descriptions, some smoking and gambling, others shouting and carrying on hectic conversation, a large number horribly maimed, sick or miserable but the majority in strangely good spirits in the midst of indescribable squalor."[48] This old courtyard, with a once-fine mansion adjacent to it, was the hostel of the beggars' guild known as *tao-fan-hui* or Society for Begging Rice. When Stott asked her servant, Ah-fu, for information about the guild, Ah-fu referred her to the hotel manager,

FIGURE 11.   This beggar headman in southern Zhejiang Province looks more like a modestly well-off farmer than an almsman. Note his warm clothing and the abundant food on the table. The wooden table is a solid piece of furniture, known as an Eight Immortals' Table, for it can accommodate eight persons. The tin on the table, however, reveals the identity of the subject, for it is the usual kind of container a beggar put on the sidewalk to collect cash alms. SOURCE: *Asia* (October 1927).

Mr. Tienli—"Sweet Pear"—who knew much about the guild next door (Figure 11).

Tienli, who in Stott's words was a "garrulous old gentleman," and who always held a yard-long pipe with a thimbleful of tobacco in its acorn-shaped bowl, was more than happy to talk. "*Ai-ya*," he said, "the *tao-fan-hui* is in every town and district in China, and well do the beggars know how to make their trade bud and flourish. . . . They are destitute only in name and appearance; for they wield an influence in Chinese life that few dare to ignore." The foreign woman's inquiry into the Chinese beggars' world intrigued the hotel manager so much that at the end of their conversation he volunteered to give Stott a tour of the neighboring beggars' den. Stott admitted that accepting the offer "took more courage than anything I had faced in China for many years."[49] But she acceded to the idea and it turned out to be a friendly visit. Not only was Stott able to venture to the center of the beggars' den but she also had the opportunity to speak at length with the beggar head, whom she described as "an entertaining and influential person—[who] willing furnished many facts."

> We passed the sentry beggar at the courtyard gate unchallenged; for my companion had duly paid his way and was unobjectionable to the guild. The inmates stopped all their various plays to stare at the "outer barbarian," but they were most polite and only too ready to show us around. . . .
>
> In two big kitchens food was being prepared for the entire community. It consisted of rice, salt chopped fish and cabbage and sweet potatoes. The share-like system was scrupulously observed, at any rate in this particular guild. The amount consumed by each person was fixed by order of the president. He was an elderly man, not without a certain dignity of appearance in spite of his filth and ragged clothing. He held the common stores, to which each member must contribute a minimum quantity of food and cash, under lock and key. If a member failed to provide his share, he was turned out to beg "on his own" after he had been given a certain number of days of grace.[50]

In comparison with Holcombe's Beijing beggars, who claimed their king could never be seen by profane eyes, Stott's informants were amicable, willing to talk, and even proud of their vocation. This kind of small-town hospitality, so to speak, helped Stott—in Pingyang and other hinterland towns she lived in or visited—to obtain some detailed information on beggars' organizations that was not readily known to the public. In short, the fact that foreigners were able to observe beggar's organizations in this vast land, from capital cities to hinterland towns, indicates that this grassroots institution had become a prominent feature of China's social landscape.

CHAPTER 5

Ruling the Street

ALTHOUGH AS A GROUP beggars were at the very bottom of the social ladder, once organized they had their hierarchy, which could be rigid at times. Throughout China in late imperial and Republican times beggar organizations constituted part of the nation's broader secret societies. The soul of a beggars' guild was the ringleader, a beggar who, in the public's eyes, had ascended to the status of a kind of lower-ranking gentry, a petty police chief, or a devil-may-care doyen, but he was the authentic and all-powerful patriarch of his group and the ruler of his turf. Much of his power was derived from personal charisma, social networking, and, most significantly, a tactical endorsement from local elites and officials.

The "Great Shaft" in North China

On June 3, 1899 some young American women taking a stroll on the city wall of Beijing near Qianmen (Front Gate) encountered a group of beggars. The scene described by one of the Americans in a letter home was nothing out of the ordinary for Chinese panhandlers, some of whom engaged in a performance for the visitors, but it was apparently an unpleasant jolt to the foreigners: "These half-covered wretches would run in front of them, form lines, fall upon their knees at their feet, *kotow* (bump their heads on the bricks), and yell and cry in the must horrible way. They stood on their heads, turned over and over, and kept up a loud noise all the while." When the women asked two well-dressed Chinese on the wall why nobody stopped the beggars, the answer was that people dare not do so because these beggars were organized into bands and woe to anyone who interfered with their business.[1]

The organized bands of beggar in Beijing and elsewhere in much of

North China (especially Hebei and Shandong provinces) were called "shaft" (*gan*) and their ringleaders, the "great shaft" (*dagan*). The name "shaft" was derived from a wooden rod that served as the symbol of the power of the ringleader. Painted in red and enclosed in a red silk bag, the shaft was placed in an eye-catching spot at the beggars' den or the ringleader's home, such as on the wall of the sitting room, where it was hung horizontally. At his in-auguration ceremony, a ringleader would worship the image of the legend-ary forefather of the begging profession and kowtow to the shaft. To ordi-nary beggars, the shaft was more than a ritual object; it was an awesome symbol of real power. Any newly admitted beggar had to kowtow to the shaft in the knowledge that should he violate any of the rules of the group the rod would be the instrument of his punishment. In festivals and ritual ceremonies, the entire group would line up to bow and kowtow to the shaft.

This worship was a way of reinforcing the authority of the ringleader. In dealing with an offense or crime, the ringleader brought the shaft to his court, where he could order it to be used to bludgeon the offender. The rule, or rather the tenet, was that even if a beggar was bludgeoned to death, no charges would be brought in court, for the ringleader was either ap-pointed by the local authorities or his status was acknowledged, and thus he was permitted to discipline his subordinates to the full extent of his authority.

The shaft, however, was regarded as a sacred symbol and used to flog beggars only on solemn occasions. Practically speaking, because mendicancy was an itinerant occupation and the shaft was too cumbersome to carry around, often when a beggar head was outside his den, he carried with him a long-stemmed tobacco pipe (*hanyanguan*, the most popular instrument for tobacco smoking before cigarettes were introduced to China in the late nineteenth century) as a substitute for the powerful shaft.[2] The pipe was made much longer and thicker than an average tobacco pipe so that it re-sembled the real shaft at home. At the same time, it was handy enough to carry around on the street and solid enough to be used to swat any unruly beggar on the spot. In addition to this function, it was, of course, a real pipe, providing the headman with the pleasure of having a smoke on the street anytime he pleased.

Although the rod was usually painted red, in Beijing ordinary beggars were called "Blue Shafts," a name used to distinguish them from a special type of mendicant known as "Yellow Shafts," who belonged to the Eight Banners, the Manchu clans that were related to the imperial family. The Eight Banners were ranked into a great variety of statuses according to the closeness of their lineage ties to the throne and also their social and eco-nomic circumstances. Following the founding of the Manchu dynasty in

1644 these Manchu kinfolk became spoiled children of the empire. After forsaking the nomadic lands of Manchuria and entering the magnificent capital of Beijing, and after being placed in privileged but not necessarily lucrative positions, some banner members became profligate and idle, and gradually lost all their livelihood. Many eventually degenerated into various kinds of vagabonds (Figure 12). Still, their aristocratic background protected them from becoming ordinary beggars. Their ringleaders were no ordinary toughs but members of the royal family who were, as a rule, stubborn and intractable characters. Members of the Yellow Shaft did not wander on the street all the time, as ordinary beggars usually did, but only begged (or rather, as we shall see, levied beggar taxes) three times a year: during the Chinese New Year, the Dragon Boat Festival, and the Mid-Autumn (or Full Moon) Festival. On each occasion, they solicited alms from businesses (mainly, retail stores); ordinary residential homes were not bothered.

The begging of the Yellow Shafts in fact involved a peculiar ritual. When they were on the streets, they usually formed a pair: one man sang while another accompanied him on a drum. Sometimes four beggars worked together to make two pairs. When the beggar stopped in front of a store and sang, he stretched his hands out with the palms facing down toward the ground; simultaneously, his companion kept the drum level. Seeing these gestures, a sensible storekeeper would walk out from behind his counter with money in hand, then, raising his hands slightly higher than his forehead he would place the money on top of the drum. The whole process was accomplished without the two parties exchanging a single word. Also by custom, the alms should not be fewer than five big coins and should be given by the shopkeeper before the singer completes his fifth sentence.[3]

The Yellow Shaft signified a royal connection, for yellow was exclusively an imperial color. A special bright yellow (*minghuang*) color was reserved for the emperor only; even his brother was not allowed to use it. Blue, on the other hand, was for commoners. However, no matter what "color" they were, the key was the "shaft," the symbol of the power of the headman as well as the instrument to enforce that power. In due time, this became an implement shared and understood by both the "yellow" and "blue" beggars. In North China by the late Qing, professional beggars were simply referred as people who were "on the shaft" (*ganshang de*).[4]

Beyond the Great Wall

The institution of the "shaft" extended beyond the Great Wall. In more peripheral and less sinicized areas, such as Mongolia and Manchuria, beggars were organized in essentially the same way as those in Beijing. That the beggars' organizations in these areas were similar and in some aspects identical

FIGURE 12.   A ragged night watchman standing on a doorstep near a city gate in Beijing, hitting a bamboo clapper and yelling. Although this man, an obscure Manchu bannerman named Old Weng, might not be exactly a panhandler, beggars often were assigned such duties by their guild. A night watchman's main task was to patrol the neighborhood every two hours after sunset. He beat a gong or bamboo clapper to announce the hours and shouted loudly and repeatedly, drawing out the last few tones so his announcement would carry far: "All is in peace and order-r-r! All is in peace and order-r-r!" Photo by John Thomson, ca. 1868. SOURCE: Courtesy of the New York Public Library. Information on the identity of the man from *The Face of China* (Aperture 1978).

to their counterparts in China proper reflects the remarkable consistency and institutionalization of beggary throughout the country.

THREE GENERATIONS OF RINGLEADERS
IN A MANCHURIAN TOWN

About thirty miles southwest of the major Manchurian city of Harbin was a small walled county seat called Shuangcheng (literally, Twin City). In the southwest part of the town was a back alley named Wealthy Wing where, ironically, was located the town's official poorhouse. Early in the twentieth century, inside the alley was a sizable residential compound consisting of a cluster of traditional Chinese courtyard houses. In the middle of the compound were nine well-painted and decorated rooms: five in the center, facing the south, and two wings on each side. This was the residence of the beggar head. Ten additional wings, five on each side, were built on the outskirts of the compound. These dwellings were for all the other beggars. A wooden board with six characters written in bold golden color, *Shuang cheng fu qi gai chu* (Beggars' Section of Shuangcheng Prefecture), hung vertically on the red gate of the compound, indicating that this was the town's official poorhouse.

According to Zhang Runqing, who was born in Shuangcheng in 1895 and was a veteran inmate of the poorhouse, the premises were a government-sponsored charity from the Qing through the Republic. But the county government gave little support to the poorhouse other than lending its political authority to the beggar head. Essentially, the county endorsed the headman and let him run the institution as he pleased. From the late Qing to 1946, Zhang Runqing had witnessed three generations of beggar heads in the county, all of whom were appointed by the county magistrate, with the consent of the local chamber of commerce, which gave the beggars a variety of financial aid.

The first beggar head was a man named Zhang Xiang, of Manchu origin, who had been the county beggar ringleader from an unknown date in the late Qing to 1914, when he died. Zhang was a skillful flatterer and it was no secret that he gained his position by fawning over the local yamen. His Manchu background may also have helped. Whatever the reason, by the end of the Qing he had established himself not only as the beggar head but also as a well-respected senior figure in town. People did not address him by the conventional term for a beggar head (that is, *tuantou* or "tramp-major" or "group chief"); instead, they called him "senior master." Or, sometimes the locals used a modern title, which connotes ridicule: "section chief" (*chu-zhang*). By custom the position could be hereditary, but it seemed Zhang was impartial enough not to pass his position to his son. Instead, the man who inherited Zhang's position was his adopted son, Guan Fuji, an actor in a local itinerant theatrical troupe.

Adoption was not a formal, legal matter in this case. Rather, it meant Guan was a trusted disciple and close retainer of Zhang. While the position of beggar head could be hereditary, it could also be transmitted through a tradition of "passing on [the ringleader's position] to a disciple rather than a son" (*chuan tu bu chuan zi*); all depended on which tradition was followed. But Guan got this position also because he had pleased the county magis-

trate and the head of the chamber of commerce: both men liked his performances in the itinerant theater. Guan was particularly good at playing the
role of a little eunuch in *Fasimen* (The Temple Gate), a popular drama
known for its erotic plot. He was also popular in the role of the beggar head
Jin Song in *Hongluanxi* (A Happy Couple), a drama adapted from the Feng
Menglong story we mentioned earlier. This was hardly surprising for what
Guan had played in the drama became a reality: for the rest of his life he was
the county's real "tramp-major."

When Guan died in 1924, Zhang Xiang's biological grandson, Zhang
Xingbang, an opium addict then in his forties, inherited his grandfather's
position. Reportedly Xingbang bribed the members of the county chamber
of commerce to get their endorsement. He ruled the beggars for more than
two decades and was known as the cruelest ringleader in Shuangcheng's recent history. Beggars, especially those from outside the town, would prefer
roaming the streets on their own and staying on the doorsteps of a Buddhist
temple rather than being under the roof of the poorhouse in his "care."
Zhang obviously took financial advantage of his position. During his tenure
he was able to completely remodel his home in Wealthy Wing, making it an
extraordinarily lavish residence. He purchased more than fifty acres (300 *mu*)
of land outside the county town and rented it out to local farmers. In 1946,
when the Communists took over Shuangcheng, the fifty-odd remaining
beggars in the town and Zhang's tenants in the countryside all pointed the
finger at him in the Land Reform campaign. Knowing his end was near, the
aged man killed himself by swallowing raw opium, a common method of
suicide among opium addicts.[5]

Like their counterparts in Beijing and elsewhere in North China,
Shuangcheng's beggar heads also had a shaft as their symbol of authority. It
was a two-foot long wooden rod, of which the top half was painted red and
the bottom half black. A half-foot-long leather thong was tied to the black
end of the shaft, so the shaft was practically a whip. Like the Great Shaft elsewhere in China, the shaft wielded by Shuangcheng's beggar head was both
a symbol of power and an instrument of discipline.

In Shuangcheng, the county government, acting on behalf of the local
elite (that is, members of the chamber of commerce), granted power to the
beggar head in exchange for his service in controlling the potentially unruly
vagabonds. The reverse was also true, that is, the local elite, acting on behalf
of the county government, made the decision as to who should hold the
shaft. Either way, the state and the elite allowed the organized band regularly
to collect tax-like alms from local residents and commercial establishments
(a subject to be discussed later in this chapter). The beggar tax was the main
source of income for the operation of the guild and as always the headman,

by force or by trickery, made sure most of the tax came into his hands. In a way, the headman was no longer a panhandler but had ascended to the status of a police chief of sorts, for he was expected to offer services that were usually provided by a police department.

The beggar head in Shuangcheng was obligated to accept any homeless person in the town into his den. He was responsible for burying "public" corpses, including corpses from the county jail, unidentified corpses found on the roadside, and the executed. He was also responsible for assigning beggars to guard the four gates of the town wall. Beggars performing such municipal duties may seem absurd. But for a town that had scarce resources for policing but abundant manpower among the destitute, it was a rational, if not even a wise, arrangement. Throughout the country beggars were called on for all kinds of governmental service that required laborers. We shall see that Shuangcheng was not alone in using this tactic to cope with street people.

"MOUNT LIANG" IN THE GRASSLANDS OF INNER MONGOLIA

By the early Republican period the Inner Mongolian town of Baotou on the banks of the Yellow River north of the Great Wall had grown into a city of about 60,000 people, but administratively it remained a market town (*zhen*) under the jurisdiction of Salaqi County. The county had a police squad of thirty men stationed in Baotou, which was simply insufficient for a city of that size. Baotou was in fact run by a five-member committee consisting of representatives from the local business community. Four of its members represented the Great Firm (Dahang), the most powerful party in the town, and the fifth represented the suburban landowners' association known as the Farm and Garden Society (Nongpushe). The committee was mandated by the Salaqi county administration to govern the city, but its "police branch" was in fact in the hands of a group of organized beggars and gangsters who called themselves Mount Liang.

The name was derived from the famous Song-dynasty rebel headquarters, Mount Liang, in western Shandong. The name "Mount Liang" had long been a synonym for chivalry and brotherhood because of the fourteenth-century novel *The Water Margin* (*Shuihu zhuan*), the most popular classic in Chinese literature on the Song rebellion.[6] Baotou's Mount Liang originated in a shanty area where temporary shelters were erected for coffins awaiting burial, hence its name, Dead Man's Ditch. By the late nineteenth century, along with the growth of Baotou as a prosperous port, Dead Man's Ditch became a crowded shantytown where a number of "drum houses" (which offered funeral and wedding services) and "black rooms" (temporary jails) were located. The residents of Dead Man's Ditch were primarily beggars, but they also included servants (for funerals), itinerant street entertainers, sedan chair and coffin carriers, and trumpeters for weddings and funerals. By the early twentieth century, the dwellers of Dead Man's Ditch all belonged to Mount Liang.

The ringleader of this fraternity, like his cohorts elsewhere, wielded an awe-inspiring shaft, which was placed on an altar in front of an image of the Ming emperor Yongle (reigned 1403–24) and the Han dynasty recluse Fan Dan, both of whom were worshiped as the forefathers of this group. These vagrants, like the Song rebels, believed that brotherhood and personal loyalty were the most important virtues for a group bound together in adversity. Unlike the Song rebels, however, the Mount Liang people were organized to serve the government for pay rather than to rebel against it. Under the direction of the ringleader, the beggars of Baotou were assigned to a variety of public services that made them more like municipal workers than street beggars. They patrolled the town and served as night watchmen. In the evening they carried red lanterns marked with the words "Great Firm" and were authorized to stop, check, and even arrest pedestrians in the late hours. Sometimes the city gate guards, while on duty, would give the gate keys to the Mount Liang people in order to free themselves for an unauthorized trip outside the town for a little pleasure: gambling.

The regular services of the beggars included picking up garbage, collecting night soil from public toilets, removing roadside corpses, and so on. They were the firemen when there was a fire and the emergency personnel at times of natural disaster. In 1918, there was a terrible plague of rats that claimed more than 3,000 human lives in Baotou, and it was the Mount Liang people who carried all the corpses outside the town to be cremated. In 1926, Baotou was officially made a county town (*xian*) and twelve years later, in 1938, it was promoted to the rank of city (*shi*). Gradually, a police department took over much of the work traditionally done by Mount Liang. For beggars, this was the beginning of the end of the heyday of Mount Liang, and some began to leave Baotou. Many joined the Senior Brothers' Society (Gelaohui), a powerful gangster organization in late Qing and Republican China, and became bandits in the Hetao (the Great Bend of the Yellow River) area.

Although in decline, Mount Liang managed to survive Baotou's administrative changes and by the late 1940s it was still a major player in Baotou's lower society, especially among beggars and pilferers. The last head of Mount Liang, Li Genluo, presided over the final stage of this organization. Li had been a soldier. Before he was wounded in combat in Lengkou against the Japanese he was a platoon leader in the Thirty-Second Army, headed by the famous commander Shang Zhen (1884–1978). After being wounded, Li returned to his hometown of Baotou, right at the time when his uncle, who was the head of Mount Liang, died. Li led a group of demobilized soldiers in driving his uncle's followers away and then took over the leadership. Although Li presided over the twilight of Mount Liang, he was proud of the once impressive lineup of his group.

"During the 1911 revolution, many of the Mount Liang people joined the army of Yan Xishan [1883–1960, a major warlord]," Li remarked nostalgically to a reporter who interviewed him in 1946. "Eight of them were promoted to the rank of regimental commander or battalion commander." At the time of the interview Li still had some unusual characters under his supervision, including a person who once served as a county magistrate under Sun Dianying (1889–1947), a petty warlord whose use of explosives to blast open the magnificent tombs of Empress Dowager Cixi (1835–1908) and Emperor Qianlong (reigned 1736–95) in order to steal their lavish treasure was one of the most notorious thefts in Chinese history. Li's feeling about his group, however, was more than nostalgia and vanity; it was about the real power Mount Liang still had at the time of this conversation. "If you gentleman have a buddy who's lost something in Baotou," Li boasted to the reporter, "I can guarantee its return within three days."[7]

Beggars' Gangs in Shanghai

HEADMAN ZHAO

To get access to a beggar ringleader was not easy, and it was even harder to get him to whisper about his group. Liu Yingyuan, the reporter who met with Li of Mount Liang, had made several attempts before he was able to actually meet the headman. Liu's final channel was Baotou's police chief, Han Jitang, who sent his criminal section chief, Niu Zhantian, to call the beggar head in for an interview. Only because Liu had such an impressive connection did Li receive him with courtesy and give him a tour of the beggars' den, which for decades had been a mysterious hive to outsiders.[8]

Likewise, in Shanghai in 1933 when two female sociologists, Jiang Siyi and Wu Yuanshu, conducted an investigation of the city's beggars, they had to make connections in order to interview one of the city's major beggar heads. In the early Republican period, Shanghai had eight major beggar ringleaders, known as the Eight Brothers. In a standard Chinese gang hierarchy known as *beifen* or "generation," they were the most senior generation, and following the Chinese custom that the given names of brothers should all share one character, in their names they all used the character *Tian* (heaven). Actually, only their last names were known: Lu, Zhou, Zhong, Wang, Shen (two), and Zhao (two). The Eight Brothers divided Shanghai into four districts (east, west, south, and north), each of which was headed by two "brothers" of the Tian generation.[9] Jiang and Wu interviewed one of the bothers, Mr. Zhao, who at the time was semiretired.

The two sociologists had made painstaking efforts, including library and archival research and field trips to beggar dens, to gather information on Shanghai's street beggars, but it was a matter of luck that they had come across a chance to interview Zhao. The two women had a mutual friend named Ms. Zhou Zhexin, whose husband was from a well-to-do family that had a family accountant who happened to know beggar head Zhao personally. Through this connection, Jiang and Wu were able to make an appointment with Zhao on March 5, 1933 at a teahouse in Nanshi (the old Chinese town of Shanghai). Their report of the meeting provides a portrait of a Shanghai street ringleader who rarely appeared in public.

When the two women and their friend walked into the teahouse around two o'clock in the afternoon, Ms. Zhou told the waiter they were looking for a Mr. Zhao. Then, a middle-aged man came out to greet them and asked the waiter to serve tea. This was Mr. Zhao, who looked quite different from the conventional image of an underground ringleader as a gangster. Here is how Jiang and Wu described him:

> He is a tall and handsome man of about forty, with a round face and big eyes. Dressed in a black serge long gown and a mandarin jacket over the gown and wearing a skullcap resembling the rind of half a watermelon, black shoes, and white socks, he looks poised, shrewd, and energetic. He speaks in a soft voice with a Shanghai accent, giving people an impression of gentleness as if he were a scholar.

Not only did Zhao look like a gentleman, but also he talked like a person who had a strong sense of public responsibility. He said that he had been willing to serve as the beggar ringleader for three reasons, all of which sounded noble: "First, for the public safety of the city; second, for our country; third, for our countrymen." Zhao was critical of virtually all parties that had tried to deal with beggars in Shanghai:

> Those people who were in charge of the [Chinese] Rehabilitation House (Jiaoyang yuan) had no experience with beggars. They only knew how to snatch beggars off the streets and put them in the house. No wonder many beggars just wanted to run away from there and later the house was closed down anyway due to a lack of funding. The authorities of the foreign concessions only know how to seize beggars and dump them in the Chinese districts. The Chinese administration doesn't do much either. Mostly, it just lets the beggars be there. Sometimes the government drives beggars out of the city, or puts them in the Vagrants Workhouse (Youmin xiqinsuo). In my view, none of these is a basic solution.

However, Zhao was not just critical, he also showed an intention of help-ing. "If you're are going to run a rehabilitation house," he said, "I am most willing to help."

Although the interview was conducted for an academic purpose and Zhao was suave enough not to expect much from any group outside the beggars themselves, he evidently thought anyone who bothered to ask de-tailed questions about beggars ought to have a charitable purpose or some kind of other plan in mind. Zhao did not volunteer himself and leave it at that. He proposed at least three measures or principles for dealing with street beggars. First, Zhao said, beggars should be treated as individuals, or at least they should be suitably treated according to age and sex. It was wrong for people to treat all beggars as if they were of the same character. Second, those who deal with beggars or run the Rehabilitation House should be ex-perienced people; Zhao clearly implied that he himself was such a qualified person. Third, funding for the institution should come from local stores, that is, the poorhouse should be "self-supported" by the age-honored prac-tice of "beggar taxes." If all these measures were applied, Zhao suggested, "there will not be a single beggar on the streets in this area."

A short biographical sketch of this beggar head is revealing. Zhao, a na-tive of Shanghai, could trace his family line back to the Ming dynasty (1368–1644), when his ancestors were beggars in the county town of Songjiang (about twenty miles southwest of Shanghai; at that time Shanghai was administratively under Songjiang). One of his ancestors served as a night watchman for the town, a common job for beggars. The legend goes that a pirate boat was captured by the county government and all the people abroad were arrested and charged as criminals, but among them was an in-nocent young man who had unwittingly taken passage on the boat. Zhao, as a night watchman close to the yamen, happened to find out the truth and managed to get it known to the authorities and therefore rescued the young man. The young man turned out to be a son of the governor of Hunan. He later passed the civil service examinations and was appointed the magistrate of Songjiang. Out of gratitude, the new magistrate appointed Zhao the headman of Songjiang's beggars. By the 1920s, the position had been passed down through the family for nine generations.

The ninth generation beggar head Zhao (that is, the person who ap-peared in the Nanshi teahouse), however, was not an immediate offspring of the Zhao family. The eighth generation headman Zhao did not have a son, but adopted his nephew (his sister's son) in order to pass on the position. The ninth generation Zhao had his primary education in a Chinese-style private school. In addition to his duties as a beggar headman, he also served as an inspector in an outpost of the tax office in Nanjing in 1921 and was a member of a detective team in 1923. At the time of the interview, Zhao described himself as having "washed his hands" of the job of beggars' headman, a term that implied that the job was "dirty" or crime related. He now owned a small teahouse in Nanshi and was the father of five children, three daughters and two sons.[10]

Zhao's roundabout suggestion that he could be the person to police Shanghai's beggars was not a baseless absurdity. In fact, at the time of the interview one of Shanghai's high-ranking police officers was a former beggar. Cheng Ziqing (1885–1956), the chief detective in the political section of the police department of the French Concession, was known as "the petty beggar of Zheng's Wooden Bridge." Cheng, a native of Zhenjiang, Jiangsu Province, had been a rice store apprentice before he became a fairly well-known street character in the neighborhood known as Zheng's Wooden Bridge (today, Fujian South Road), a notorious beggars' den, hence his epithet. Like Zhao, Cheng had only three years of primary education in a Chinese-style private school, and he knew no French. But his connections with Huang Jinrong (1868–1953), one of the top three gang bosses in Republican-era Shanghai and also Chiang Kai-shek's senior—and mentor—in the gang hierarchy before Chiang rose to political prominence, earned him a post in the police department. When the Communists took over Shanghai in May 1949, Cheng had been in the police department for thirty-seven years.

This "petty beggar" indeed left a not-so-petty mark on modern Chinese history. In the evening of July 30, 1921, when the inaugural meeting of the Chinese Communist Party (CCP) was being secretly held in a tiny (about 180 square foot) living room in an ordinary home in the French Concession, a middle-aged man dressed in a long gray gown stepped into the house, pretending to be looking for a Chairman Wang. Alerted, the Communists at the meeting quickly fled the house and left Shanghai for Jiaxing, in Zhejiang Province. The Communists (including Mao Zedong) thus escaped the police search that came only a few minutes after the man's suspicious appearance, and concluded their secret meeting in a rented pleasure-boat on Lake Nanhu.[11] The intruder was Cheng, who later told a colleague in the police department that according to intelligence he had at the time a foreign "red element" (referring to the Comintern agent known as Maring) was convening a meeting in the house, but he was unaware that this was the first national congress of the CCP.[12] That evening, if Cheng had been more circumspect, he might have been able to throttle the Communist Party at its birth. The "petty beggar of Zheng's Wooden Bridge" apparently was too reckless, but he nevertheless quite dramatically altered the progress of the meeting that has been described in China since 1949 as an event in which "heaven was separated from earth" (*kaitian pidi*), that is, an epoch-making event.[13]

THE HIERARCHY

Zhao, as one of the Eight Brothers, was at the pinnacle of the hierarchical world of Shanghai beggars. From the top of the structure each of the Brothers appointed and controlled about six so-called Big Heads (*da toumu*), each of whom in turn had about five Little Heads (*xiao toumu*). According to their places of origin, Shanghai's beggars were divided into five different groups (*bang*): Fengyang (of Anhui Province), Huiyang (of Henan Province), Shandong, Jiangbei (northern Jiangsu Province), and Shanghai locals (*jianghubang* or *benbang*). Each group had a Senior (*laoda*) to represent its interests and to communicate with the Brothers.[14]

The main responsibilities of all these ringleaders were, in addition to supervising beggars, "fund-raising" and distribution. The primary source of income for the beggars was the alms of stores, and hence the importance of begging turfs. The ringleader's job was to contact the storekeepers in his district and negotiate the amount of "tax" that each store or shop was to contribute (which was mainly based on the size and type of the store or shop, and usually no less than three silver dollars every six months).[15] On the second and sixteenth days of the second and eighth months, allowances were distributed among the beggars according to their begging performance during the year. The favorite spots for this great gathering were the desolate old drill ground in Nanshi and deserted temples in Zhabei.[16]

Under the direct control of the Brothers, the Big Heads' responsibility was to patrol the streets to supervise the beggars under their jurisdiction, especially to prevent beggars from disturbing the stores that had paid the "tax." The Little Heads' duty was usually to act as night guards for stores that paid large amounts of money ($80 or more silver dollars annually). The lowest beggar head was called an Uncle (*yeshu*). The Uncle was not appointed by the ringleaders but was an experienced beggar who achieved his power among new and child beggars by fighting and toughness of personality. His position in theory was below the Little Heads but his actual power was close to that of the Big Heads. He had a few followers known as Little Users (*xiaoyong*), who were mostly children, and he himself in turn had a gang boss as his Master (*laotouzi*), who was usually not a beggar at all but a local tough. At the very bottom of the hierarchy were ordinary beggars and the Little Users.

A new beggar in Shanghai first had to find out who was the headman of the area where he or she wanted to beg and secure his permission. This involved a ceremony to bind the newcomer as a follower of the ringleader. Gifts, usually cigarettes (the most popular brand was "Great Britain"), were presented as a token of respect to the leader by the new beggar. At a lower level, a Little User usually gave 360 sesame cakes as a gift in order to be accepted. The entrance fee apparently became inflated by the 1940s, as it generally involved the novice offering "ten dollars, the first two months of alms, and kowtowing twice" to his Senior (laoda).[17] Unacknowledged beggars were bullied by other beggars and driven out of the area.

Once accepted, a beggar had to obey the rules of the guild, which included not disturbing stores that had already paid their "tax," not entering other beggars' areas, not raping and stealing, and so on. Violators were punished ruthlessly, tortured, and even murdered. Beggars who kept a perfect record for the whole year were rewarded with a double allowance in the second- or eighth-month distribution. The beggars' rules also included a sort of insurance or, to use a contemporary phase, a "social security tax." Beggars were expected to contribute a certain percentage of their daily gains to the beggar heads to be saved for emergency needs, and they were entitled to use the funds in case of sickness or death. This rule obviously benefited the beggar heads most, but it also gave an ordinary beggar a sense of security. Some beggars were therefore not willing to work in factories or workshops that were set up for vagrants, feeling that "those factory owners and hypocritical gentlemen exploited them more than their heads did."[18]

Exactly how effective the system was may never be known. Insufficient information about beggars' organizations sometimes led to exaggeration. It was said that the ringleaders were able to call together all beggars in Shanghai in ten minutes, which, considering the size of the city and its complicated transportation system, was quite unlikely.[19] But the beggar heads clearly knew their domain. For instance, beggar head Zhao was able to estimate the total population of beggars in the city, which was not an easy task, for even municipal officials had never come up with an authoritative figure. It turned out that the number he quoted tallied with the figures reported by other, more "scientific" sources such as surveys by the government and sociologists.[20] The American journalist Ernest Hauser satirically pointed out in 1940 that a Shanghai beggar head was able to locate missing items: "For all his hollow hands, His Majesty might have extended a helping hand to you, at times: if you had left a brief case in a public rickshaw, for example, he was the person to see."[21]

Still, that there was a hierarchy among the beggars should not lead one to conclude there was a centralized system within which every level was clearly ordered nor that every beggar felt authority from the top. The "cell" of this beggars' "body politic" seems to have been the Uncle, who tended to be more or less independent, and consequently the structure of begging was to some extent decentralized. The Uncle had his own followers (the Little Users), and monopolized begging within a block or a few alleyways. Since he had his own "back-ups" among local bullies, such as members of the

Green Gang, the most powerful mafia in Republican-era Shanghai, few people dared infringe upon his turf.

For a new beggar or a Little User, the Uncle was the boss, guide, exploiter, and protector. To become an Uncle was a future they had hundreds of reasons to dream of. Once becoming an Uncle, a beggar did not have to beg. His income came from several sources: (1) The Little Users had to give their uncle a certain daily fee, which varied from 20 to 50 percent of their daily income. A beggar who failed to submit the fee without reason would be tortured. (2) Like storekeepers, who paid the "beggar tax," street peddlers who set a food stand on a street corner or alleyway entrance had to pay a "tax" to the Uncle in order to avoid trouble (such as Little Users eating at a food stand without paying or even throwing the stand into the Huangpu River). (3) Weddings, birthday parties, and other events in the turf such as moving or store openings were good opportunities for the Uncle. He came to say "congratulations" and other sweet words and ask for money. (4) Other events in the neighborhood, such as the changing of a shop's signboard, gang negotiations in a teahouse (*chi jiang cha*), and scuffles also presented an opportunity for the Uncle to beg or extort. (5) In summer, fruit stores (which were very common in Shanghai) often piled up fruit on the sidewalk in front of the store and hired an Uncle to watch the goods overnight. The Uncle took the money and assigned a Little User to do the job. On the next day, as a reward, the Little User's daily fee would be waived. (6) Having served as a Little User for a few years, a beggar might feel strong enough to become independent, but he had to give his Uncle about 4–5 silver dollars in order to "graduate." Once released from his boss, the beggar could recruit his own Little Users (that is, become an Uncle himself) and start to built his own turf.[22]

Iron Fist and Rice Bowl

No matter how beggar guilds were structured, the central figure in each organization was the top ringleader or, as he was often sensationally called outside the mendicants' world, the "beggar king." Chester Holcombe asserted that "the beggars' officers were elective" and satirically commented that "so far as I have been able to learn, the mendicants of the capital are the only Chinese in the empire who are permitted to exercise the privileges of the ballot."[23] It is a bit too rosy to say that any beggar head came to power via an election. As we have seen, beggar headmen were often appointed by the county magistrate. The process of winning the chieftainship often involved a recommendation from a *dibao* (local constable) or a member of the local gentry, thus a connection with local officials or bigwigs was essential. Connections with broader gang organizations, such as the Green Gang in Shanghai and the Gowned Brothers in Sichuan, were also part of the game.

On the other hand, the beggar headman did have grassroots support among local beggars, and this was often a prerequisite for winning official backing. There were certain qualities, other than having gang connections, that made a beggar stand out from his peers and facilitated his rise to power. One was personal charisma. Toughness and aggressiveness, organizational skill, and some sort of chivalrous spirit toward fellow beggars were usually also crucial. As we have seen, once a beggar was acknowledged as a ringleader, he could pass the position on to his offspring or relatives (such as a nephew), but a weak successor was subject to being replaced by a stronger rival.

The qualities of a beggar head also depended on brawn and, sometimes, unusual physical experiences. The rise of two headmen in Chengdu is revealing in this regard. Wen Bin, who was about forty years old in 1948, had been a solder, a peddler, and a thief. His left hand had been chopped off in a bungled robbery and after that he became a beggar. The handicap, however, served as evidence of his experience and toughness in the eyes of his follow beggars. In his ample experience of wandering around the country he learned the particular skills and knowledge of the world of "rivers and lakes" (*jianghu*). He soon became the headman in the most desirable begging area in east Chengdu. He was said to be observant, eloquent, and quickly adaptable to any circumstance. He was agile and brave, while at the same time versed in the ways of the world and sophisticated in handling public relations, an essential quality for leadership of this nature.[24] In another case, a beggar head nicknamed Food Jar, who haunted the City God temple near the northern gate of Chengdu, was renowned for his unusual ability. Food Jar's surname was Fan, a homonym of the word "food" (*fan*, literally "rice" or "meal"). He earned the nickname through his rare ability with food. He could fast for three days and not show a sign of physical weakness, but he could also eat as much as two to three days' worth of food at one sitting. On that ability he often gambled with local hooligans. Once, at the bridgehead of the Wanfu Bridge he bet with a busybody, besieged by bystanders, that he could swallow twenty raw eggs at once: he did so, and looked perfectly happy. Food Jar understandably became a well-known character in the neighborhood and his real name was soon forgotten.[25]

An effective headman indoctrinated his fellows in ethics or at least a code of conduct, so that discipline was morally grounded. His lectures also aimed to inspire them with the heroic legends of the forefathers, to encourage them not to lose faith in the beggar's life and, moreover, to act with professional pride. But overall the beggar head was not a clergyman; his rule was essentially penal. The beggar head possessed an almost absolute power over his subjects—to the extent he might punish an unruly beggar with death. The following ten rules, observed in a beggars' guild in Laohekou in the middle Yangzi River valley province of Hubei, were typical:

Rule 1 Violation: Stirring things up [that is, spreading malicious gossip leading to trouble among members]. Punishment: cutting off the tongue.

Rule 2 Violation: Betraying a fellow beggar. Punishment: Cutting off a finger.

Rule 3 Violation: Telling the owner of lost property the location of that property. Punishment: Slicing off a heel.

Rule 4 Violation: Stealing from a fellow member. Punishment: Cutting off a hand.

Rule 5 Violation: Stealing from a friend or a neighbor. Punishment: Cutting off a toe.

Rule 6 Violation: Falsely accusing a fellow member of theft. Punishment: Gouging out an eye.

Rule 7 Violation: Bullying a visiting beggar. Punishment: A cash fine.

Rule 8 Violation: Sexually harassing or assaulting the wife or daughter of a fellow member. Punishment: Drowning.

Rule 9 Violation: Sexually harassing or assaulting fellow women members. Punishment: Death.

Rule 10 Violation: Stealing outside one's turf. Punishment: Death by being sliced in half at the waist.

Each violation was coded in argot. For instance, violation of Rule 3 was called "Bringing a horse to the manger," and of Rule 8, "Bullying the flower and killing the willow."[26] Little is known as to whether these rules were actually carried out. They may have served more as a warning and a set of moral guides than as ironclad laws. But there should be no doubt that discipline of this nature was the main pillar supporting beggars' guilds nationwide. Shanghai's beggars, for instance, also observed rules such as not begging at stores that paid the protection fee, not invading other beggars' turf, not disrupting public safety on the streets, not engaging in sexual misconduct with fellow beggars, and so on. Punishment for violating the rules included "making a wonton" (trussing up a person in the shape of dumpling and denying the culprit food for a day), beating, deportation (expulsion from the begging territory), torture, and death.[27]

At the same time, the beggar head was responsible for taking care of the basic needs of the beggars, essentially, as we have seen in the Shanghai case, supplying them with daily food and shelter and assuring the truly sick had rest. He was also responsible for maintaining the begging order in his turf and negotiating with parties outside the guild. One might say that one of his hands was clenched into an iron fist while the other held a rice bowl. There was, in short, a control-and-concern dualism in the beggar head's relations with his fellows. By late Qing and Republican times it had become a pattern nationwide that the government and the business community relied on the beggar head for keeping local vagabonds in order.

Yet this "solution" to the social problem of mendicancy could not have existed without a certain type of social contract between beggars and the general society they daily encountered and relied on, nor without a certain degree of governmental endorsement. The key to the functioning of the headman's power, as well as to the operation of the guild in general, was the so-called beggar tax.

The Beggar Tax

Beggar taxes, as the name suggests, were payments society had to offer to alleviate the problem of the street poor, at least temporarily. No official code legitimized these "taxes," yet for those who were involved, these contributions were authentic taxes that they virtually could not avoid. In the end, it was the Chinese "middle class"—shopkeepers, artisans, small-business owners or operators, and urban residents of various sorts—who bore the largest share of the burden of regularly supporting the never-ending army of mendicants in modern China.

The practice of shops and residences paying protection money to beggars was such a widespread and public matter that it was often observed and recorded by Westerners who lived in various parts of the country in the late nineteenth and early twentieth centuries. They offered diverse yet consistent accounts of this custom. The following accounts from their memoirs may sound repetitious, for they are so similar that, for a moment, they look even like acts of plagiarism. But they were all based on the authors' many years of residence and study in China, and some of the accounts are based on personal experiences and ethnographic observations. The seeming redundancy of the depictions reveals precisely the ubiquity of this key operation of beggars' organization in the century prior to 1949.

Wells Williams (1812–84), a professor of Chinese language and literature at Yale College, wrote about the "poor-tax" soon after the Opium War (1839–42):

> This class is under the care of a headman, who, in order to collect the poor-tax allowed by law, apportions them in the neighborhoods with the advice of the elders and constables. During the day they go from one door to another and receive their allotted stipend, which cannot be less than one cash to each person. They sit in the doorway and sing a ditty or beat their clap-dishes and sticks to at-

tract attention, and if the shopkeeper has no customers he lets them keep up their cries, for he knows that the longer they are detained so much the more time will elapse before they come again to his shop. . . . Many persons give the headman a dollar or more per month to purchase exemption from the daily importunity of the beggars, and families about to have a house-warming, marriage, or funeral, as also newly arrived junks, are obliged to fee him to get rid of the clamorous and loathsome crowd.[28]

Later, John Macgowan (d. 1922), a Briton who came to China in 1860, reported:

> The begging fraternity is under the control of a head-man, to whom the man-darin has delegated very extensive power. As it would interfere with the business of the shopkeepers to have the ragged crew pestering them during business hours and driving away customers by their presence, this man contracts with each of them for a monthly payment, which he collects from them. To show that such an engagement has been entered into he pastes the beggar symbol, viz., a gourd, over his door, as a sign that the house has been made free from beggars.[29]

In 1882, Herbert Allen Giles (1845–1935), a British diplomat and sinologist, summarized the situation very well: "There is a beggars' guild in every Chinese town of any size. Its members levy regular contributions from the various shopkeepers, who thus purchase an immunity from molestation."[30]

These reports generalize about the practice without giving specific locations, but more localized observations are available to substantiate the details. In Guangzhou, it was a custom, as John Gray reported in 1860, that

> twice annually, in spring and autumn, the beggars of Canton [Guangzhou] are entertained at dinner in one of the public halls of the city by wealthy shopkeepers. These entertainments are given by the tradesmen on condition that the beggars of the guilds will come to them for alms not daily, but on certain specified occasions. . . . Charity of this sort is of very great antiquity.[31]

In fact, the dinner Gray attended was the less substantial part of the charity. The real deal behind the entertainment was the protection fee. By the late nineteenth century Guangzhou's beggars belonged to a guild called the Hall of Guandi, headed by Chen Qifeng, a vagrant from Henan in the Yellow River valley who built his turf near the Hualin Monastery in west Guangzhou. Early in the Republican period, Chen had firmly established himself as the city's undisputed beggar chieftain. His power base was essentially the age-honored tax system, which was tacitly backed by the local police. The beggar tax in Guangzhou was budgeted into five equal portions: an allowance for major beggar heads, an allowance for the local police, and three for the beggars themselves, consisting of daily expenses, medical expenses, and funeral expenses. Although it looked like 60 percent of the tax went to the beggars, the reality was that the headmen of all ranks grabbed the most.[32]

Justus Doolittle, an American missionary, wrote an account in 1865 of his fourteen years' residency in Fuzhou, a city about 500 miles northeast of Guangzhou.

> A head man of the beggars may make an arrangement with the shop-keepers, merchants, and bankers within his district that beggars shall not visit their shops, warehouses, and banks for money for a stipulated time, and the beggars are obliged to conform to the agreement, if native beggars. Religious mendicants, or refugees, exiles, etc, from other provinces, who take to begging for a living, do not come under these regulations. The head man receives from each of the principal business firms with which he can come to an agreement a sum of money, varying, it is said, from a few to ten or twenty dollars per annum, as the price of exemption from the importunities of beggars; and in proof of this agreement he gives a strip of red paper, on which is printed or written a sentence to the effect that *"the brethren must not come here to disturb and annoy."* This paper is pasted up in a conspicuous part of the store or bank, and the money is taken away and *professedly* distributed among the beggars concerned, though it is sagely surmised that he appropriates the lion's share to his own use. After a business man has made this agreement with the head man of the beggars, should any native beggars apply for the usual pittance, it is only necessary to point to the red slip of paper and bid him begone.[33]

Both Guangzhou and Fuzhou are southern cities, but this was certainly not exclusively a southern custom. Up in the lower Yangzi region, in cities like Hangzhou and Ningbo, every year when winter drew near,

> the [beggar] king or his officers will offer terms to the shopkeepers. If they compound by small annual tax, the shop is exempted from the molestation of these professional beggars, and a paper to this effect is prominently pasted near the counter. If the shopkeeper refuses this tax, his life is a burden to him. The beggars, singly or in families, daily visit him; and undaunted by shouts, or oaths, or shavings thrown in their faces (greater violence than this few would dare to offer), continue their drawling appeal, till the shopkeeper in despair tosses them a copper cash (the twenty-fourth part of a penny); and they leave, but only to return the next day, or the next week at the furthest.[34]

Exactly the same practice was observed in another lower Yangzi River valley city, Suzhou, where the beggar head's business was to protect shops from beggars who might come so often and be so persistent as to interfere with business. In the 1920s, the protection fee for a store ranged from 100 or 200 cash per month to as much as over 1,000. New stores, especially pawnshops, were also expected to pay a fee at their grand opening. The rule was that "the beggars know well the sign that tells when the money has been paid and that they do not visit those places." Some of the stores arranged the second and the sixteenth of each month as "begging days" for mendicants to call upon them.[35]

Along the Yangzi River westward into central China, in cities like Han-kou, an almost identical practice was observed in the late Qing:

[The headmen] divide the streets of the city among beggars, who then go in little companies to make as much as possible out of the district allotted to them. They go about with sticks and gongs; entering shops, they make so much noise that the buyers and sellers can hardly hear one another speak: this makes the shop-keeper so anxious to get rid of them that he gives them a cash, and then they go away at once.

Some of these shopkeepers make an agreement with the headman of the dis-trict, by which they pay him a certain sum every year on condition that the beg-gars under his control shall not come to beg of them. He takes the money, di-viding part of it among the beggars, and, of course, keeping a good share for himself. He then gives the shopkeeper a strip of red paper to paste up by his door, on which is written a Chinese sentence meaning, "The brethren must not come here to disturb and annoy." After this, if any of the professional beggars come to that shop they are shown this strip of paper and told to go away, which they usu-ally do at once. Should they persist in begging, the shopkeeper may beat them and drive them away, which he would not dare to do unless he had this proof of an agreement between himself and the king of the beggars.[36]

Although the schedule for collecting the tax may have varied and details were worked out case by case, the general rule was that the second and sev-enth months of the lunar calendar were the time for beggars to collect the payments, the usual amount of which in the late Qing was three thousand cash for shops and two thousand cash for residences.

In the "tax season" in the lower Yangzi River valley, the beggar head of the town, together with a couple of his confidants, each carrying a cotton bag over his shoulder, went door-to-door collecting the tax. Once a shop or a household paid, it received a two-part receipt known as a "beggar slip," which was pasted on the door. The first part of the receipt, to be posted on top, was a sheet of diamond-shaped green paper on which two characters, *Feng Xian* (acting on his honor's order), were written, indicating that this was an officially sanctioned action. The second part of the receipt was a rect-angle of red paper of about seven *cun* (1.3 inches) long and a little over one *cun* wide, which was pasted vertically underneath the green paper. It bore a sentence in black ink: "The Spring [or Autumn] Beggar Tax of Two [or Three] Thousand Cash Has Been Paid."[37]

The schedule for local beggars was intentionally set before the traditional begging season, that is, the second and eighth lunar months, when vagrants from other places came to town for alms. The calendar reflected the rhythm of rural life: the second lunar month was the slack interlude between the Chinese New Year celebration and the spring sowing season and the eighth month was the time for the autumn harvest. By that time those who had paid the local beggars their due would feel it was well worth the money, because the targets of the outside vagrants were those who had not paid the tax. These beggars, who came in groups that varied from three to six persons, looked for shops and homes that did not have a receipt on the door. Once a target was found, the beggars would throw an iron dart-like weapon onto the counter of the store and declare: "This is a travelers' escort from far away. I came to your noble place and became ill. Thus, here I 'pawn' my dart in your store for cash." His fellow beggars, wielding all sorts of swords and spears, would then commence to put on a street show in front of the store. Other beggars might perform acrobatics, such as balancing a chair, a long stick, a door plank, or a table on the nose or forehead. Still others might just sit at the entrance of a store and start playing the Chinese violin (*huqin*) and sing arias from Peking opera. Any of these performances would draw a crowd and interfere with normal business. To end the harassment, the shopkeeper had to pay at least 100 cash to each beggar. Trying to bargain or showing any reluctance to pay would only cause the beggars to demand more, as if they were making bids at an auction.[38]

That shopkeepers had to rely on their own wits rather than the legal or administrative system to maintain a minimal level of social order necessary for conducting business reveals the impotence of the state in coping with the mounting social problems caused by poverty. Even in Beijing, right under the nose of the emperor, beggar taxes were flagrantly levied. In 1906, for example, a fee of 10 taels of silver was demanded by the beggars' guild when a store of an ordinary size opened for business. If the store was a large one, the assessment was correspondingly increased.[39]

China's most Westernized city, Shanghai, was not exempt from this indigenous institution. The practice of the beggar tax was duplicated in every detail in this treaty port. Indeed, there was perhaps no other custom that better demonstrates the affinity between mendicancy in Shanghai and that in the rest of China than the beggar tax. Since begging in Shanghai in the 1920s and early 1930s was organized under the Eight Brothers, who divided the city into four areas for mendicancy, a professional beggar always had a clear idea where he or she could beg and not infringe on the territory of others. The beggars' guild had an income from stores that paid them on a regular basis. Twice a year, in spring and autumn, beggars went to stores to collect the "beggar tax," and just as in the Yangzi River valley, once the "tax" had been collected, the beggars gave the store a "receipt" consisting of two pieces of colored paper that the storeowner would post in a conspicuous place in the store. One was a diamond-shaped green glazed piece of paper with the big character *KAN* ("look" or "attention") on it. The other was a red rectangular glazed piece of paper with a notice reading: "All beggars and tramps: No Begging!" Stores that posted these receipts were relieved from further begging and soliciting. The beggar tax varied from a few dollars to twenty dollars early in Republican period, depending on the size of the store. Most storeowners felt it was worth paying a few dollars twice a year to avoid repeated encounters with beggars over the year. Some even paid as much as eighty dollars a year to the beggars in exchange for their service as night watchmen, at a time when an unskilled laborers earned about eight to ten dollars a month.[40]

There were several reasons for the prevalence of the beggar tax. First, as the Chinese saying put it, people are "less afraid of a barbarian than a beggar." Being totally impoverished, beggars had nothing to lose, which, ironically, made them free to engage in a mild form of social terrorism. Second, paying the tax freed the shopkeeper to engage in business unmolested. If a beggar persisted in begging at a shop that displayed a tax receipt, he might be beaten by the shopkeeper and driven away. Punishment from the beggar head would certainly be more severe. According to one report, "it is affirmed that the head man might, if the beggar repeatedly violated the agreement, flog or beat the culprit to death, and no notice would be taken of the matter by the higher authorities."[41] If the violators were from out of town, it was the beggar head's responsibility to drive them away, which he would almost always do in order to keep his credibility.[42]

Finally, as mentioned earlier, the institution of the beggar tax was supported, sometimes only through tacit agreement, by the authorities, who acquiesced in order to contain the problems associated with poverty and vagrancy and evade the unpleasant work of dealing with beggars. There was also an important budgetary reason behind the government's acceptance of the protection fees: the "right" to levy the beggar tax was granted as a trade-off for various services from beggars. We have already seen beggars performing some municipal duties in Baotou and Shuangcheng in Republican times. Indeed this sort of arrangement was only a continuation of a Qing-dynasty practice.

Local government in the Qing period was not provided with centrally collected taxes and had no tax revenue of its own. Its budget was met by so-called base customs (that is, a variety of customary fees and services).[43] As part of the "base customs," beggars were at the county yamen's beck and call. Commonly, beggars attended the magistrate when he was traveling in town. They carried his sedan chair, bore official standards and other regalia, and struck a gong to announce his coming so street vendors and pedestrians could retreat. They performed similar duties when a high-ranking official passed through the county. If the official traveled via the waterways, beggar were called on to serve as boat trackers; if he traveled by land, more beggars were needed as porters and to serve in the contingent of marchers required to make a suitably imposing procession. On these occasions, the beggar head was always on the spot to supervise. The beggars called up to duty were usually young and able-bodied, and once they were lined up and clad in uniforms, it would have been hard to guess they were just street people temporarily drafted into government service.[44]

When labor was needed on a more regular basis, again beggars were drafted. For instance, in Yangzhou, a major hub on the Grand Canal, which transported tax grain to Beijing, beggars were regularly called upon to pull the boats that passed by the town on their way to the capital. The physical exertion demanded by this kind of labor often caused the death of elderly and undernourished beggars. This led to the provincial government banning the practice in the early Qing. An official stele was erected on the waterside to announce the prohibition, an indication of the severity of the problem. Nonetheless, the practice was soon revived and by the end of the Qing period it was once again common (Figure 13).[45]

FIGURE 13. A drawing from a late nineteenth-century pictorial of yamen runners in Yangzhou, along the Grand Canal, catching beggars on the street and forcing them to serve as unpaid (corvée) laborers. In the background a group of beggars is towing a government boat transporting rice to Beijing. SOURCE: *Dianshizhai huabao* (The Dianshi Study pictorial).

The custom throughout China of using beggars as corvée labor was tenacious because organization was in the hands of local beggar headmen and because it served the purposes of the county yamen. It would have been beyond the limit of the yamen's budget to hire laborers to do the myriad jobs it required.[46] Although the county government did not compensate the beggars, it allowed them to exact protection fees from local businesses, something that benefited both parties: the government saved its budget and the headmen enhanced their position. Moreover, the beggar guilds were legitimated. The beggar tax, of course, supported more than the cost of the corvée duties; it fed the whole crowd of beggars in general. Ultimately, by lending the mendicants the power to "rule" the street, the Chinese state had quietly shifted a formidable financial burden to society.

CHAPTER 6

The Wisdom of Mendicancy

JUSTUS DOOLITTLE, who lived fourteen years in the southern city of Fuzhou, observed beggars' activities on the streets around 1860:

> Sometimes the beggars visit the stores or shops in companies, with loud entreaties for pity, pounding on the floor or the counter, or making a deafening noise with gongs, in order to expedite the giving of a cash. A single lusty beggar with his lungs and staff, or gong, will make such a noise as to interrupt business entirely by drowning conversation, so that the shop-keeper, in a kind of self-defense, tosses him the cash he demands, when he goes away to vex and annoy another shop-keeper in a similar manner. Some beggars carry a tame snake with them coiled about their persons, or held in their hands, or fastened on a stick. Others have a heavy brick or large stone, with which they pound their bodies, either standing or after having laid themselves down on their backs in the street before the shop whence they expect the pittance. Some have a monkey which they have taught to perform amusing tricks; others, on presenting themselves in or before a shop, commerce a song in the Mandarin or in the local dialect, keeping time with bamboo clappers held in one hand.[1]

These are rather diverse begging methods, but they do not exhaust the highly elaborate spectrum of begging techniques in China. Beggars might have needed to adjust to local culture and customs, for in a country of China's size, regional diversity is to be expected. Yet, from the time of the empire through the Republic, the methods of mendicancy persisted with remarkable similarity across the country. This chapter first focuses on begging methods during festivities and life-cycle events, which were prime pickings for mendicancy, and then takes Shanghai as a case study to illustrate how various begging methods were engendered and exercised in an urban environment on an average day.

The God of Fortune Has Arrived!

The culture *on* poverty in China has produced some ironies. How could ragged and filthy beggars be associated with fairy-like figures who can pass messages between the real human world and the mysterious dominion of gods, deities, and ghosts? How could the poorest group in society be associated with the God of Fortune, who was (and still is) arguably the most welcome deity in Chinese culture? Ironic as they are, such contrasts for centuries made possible a primary method of begging in China. Partly through manipulation by beggars and partly out of the wishful thinking of the public, the image (sometimes it was only an inkling) of beggars as mysterious was most evident on the occasion of festivals, especially during New Year, when worship and communication with deities and supernatural beings were the main objectives of a set of elaborate rituals and celebrations.

From the early twelfth lunar month to the Lantern Festival (the fifteenth day of the first lunar month), preparation for and celebration of the New Year lasted for more than a month. In some ways this resembles the holiday season from Thanksgiving to the New Year in North America. As mainstream society was in the mood to celebrate and enjoy the festivities, this was the high season for mendicancy. Throughout the country beggars were an active and visible part of all the festive events.

One of the major preparations for the New Year was a ceremony called "sending back the Kitchen God." It was customarily believed that the Kitchen God, who resided by the cook stove of every household, watched over the family all year around until the twenty-fourth day of the twelfth lunar month, when he was sent back to heaven to report on the family's behavior to the Jade God, the supreme god in the Taoist tradition. On New Year's Eve, the Jade God would assign a new Kitchen God to the family. It is therefore important to please the Kitchen God in his final days on duty.[2] During the year, the image of the Kitchen God was no more than a printed picture posted on the kitchen wall or a ceramic figurine placed over the stove. But in the "sending back" ceremony, the Kitchen God was "incarnated" in street beggars who dressed up as deities, mostly the Kitchen God and his wife (the Kitchen Goddess) and their runners. These beggars sang, danced, and chanted in residential areas, as if they were deities on their way back to heaven. In the festival mood of the New Year's celebration, residents were more willing than usual to give alms to send the Kitchen God incarnate, or the beggars, away.[3]

After the twenty-fourth day of the twelfth month, beggars took one week off, probably to prepare for their own celebration. But from New Year's Day on they reappeared on the streets. Ironically, this time beggars were the incarnation of the God of Fortune (Figure 14), who was welcomed with ceremony by virtually all families on the first few days of the year (the exact date varied from place to place). Beggars solicited door-to-door, crying *Caishen dao* ("Here comes the God of Fortune!"), and giving people a picture of the God of Fortune, which could be an image or just two big characters, *CAI SHEN* (the God of Fortune). In the mood of the New Year and for the sake of auspiciousness, people would take the image and give a tip to

FIGURE 14. An image of the God of Fortune circulated in Beijing during the Qing period. Among his attendants are the legendary Profit Deity (upper left) and the Fortune Boy (upper right). SOURCE: Wang Shucun, *Zhongguo minjian nianhua* (Chinese New Year folk pictures).

the beggars. Shopkeepers would particularly see this as a good omen for their business in the coming year and would grasp the Caishen slip in haste while throwing a few copper coins to the beggars.[4]

Beggars' masquerading as deities was one of the principle techniques of mendicancy in China, and the role of the God of Fortune was by far the most common one in the endeavor. There were a few regional variations in terms of the specifics of this technique, but all were alike in concept throughout the country. The date for receiving the God of Fortune, for example, was the second day of the first lunar month in most parts of the country. Also, from north to south, the image of the God of Fortune was usually sent door-to-door by beggar boys. There were at least two reasons why child beggars had a particularly good chance to get alms on this occasion. A principal custom of the New Year was for adults to give "year money" (*yasuiqian*), wrapped in red paper (or in more recent years, put in a red envelope), to the children as a token of wishes for an auspicious new year. Although it was usually children of a family member or a close friend who received the lucky cash, a beggar child was more likely to take advantage of the custom than a grownup beggar. Another custom was that beggar boys were perceived, wishfully on the part of almsgivers, as reincarnations of the Benevolent Fortune Boys (*Zhaocai tongzi*), the famous juvenile attendants of the most popular Buddhist goddess in China, the Goddess of Mercy (Guanyin). A paradigmatic image of the goddess has her sitting on a lotus throne—a round, legless seat rimmed with water lilies (lotus flowers)—holding a little white jade vase full of dew in one hand and a willow twig in the other. The goddess, it was believed, dips the twig into the vase and then spreads dew drops. A few drops running down from the green leaves extinguish the wildest fire and cure every disease. The Fortune Boys, who are around the age of ten, stand on both sides of this resplendent goddess.

Regardless of who were the messengers, the ritual involved a few commonly known conventions. In case one does not want to give alms when the sender of the God of Fortune arrives, one should not say "No, I don't want it," for the superstition goes that if one does not want *it* (the God of Fortune), fortune will not come. Instead, one should say, "We already have it." In some cases, beggars masquerading as messengers of the deities did not even need to ask for money. In Chengdu, Sichuan, for example, a folk belief held that "if the God of Fortune is silent, you will have good fortune in the new year; if the God of Fortune speaks to you, you will have bad luck this year." Thus, once the masqueraders appeared at the doorway, the residents hastened to give money before the "God of Fortune" even started asking for alms.[5] A poster of the god, whether it contained an image or just calligraphy, should be placed on the wall or the door upside down (sometimes the beggar would post it for the resident). This is because the Chinese word for "upside down" (*dao*) is a homonym of "arrive" (*dao*), thus an upside down God of Fortune symbolizes "the God of Fortune has arrived."

Soliciting alms during the New Year celebration was joyful, or at least the intention of beggars was to entertain people during the most important festival of the year and get alms in return. As beggars put on some imaginative makeup and poured out onto the street as a group, the ritual for the God of Fortune and other deities resembled a parade. A few regional variations in the late Qing and early twentieth century demonstrate the creativity of mendicants. In Chengdu, beggars used copper powder to paint their faces golden to symbolize wealth and wore black paper hats to symbolize official-dom. The latter personified the Chinese metaphor "black gauze cap" (*wushamao*), meaning "official." In much of the imperial period since the Song dynasty (960–1279), Chinese officials of all ranks wore a black gauze cap as part of their official attire. The beggars' appearance—golden faces and black caps—embodied the most favorable combination of best wishes for, as the Chinese adage put it, "making a fortune and being promoted to officialdom" (*shengguan facai*).[6]

Some beggars, such as those in Shaoxing, Zhejiang and Quanzhou, Fujian, had a more creative symbol for fortune. They carried a branch of fresh, green cypress, on which a few copper coins were loosely tied, much like hanging ornaments on a Christmas tree in the Western tradition. This branch symbolized the so-called *yaoqianshu*, a legendary tree that sheds coins when shaken. When the beggar shook the tree (or, rather, the branch or stem), the coins jingled and he or she sang "lucky songs" (ditties and rhymes that express good wishes) or uttered some words of blessing to prospective almsgivers, wishing them to have a yaoqianshu, so money would flow into their pockets like fruit grows on a tree. In return for such a blessing, people offered cash, rice, or New Year cakes.[7] In Quanzhou, the lucky song offered ten "best wishes," sung to the rhythmic shaking of the stem:

> Shaking the money tree: here are the red umbrella and golden chair;
> Shaking the money tree: the money that drops buys land and rice fields.
> The first shake brings prosperity,
> The second shake brings wealth,
> The third shake brings noble twin sons,
> The fourth shake brings four generations of high-ranking officials,
> The fifth shake brings five sons and two daughters,
> The sixth shake brings the six states together under Prime Minister Su,
> The seventh shake brings seven sons and eight sons-in-law,
> The eighth shake brings the Eight Immortals down to earth,
> The ninth shake brings the nine imperial ministers,

The tenth shake brings ten sons and ten daughters-in-law.
Gong xi fa cai—May you have a great fortune![8]

In Kaifeng, the city on the banks of the Yellow River that in the eleventh and twelfth centuries was the capital of China, beggars usually appeared in pairs during the holidays. The main character of the pair was a child beggar disguised as a turtle. A yellowish straw bag covered his whole head, with only a hole left at the nose for breathing. On the bag a picture of a turtle was drawn in white limewash. As if the scene were not clear enough to send the message that this child was playing a turtle, two characters, *wang ba*, (literally "Wang Number Eight," a slang expression for "turtle" and also a cuss word), were written on the headgear. An adult beggar walked behind the "turtle," holding a straw string, the other end of which was wrapped around the child's neck like a leash, as if he were taking the "turtle" for a stroll. The two roamed the streets, in the name of "collecting bad luck" (*shou huiqi*). Supposedly, the "turtle" was the receiver of local residents' bad luck, and the two were taking it away, much like garbage men haul away the trash. In a festival when good omens and auspicious wishes were the foremost desire of the people, only beggars in search of alms would follow such "self-destructive" methods. As a Chinese saying has it, "One does not feel itchy if one has many lice." The assumption was that one cannot be more unlucky than being a beggar, so it would be a small matter for a beggar to endure a bit more imaginary "bad luck."

The turtle beggars cleverly exploited the popular mentality and psychology to the maximum. Their main targets were shopkeepers and the amount of alms they expected depended on the size of the shop, but the custom was that copper coins should always be given out in eights: eight, eighty, eighty-eight, or eight hundred. The word "eight" (*ba*) in Chinese rhymes with the word "booming" (*fa*; in Cantonese the two words are almost homophones), thus "eight" was seen as a lucky number connoting "making a fortune," which was of course a particularly important matter for shopkeepers. Moreover, the limewash sign, "Wang Number Eight," was a play on words. This slang term for turtle also meant "cuckold." The sign was therefore another self-destructive act of beggars making fun of themselves, but it also clearly hinted at the customarily appropriate number of copper coins. In any event, once the pair received some alms, they sang a few auspicious words and left.[9] In Manchuria, beggars simply masqueraded as green turtles holding an abacus. Since both the color green and the turtle symbolize a cuckold, the symbolism of the costume was unmistakable. The beggar would come to a store, making noise with the abacus as if he were adding some sums and joking to the shopkeeper or shop assistants, "Let's clear up our accounts!" Since paying off all debts accumulated during the year before the New Year was a custom virtually everywhere in China, the implication here was salaciously witty: "I admit that I am a green turtle because my wife has slept with you over the year. Now on New Year's Eve you should at least give me some pocket money to compensate me." The buffoonery and quipping tended to amuse shopkeepers.[10]

A similar custom could be found in Yangzi delta cities like Suzhou, where turtles abounded in the region's paddy fields and waterways. Beggars simply put authentic turtle shells on top of their heads and danced through the streets during the New Year. In Songjiang, for another example, beggars, stripped to the waist, used a red string to tie a tortoise-shaped straw cap on their heads. They wore straw eyeglass frames on their noses, held a broken palm-leaf fan, and sang "The tortoise comes on the street, business is booming!"[11] Also in Suzhou, beggars dressed in broken armor to masquerade as Zhong Kui, the exorcist par excellence in Chinese popular religion since the Song dynasty. By this masquerade beggars served as a deity to scare away evil spirits and demons in the New Year.[12]

As part of the entertainment, they sang a variety of ditties and rhymes, a practice known as "chanting happy songs" (*nian xige*).[13] The theme of these songs was always "money and fortune." One of the songs sung by beggars in Houkou runs:

> The God of Wealth is walking in your door.
> Congratulations! You will make a great fortune.
> A noble son will be born in your lucky house.
> Fortune and luck come together.
> Give quickly, to make a fortune quickly
> —you will have good business year round.
> Give one *sheng*, you purchase Nanjing;
> give one *dou*, you purchase Hankou;
> give one *hu*, you purchase land and build a house;
> give one *dan*, you purchase a "merry-go-round."
> Give quick! Give quick!
> You purchase mules and horses.[14]

In Shaoxing, a New Year's song called "With the Stream" (meaning, everything is as smooth as the flowing current) was a kind of song-and-dance duet, in which one beggar held a bamboo basket and the other had a huge "golden ingot" made of paper. The two beggars stood in front of the door of a household, throwing the paper ingot back and forth to each other and singing:

> Making a great fortune in the New Year, golden ingots are floating in.
> With the stream!

Big ingots: Piled up in your warehouse.
With the stream!
Small ingots: To buy land.
With the stream!
Pieces of silver: To erect buildings.
With the stream!
This year: To build three front halls.
With the stream!
Next year: To build three back halls.
With the stream!
In between the halls: To build a pavilion full of sweet-scented osmanthus
    flowers.
With the stream!

. . .

Stand up to scoop up the New Year's cakes [from the water].
With the stream!
Your son's cake is the one for the Number One Scholar [that is, the
    highest status].
With the stream!
Your daughter's cake is the one for the Dragon and Phoenix [that is, a
    perfect marriage].
With the stream!
Your wife's cake is the one for fortune and longevity.
With the stream! [15]

In the mood of the New Year and for the sake of luck, most people offered alms to beggars when asked, not unlike the charity extended to homeless people during holiday seasons in the Western tradition (Figure 15). But in China charity for beggars was in part associated with the folk notion of homeless people as mysterious. For people outside the world of vagrancy, beggars' wandering life and eccentric behavior, their unknown past and unpredictable future, their strange chants and weird attire, and so on, all contributed to the notion that they were connected to an unknown and, perhaps, awesome world, and were somehow mystical and spiritual. As we have noted, in the popular imagination the God of Wealth appears as his opposite: the poor beggar. Alms given to beggars would bring luck and forestall disasters; thus, awe for gods was transformed into mercy for beggars. In a way, beggars in China played a role in linking up ordinary people and spirits, and in New Year's festivities they became a sort of deity intermediate between man and ghost. [16] No matter how factually ungrounded the belief may have been, that beggars masqueraded as deities or messengers of deities reflected their acumen in manipulating superstitions, folk beliefs, and iconic symbolism and seizing the opportunity for alms presented by festivals and rites.

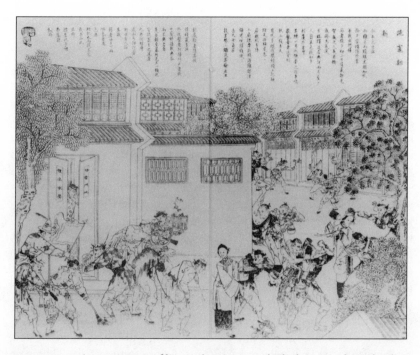

FIGURE 15. A street scene of beggars' activities, which the artist claims he drew from what he saw on "the second day of this [Chinese] New Year [ca. 1895]," presumably in the "Chinese city" of Shanghai. In the foreground from left to right: beggars are sweeping the doorway of a wealthy home; a beggar wears a turtle hat while holding a palm-leaf fan; a beggar holds a "money-shaking tree"; a beggar plays an "ox," led by another beggar; a woman beggar's basket is dropped by accident, breaking her rice bowls; two beggars are fighting over a begging turf; a woman beggar and her partner are performing a flower-drum song. In the background, a number of beggars are running around with "money-shaking trees" or "golden ingots" in their hands. At the corner of a house a beggar is holding a wooden board with two characters on it, proclaiming it to be a "golden brick." The beggar next to him is wielding a clapper to make "sound effects" for the show. SOURCE: *Dianshizhai huabao* (The Dianshi Study pictorial).

Red and White Events

The New Year was, of course, a once-a-year opportunity for beggars. Although solicitations like those we have discussed could be found in other annual festivities also, none was nearly as widespread and intensive as those during the New Year. However, there was another major begging opportunity, one that did not follow the calendar: begging at life-cycle events, which were much more frequent than once a year.

During "happy events" (*xishi*), such as weddings, the birth of a child, the grand opening of a business, anniversaries, and so on, the celebrating family by custom welcomed all people who came to offer their congratulations, even if the congratulators were strangers to the family. Likewise, at funerals, most bereaved families would receive everyone who came to offer condolences and pay their respects to the dead. These two sorts of occasions, known as "red" (weddings, births, birthday celebrations, and so on) and "white" (funerals and anniversaries of the deceased) events, and the customs associated with them, were fully exploited by beggars. It was part of the major responsibility of a beggar head—in fact it was a test of his ability—to know ahead of time the relevant forthcoming events on his turf so he or his underlings could be on the spot at the right moment to congratulate or to mourn. People outside the beggars' inner circle thought that "beggars seem to have an intelligence department of their own that gives them precise information as to every marriage that has been arranged, and the exact day and hour when it is to come off." [17] The secret was that beggars had their sources of information. These included domestic maids and servants of the well-to-do families in town, shops that provide wedding and funeral services, and, more reliably, the Date Selection Hall, astrological fortune-tellers who gave guidance on picking the "right day" for a life-cycle event. [18]

It was tacitly understood that the family should receive and offer a gratuity to these uninvited guests, and most families did so for the sake of propriety and auspiciousness. In time this became a firmly established custom nationwide. Even students sitting for the civil service examinations had to prepare a tip for beggars. A candidate who successfully passed the examination at the county or provincial level expected to be enthusiastically, and noisily, received by his landlord with popping firecrackers and hearty congratulations. Among the first to offer congratulations was the town's beggar headman, who, etiquette dictated, in return should receive cash alms. [19]

Begging on these occasions could be very precise and ritual-like. In Wuhu, Anhui Province, by custom well-to-do families who were going to have a "happy event," mostly weddings, should send a red-colored invitation (red being the color of luck and happiness) to the beggar head. On the day of the event, the headman would send eight beggars—seven men and one woman—to the family to congratulate them. The gender composition of the group was deliberately chosen to re-create that of the Eight Immortals; in other words, this beggar delegation was perceived as the incarnation of the favorite band of deities in Chinese popular culture. The beggars brought gifts, customarily of four kinds: a cake, a bun stuffed with jujube paste, a pair of red cradles, and a string of small firecrackers. Upon entering the door, they also presented the host with a red envelope containing three copper coins, each symbolizing one of the three best cosmological fortunes in folk culture: luck, wealth, and longevity. To receive the beggars, the householder would set a table in the courtyard for them. Tea, tobacco, and appetizers were offered before dinner was served. As each course of dinner was served, the beggars sang impromptu and witty ditties, often taking the food as a subject of each ditty for good wishes. For example, when chicken was served, the song might be:

> The phoenix spreads its colorful wings,
> Symbolizing the happiness of your family on this lucky day.
> The Eight Immortals are invited in to dispel evil spirits,
> Everything will be smooth and prosperous.

The song accompanying a dish of fish might be:

> Golden carp jumping through the Gate of the Dragon
> Symbolize the joyfulness in every room of your home.
> All dragons in the universe are gathering here,
> To wish and sing a song for peace in the world.[20]

After the dinner, the host family was expected to give cash and a large piece of cake to the head of the delegation for him to bring back to his fellows in the den or guild. The key to this formality was of course the amount of cash alms, which was calculated according to a fixed formula: the estimated cost of the banquet per person multiplied by the number of people in the guild who did not show up.[21]

In most cases people considered alms for beggars as a part of the expected expenses and budgeted accordingly. Like the beggar tax, alms were often given to the headman in a lump sum in exchange for his protection, which was always effective. Should a family distribute alms to beggars on an individual basis, the family was "giving money to ask for trouble," for it could never satisfy an endless torrent of beggars. The fees obviously varied by time and location. A personal accounting book of Zhang Lianfang (b. 1905), a Shanghai-based businessman, shows that when he got married in October 1927 in his hometown, Sijing, a small town near Shanghai, the fee for the beggar headman was one silver dollar. The family also spent 4.8 silver dollars to hire three trumpeters—trumpeters were often beggars. This was out of a total budget for the wedding of $65.25.[22] In Chongqing, China's wartime capital, the protection fee for a wedding equated to ten–odd silver dollars in the late 1940s, ten times the amount expected in the town of Sijing some twenty years earlier.[23]

Ou Yangping, a local magnate in Chongqing, recalled his experience with beggars when he got married in 1947. The wedding included a dance party and a Western-style banquet at Queen's Restaurant, the city's most popular venue for weddings. Ou was busy greeting guests and did not notice that not a single beggar was at the door of the restaurant, which in fact was unusual since he had not taken care of the headman. In the evening, the Ou family had a Chinese banquet at home as part of the wedding. Before the dinner started, Ou was told there was a visitor at the door who had come to offer congratulations and give a wedding present. Ou went out to receive the uninvited guest. He was a man in his thirties, dressed in a clean cotton coat in the Sun Yat-sen style; his face had the typical look of an opium addict. As a way of showing awareness of his position, the man politely did not step over the threshold when he handed Ou a cheaply mounted scroll painting. "Our brothers all congratulate Mr. Ou!" the man said. "We've warned our brothers not to bother you at Queen's, and neither are they allowed to bother you here at home." Ou unfolded the scroll and saw inside a piece of red paper on which was written with brush in black ink a couple dozen nicknames: Cripple Zhang, Blind Li, and so on. Ou immediately realized that he had forgotten to take care of the beggars and the headman was giving him "face" by not harassing the wedding. As a savvy and street-wise man, he knew how to handle this and show his appreciation. Politely accepting the gift, Ou summoned a servant who had some connections with the Gowned Bothers (a powerful secret society in the region) and instructed him: "This fellow is a beggar headman. It is not proper to entertain him in the house. You should take him to a restaurant and give him a good meal and offer some money. Be sure not to be rude or offend him in any way!" Ou was pleased that his effort succeeded: not only was his home left in peace, but it also seemed that ever since then his wife was somehow exempted from beggars importuning. If a beggar was going to approach her on the street, another one would come out shouting at the beggar: "Are you blind? Can't you see this is Madam Ou?" [24]

Although Ou had overlooked the beggars as he prepared for the wedding, he in fact knew very well what usually happened at weddings at Queen's should a deal have not been previously arranged with the local beggars. The most filthy beggars would block the entrance and others would lie down on the street right in front of the wheels of the wedding car. Such harassment was not peculiar to this place or to the city of Chongqing but was the norm across the country. Those who ignored beggars or were reluctant to comply with the custom would almost certainly bring themselves trouble and embarrassment. Typically, an unruly and ragged crowd of beggars, which could easily number in the hundreds, would appear on the scene precisely at the pivotal moment of the event—when the bride's sedan chair was about to arrive—shouting and whining and begging, until it was impossible to continue the event and the host was forced to pay the demanded fee.

Sabotage and harassment were, on the other hand, not as unrestrained as they may have looked and did not go beyond making an embarrassing scene. Despite the discord, as one observer summarized the usual situation, "no person is touched and not an article is stolen." [25] This in a way reflected the maturity of the organized extortion, for no criminal charge could really be made against the beggars. Thus even in Shanghai, where the modern police establishment was one of the best in the country, beggars sabotaging life-cycle events was not uncommon. As a matter of fact, because of the population density of the city, this could be especially devastating. For instance, a merchant, Yang Gengguang, married a courtesan in 1935, and on his wedding day he could not get out of the luxurious Yipingxiang Hotel (founded in 1883) on Tibet Road in the International Settlement because it was encircled by a mixed crowd of beggars and others seeking gratuities. He was finally rescued not by the police but by his friend Du Yuesheng (1888–1951), one of Shanghai's top gang bosses, who effected the release by giving the crowd a total of $3,000.[26] Du earned a reputation for being supportive of his friends and benevolent to the poor.[27] In another case, the mansion of a wealthy family who were holding a funeral parade (known as *da chusang*, or grand funeral) was besieged by beggars for a whole day because the beggar guild was unhappy about the amount of gratuities it received. Policemen were called in, but they failed to drive away the crowd. The siege was lifted only after the family gave the beggars what they asked for.[28]

Indeed, because dignity and auspiciousness were of such great concern to most families, beggars could subvert an event without an organized effort—a single beggar could easily spoil things simply by making a scene. The following is typical. A beggar approached a wedding ceremony singing a flower-drum song full of blessings:

> Pow-pop-pow, Pow-pop-pow are the sounds of the happy firecrackers:
> The Zhang family is having a wedding ceremony.
> The door is decorated with happy couplets and colorful silk strips:
> Outside the door the heads of the carriages are like dragons and the
>   traffic is like a stream,
> Inside the door there are four treasure bowls on each side.
> The Trio of Fortune, Wealth, and Longevity are the best men,
> The Four Great Attendants of the Buddha serve as the door guards.
> Eight virgin lads and eight jade girls are playing pipes and flutes.
> The groom and bride stand shoulder to shoulder:
> Kowtow to heaven and earth, then, kowtow to father and mother.
> Let me wish the couple happiness together forever!
> Let me wish the couple to have many sons and grandchildren!

These good wishes offered as a form of entertainment could be considered a quite civilized way of begging. But if the family ignored the beggar, he or she could sing a song that would immediately sour the happy atmosphere. A naked curse might be too offensive, but the beggar could still sing a song to humiliate the family, and the bride was always an easy target:

> Entering a well-lit bridal chamber,
> One sees that the bride's feet are eight-inches long.
> Old buddies, come over to measure her feet:
> Are they not eight-inches long?

> Entering a happy bridal chamber,
> All of a sudden one hears the bride farting.
> Old buddies, come over and smell the gas:
> Is it a fragrant fart or a stinking one?[29]

This kind of ritual sabotage was a very effective begging tactic. Here, as Philip Kuhn points out, "respectable society" was most vulnerable to an attack of "social outcasts" who "seemed to care neither for social 'face' nor for cosmological fortune" since they had already been profoundly unlucky.[30] Because of the importance of "red and white" events in Chinese society—they particularly involved social status and face—most families, including some that were financially constrained, spent a fortune for these occasions, and the dense population of Chinese cities made "red and white" events so frequent that they became one of the major and regular sources of beggars' income.[31]

Moreover, by the late Qing many life-cycle services in big cities had been simply taken over by beggars' guilds. Since guilds had played the role of maintaining order at weddings and funerals, it was a natural step to employ beggars for a variety of services called for by these events. In particular, life-cycle events required, in addition to family members, a large number of people to make up a parade. Virtually no other group but local beggars was always readily available for that purpose. In Beijing, beggars ran a funeral service known as pole houses (*gangfang*). The word "pole" (*gang*) referred to the stout carrying pole for transporting coffins, but it recalled the "pole" or "shaft" (*gan*) that symbolized the power of guilds discussed in Chapter 4. The so-called houses provided two services: rental of paraphernalia and labor. All kinds of paraphernalia for funeral ceremonies and processions were available for rent, such as gongs (for announcing and clearing the street before a procession), parasols, big fans, flags, pennants, placards, sign boards, carts, sedan chairs, embroidered silk coffin covers, and so on. The labor part included carrying coffins, bearing flags and placards, or simply walking in the procession. The public regarded jobs and errands involving funerals as definitely low and somewhat menacing, thus it seemed logical that the most unfortunate group in society should be hired to do them (Figure 16).[32]

FIGURE 16.   A funeral procession around 1926. The deceased probably died at an old age and therefore the funeral was, according to custom, celebrated as a "happy event" (that is, a celebration of longevity). These red-robed "musicians," who are cheerfully playing, were provided by the beggars' guild. SOURCE: *Asia* (October 1927).

Beggars providing funeral services, like other modes of begging, was essentially an urban phenomenon. The sinologist Arthur Henderson Smith (1845–1932) noted in the late nineteenth century: "In city processions flags, banners, umbrellas, screens, and handsome wooden tablets shining with lacquer and glittering with gilt are carried in great numbers before and behind the coffin of notables, but the bearers are not infrequently dirty, ragged beggars, straggling along without aim and without order. Little or nothing of this is to be seen in the rural districts."[33] In large cities this "beggars-as-honor-guards" racket was a serious business and often uniforms were temporarily given to the beggars who marched in processions. In the southern city of Canton (Guangzhou), the attire for wedding processions was a set of red clothes with yellow edges, plus a yellow straw hat edged with red lace. For funerals, the attire was a set of white clothing with blue edges, plus a yellow straw hat edged with blue lace.[34] Once dressed up, the procession of beggars looked quite respectable.

These life-cycle services provided by beggars continued well into the Republican period. The Shanghai Municipal Bureau of Social Affairs complained in 1935 that although a petition of the guild for official registration of the business with the bureau had been rejected in 1929, it was still providing these services.[35] The perseverance of this trade was not just due to the usual impotence of Chinese authorities in handling beggars, but also to the fact that there was a ready market. Hiring beggars was cheap. Thus it was easy to gather a large number of beggars to form a grand procession and stoke the vanity of the family. In a city where Western-style funeral homes were available but expensive, this traditional service fit the bill.[36] But a more cultural reason behind the tenacity of the service was also noted, as Amelia Stott wrote in 1927:

> When passing through Peking [Beijing] one autumn, I found a strike of beggars in full swing. The reason was that one of their "top-knot" men had been arrested. One might suppose this to be a welcome and highly desirable strike. But not so, as it turned out. It was just in the middle of the principal wedding season, and the absence of minstrels gave trouble to old-fashioned Chinese families. Foreign brass bands could be hired, of course; but the mysterious death of a young bridegroom was cleverly used as propaganda by the *tao-fan-hui* [beggars' guild], which attributed the tragedy to the employment of the evil foreigners' "fashion" and predicated that any marriage unattended by the time-honored beggar minstrels would be one of woe and disaster. Besides prophecies of ill, so many other annoyances beset the citizens of Peking as a result of the strike that it ended in favor of the *tao-fan* [beggars]. They did not resume work and banish anxiety in regard to marriage good luck until a deputation had visited them and solemnly promised to negotiate for the release of their imprisoned leader.[37]

Here, in the face of competition from new trends, beggars were vigorously marketing their services, and it seems that at least in this case the "time-honored beggar minstrels" still held the upper hand in the early Republican years.[38]

Begging in Shanghai: Strategy and Tactics

All of the techniques and tactics, including "social terrorism," wielded by Chinese beggars were most effective, and in some instances only possible, in a densely populated urban environment. China's largest and most populous city, Shanghai, is therefore an ideal case to illustrate the various begging methods that could be found throughout the country. The prosperity of modern Shanghai created a favorable environment for mendicancy; some people went so far as to call it a "paradise for beggars."[39] From 1917 to 1947, a number of investigations of Shanghai's beggars, conducted by sociologists, social workers, Christian activists, journalists, and others, inventoried the various popular begging methods in the city: depending on who did the counting, the number varied from seven to twenty-five. Each tactic or technique had a name in the beggars' argot. Still, none of these investigations was inclusive of all begging methods in the city. Most begging tactics in Shanghai were universal in China and existed for centuries.[40] Even the terminology—the words used in importuning and the argot—was identical or akin to that in other cities.

Shanghai early in the twentieth century was not only China's most prosperous city, it was also its most crowded. In 1935, the population density in the International Settlement and the French concession—the core of the city—was 51,317 and 48,747 persons per square kilometer, respectively. By the early 1940s, the population density per square kilometer in these areas had increased to 70,162 and 83,599 persons respectively. The 1953 census found that the average population density per square kilometer in the city proper, which mostly consisted of the former foreign concessions, was 46,500, and seven out of the city's twenty-one districts had an average population density over 100,000 per square kilometer. Population densities in Nanshi (the old Chinese city) and the downtown area around Nanjing Road were as high as 159,000 and 148,000 respectively.[41] The begging methods discussed below can be better understood with such a population density map in mind.

"FOLLOWING A DOG"

It might seem self-evident that one of the most conventional ways of begging on the streets was to follow pedestrians, calling them "master," "madam," "uncle," "aunt" or the like and asking for money. With perhaps only a modification in the way pedestrians are addressed, mendicants all over the world beg on the street in this fashion. But the plea did have its techniques. Although any pedestrian might be the target, women were preferred, for they were thought to be more tender-hearted and easier to be persuaded than men. One of the frequently used entreaties went something like this: "Madam, miss, for mercy's sake, please do something good. No money is spent in vain—it goes in the open and is returned in secret. A good turn gets a good reward. Oh, show your kindness! Open your golden dragon-like [noble] hands! Please give a copper coin so a poor person can have a bowl of gruel."[42] But regardless of whether the beggar's target was a man or a woman, all versions of standard begging entreaties aimed to make people feel flattered, sympathetic, disturbed, or unsafe (in the sense that "God might punish me if I am unsympathetic"). Any one of these feelings might prompt a person to give alms.

A beggar who used to beg in the Temple of the City God in Shanghai's old Chinese city once recalled, with obvious pride in his knowledge of human psychology:

> Begging had its techniques. For example, to old women, I called: "Good madam, like the Goddess of Mercy [Guanyin]! Mercy! Salvation for all living creatures! Madam, reward a poor person! I wish you, madam, double fortune and happiness and long life! Have great offspring!" I loudly repeated these chants like crazy. Because pilgrims came with the idea of doing good deeds, once they heard my chant they all gave money and had an easy conscience. When I followed a young lady of about age seventeen or eighteen I quickly changed my tone, saying: "Good miss, I hope you will have a good husband and soon give birth to a lively baby." Young ladies are always sensitive to the mention of things like this, especially in front of a crowd. When I yelled these words they got really embarrassed and their faces turned red. But their annoyance made me chant even louder. In order to end the harassment, they gave money right away.[43]

Persistence was essential to this mode of begging. The American journalist Ernest O. Hauser related in 1940 that Shanghai beggars "would follow you for two or three blocks, murmuring pleas in the first block, obscenities in the second, curses in the third. And . . . in the fourth block they were likely to transfer some of their lice to your coat."[44] But an experienced pedestrian might get rid of a persistent beggar by simply crossing a street if he happened to be at the boundary of the beggar's turf. For example, the block from the Central Theater to Avenue Edward VII (today's East Yan'an Road) in the French Concession formed the border between two begging zones. Beggars would not continue to follow their objects if the pedestrian crossed to the other side of the street. A savvy Shanghainese therefore knew how to get rid of a beggar simply by walking across the street.[45]

In the beggars' argot, this type of begging was called "following a dog" or "driving swine."[46] Dogs and pigs were the creatures that figured most prominently in Chinese cursing. Here beggars had elevated themselves to the position of master and lowered their marks to the position of dirty and slavish animals. When one investigator learned of this argot, he was offended. Comparing almsgivers to animals, he declared, only shows these panhandlers to be the most nasty and ungrateful people in the world.[47] But it is more reasonable to see this as just another example of the Ah Q–style "psychological victory" portrayed by the writer Lu Xun (1881–1936).[48]

"GROUND PETITION"

A "Ground petition" (*gao dizhuang*) referred to an appeal written on a piece of paper or a sheet of cotton cloth and placed in front of the beggar, who usually sat on a sidewalk bowing or kowtowing. Petitions were also written in chalk directly on the sidewalk (Figure 17). Investigators believed that the

FIGURE 17. On a day early in the summer of 1949 a man begs on a busy Shanghai street with his appeal written in poetic lines on the sidewalk, telling of his hunger and sadness and imploring passersby to donate pennies as a way to "cultivate the fortune field," a classic metaphor for charity (with the implication that charity will be rewarded by God). Photo by Sam Tata, taken when the Communists seized the city. SOURCE: *Shanghai 1949: The End of an Era* (Batsford, 1989).

gentleness of this method made it popular among women, children, and the handicapped. The petitions were in all kinds of calligraphy and in both Chinese and Western languages.[49] In 1934, a reporter for the *Shanghai Evening Post and Mercury* copied word for word on a street corner what he called "one of the specimens of those 'petitions' written [in pidgin English] on the sidewalks": "I, Wong Ah-pao, am native of Nanking. I studied in the Changming High School. I come Shanghai look my friend and no find him. Now I have no money. No money no can buy food therefore hungry. Thank you if you give me coppers. Sincerely, Wong Ah-pao (signed)."[50] This paragraph of course aimed to appeal to members of Shanghai's sizable foreign community, which numbered about 60,000 at the time.[51] Since not all of them were native English speakers, using pidgin English was not uncommon even among foreigners. Petitions in Chinese were often written in an elegant style with beautiful calligraphy. The stories of the "petitioners" varied, but they almost always contained the theme that the person came from a decent family but had fallen to the rank of a street beggar due to a misfortune or a series of misfortunes beyond his or her control. Many of them claimed the petitioner came from a literati or intellectual family—to use the Chinese idiom, a family with the "aroma of books" (*shuxiang zhi jia*)—for such a background was the most esteemed in China. This was followed by a tortuous route that reduced the petitioner to indigence and eventually begging on the street.[52] Although there was no lack of genuine stories of this nature, most of these petitioners were professional beggars who understood the general social esteem for intellectuals and so took it as an effective way to arouse compassion. Such petitions were always handwritten by a true "intellectual," often a professional letter writer. As for the beggar, he or she had to memorize the story and be able to recite it fluently, confidently, and with sincerity—in case he or she was queried by an inquisitive potential almsgiver.

DIGNIFIED BEGGING

The discussion of ground petitioning brings us to the tactic of using dignity as a way to beg. While the public in general despised professional beggars, it tended to sympathize with those who had suddenly sunk to the status of street people. Therefore, portraying oneself as a decent, but down-and-out, person could be an effective way to stimulate compassion. Tao Jiuyin, a well-known Shanghai journalist in the 1940s, summarized ten major begging methods in the city in the decade following the outbreak of the Sino-Japanese War in 1937. At least three were a sort of "dignified begging." One method that seemed to be more effective than ground petitioning was for a whole family, dressed in good clothing, to kneel on the sidewalk in an orderly fashion: the senior persons in the front, juniors in the back, men to the left, and women to the right. All looked solemn and sad but kept silent. The message was clear: a dignified family struck by sudden misfortune or perhaps a catastrophe, with no way out but begging; they were such novices that they only knew this awkward way of begging. In another version, men and women begged for "travel money" in front of Sichuan and Cantonese restaurants. These people, who spoke Sichuan or Cantonese dialects and were supposedly natives of those provinces, claimed to have no money to leave wartime Shanghai and go back to their hometowns. This begging tactic had at least two sound foundations: Cantonese and Sichuan restaurants were enormously popular and numerous in Shanghai, which means there were many spots for these panhandlers, and the provinces were far from Shanghai, which means a considerable amount of money was needed to return home. Yet another kind of dignified begging related to the war involved men dressed in tattered military uniforms, posing on the sidewalks as demobilized soldiers of the Nationalist Army. In particular, they wanted to be taken for members of the Nineteenth Route Army, which in the autumn of 1937 fiercely fought in Shanghai against the Japanese invasion. The public's patriotic fervor made these men more sympathetic figures than, say, homeless Vietnam War veterans who appealed for help on the streets of American cities.

"Dignified begging," like most other kinds of begging, was not limited to Shanghai. Because of the nation's profound literati tradition, the image of a learned man reduced to poverty was particularly compelling to many people. For example, in the Double Spring (Shuangqun) Teahouse, a popular spot with Chengdu's intellectuals, an unemployed teacher made a living simply by begging from the customers in English: "Excuse me. I am hungry. Please give me a little money to buy Gao-Kui [*guokui*, a type of bread]."[53] Despite the fact that all customers in the teahouse were Chinese and there was definitely no need to use a foreign tongue, the very fact that someone who could speak English ended up begging convinced many people to open their purses.

If one was not up to speaking a Western language, then classical Chinese could be an asset. There were so-called poet beggars who successfully generated considerable sympathy in many parts of the country. These men usually dressed in an unlined long gown, which, although faded and worn out, served as the emblem of an old-fashioned educated man, like Lu Xun's famous protagonist Kong Yiji.[54] Like true gentlemen, these beggars pled for help quietly, using chalk to write poems, aphorisms, or worldly-wise sayings on a wall. They made no oral appeal, as if silence conveyed yet another notion: giving alms or not is up to your own conscience.

Other poet beggars were more pragmatic. In Yangzhou, Jiangsu Province, these men took advantage of the popularity of the gaily painted pleasure boats that plied the famous Slim Western Lake.[55] This resort featured classic Chinese garden scenes of willows and pavilions, an ideal setting for men of letters to pass the time in aesthetic retreat. In fact, poet beggars, walking on the lakeside, followed the excursionists in the boats and applied an ingenious method of extracting alms. They tied a pyramid-shaped white cotton bag to a long, thin bamboo pole, much like the net lepidopterists use to catch butterflies. With this device in hand, they could reach the boats on the lake with ease. One may say that the beggars were considerate of the sightseers and did not want to spoil their enjoyment of the picturesque lake. Instead of the conventional shouting of "ladies, masters—please have mercy," they recited classical poems. In a relaxed and confident manner, they quoted from *Poems of the Thousand Households*, a thirteenth-century popular anthology. This proved to be more effective than the usual plea. As they recited Tang-dynasty poems such as "Two yellow orioles twittering on the emerald green willows / One line of white egrets ascending to the bright blue sky," few could resist dropping a few coins into the white bag. Yangzhou's teahouses were another spot where poet beggars plied their trade. The writer Ye Lingfeng (1904–75) recalled that on a visit to Yangzhou in the early 1930s, he and his friend, Hong Weifa, were having an idle chat in a teahouse near the lake when a beggar approached the table and recited a poem of Du Fu's (712–70): "It is the right time when Jiangnan is picturesque / I meet you gentleman again in the season when flowers are falling." This piece was written for Du's friend, Li Guinian, and the lines the poet beggar had recited fit the situation perfectly. Hong could not help but clap and shout "bravo!" And he gave the "poet" two silver coins, enough for a few days of meals.[56]

"HEROES AT THE BRIDGEHEAD"

As we have seen, there was no clear line that demarcated beggars who wandered on the street seeking alms and beggars who offered some sort of service in return for a gratuity. The latter included such things as opening the door of private cars in front of a hotel or a theater, carrying passengers' baggage on the docks, and so on.[57]

One of the most common ways of begging in Shanghai was to be a helper on the bridges over Suzhou Creek. In the first half of the twentieth century, on the eastern end of Suzhou River, which was about two miles in length, there were eleven heavily traveled humpback bridges that connected the central part of Shanghai to the northern parts of the city (Yangshupu, Hongkou, and Zhabei).[58] On both sides of the bridges there were always beggars who waited to help rickshaw pullers and pedicab drivers push their vehicles up the bridge. With a helper, the vehicle smoothly reached the top of the bridge. But before it could run down the other side of the bridge, the beggar would ask the customer for a tip, usually a copper coin. Rainy days were especially good for business because the slippery paving made it harder than usual for rickshaw men to pull their vehicles up the bridge. In heavy rain, a helper could earn 30–50 copper coins in two to three hours.[59] In the beggars' argot, this type of begging was jokingly called "Zhang Fei pushing

Zhuge Liang," a humorous metaphor and, more significantly, one that reflected beggars' self-esteem.[60] In Chinese popular culture, the heroic warrior Zhang Fei (d. A.D. 221) often served as a handcart puller for Zhuge Liang (A.D. 181–234), the most famous military strategist in Chinese history. Here, since the rickshaw rider was "Zhuge Liang," the beggar had become the valiant hero, Zhang Fei.[61]

MIDNIGHT BEGGARS

For its bustling nightlife Shanghai was nicknamed "the city without night." Theaters, cinemas, nightclubs, and other places of entertainment that were spread throughout the city often remained open until midnight or early morning. Among the crowd that always congregated in front of the theaters were beggars. Their targets were fairly clear: rich courtesans and young dating people. Usually, rich women in Shanghai only carried silver coins in their purses since they regarded more frequently circulated copper coins filthy. This, of course, was good for the beggars. An author described so-called midnight beggars in Shanghai around 1917:

> It is a great opportunity for the [midnight] beggars when a theater empties after a show. On that occasion, as long as the beggars follow the courtesans' rickshaws most closely, they can get a considerable amount of income. In most cases, courtesans go to the show to look for a date and to be in the limelight. When they are not lucky enough to meet a favorite young man, they are surrounded by dirty and smelly monsters who are always reluctant to leave. For the sake of the "limelight" and for snaring a young man, these courtesans generously give one or two silver coins in order to get the beggars to leave as quickly as possible. Some courtesans, who are afraid that the beggars will not leave quickly enough and want them to walk off immediately, give a good amount of cash. The beggar who gets the money then heads away to "take care" of other people.[62]

When Shanghai became more cosmopolitan in the 1930s and 1940s, nightclubs also always attracted a swarm of beggars who waited in the front in order to waylay the rich patrons. Occasionally, Russian beggars were found in these places.[63]

SQUATTING OVER A DITCH

Shanghai's beggars exhausted all possible public places for mendicancy, including public lavatories. Shanghai in the 1940s had about five million people, but only 139 public lavatories, mainly designed for pedestrians, an average of nearly 36,000 residents per lavatory.[64] The situation was in fact more appalling because most of the city's residential homes did not have flush toilets.[65] The public lavatories were particularly crowded in the morning and some residents, especially men, used them daily. One should also bear in mind that everyday the city had tens of thousands of visitors.

The shortage of toilets was exploited by panhandlers to extort alms. These public facilities consisted of a ditch that was compartmentalized into a number of spaces—without doors—for people to squat over. If a space was occupied, the next person just had to stand by and wait his turn. For some male beggars it became a daily routine to go to a public lavatory and occupy a space there. The beggar would not yield the space until the next person in line reached the point of emergency, and then the beggar would start asking for money "to buy cigarettes." The person, with little room to bargain, could get his turn only by surrendering a copper coin or two. Having got money from the desperate man, the beggar would wait to find another space to squat and start the game all over again.[66]

Such extortion was a long-standing practice and was occasionally mentioned in popular literature, such as the Mandarin Duck and Butterfly type of novels, in the early twentieth century.[67] But it became a reinvented method of begging in the early 1940s. When a journalist disguised himself as a newly arrived beggar and asked an experienced beggar in a street for advice, "squatting over a ditch" was among the first techniques the beggar veteran taught the new arrival. The trick remained the same, but the suggested "money for cigarettes" had grown to twenty to thirty cents.[68] "Squatting over a ditch" is one of the most revealing examples of how urban congestion could serve the purpose of mendicancy.

DEBT COLLECTING

Beggars also took advantage of the sometimes difficult and uncomfortable job of collecting debts. When the two parties, the lender and the debtor, were friends or at least acquaintances, it was not unusual for the lender to hire a beggar to collect the debt. Typically, the loan was given as a courtesy and, almost as a rule, the lender would never ask for interest, nor in most cases even a receipt. Although the person might be reluctant to lend the money, he would feel *buhaoyisi* (embarrassed) not to show his generosity when a friend asked for help. Customarily, it was the debtor, not the lender, who proposed a date for repaying the loan. The whole deal therefore was based on the presumption of trustworthiness and the notion of face, with little or simply no paperwork.

However, the debtor, as the two Chinese categories of human types have it, might not be a *junzi* (man of integrity) but a *xiaoren* (mean person). More often than not, he took the courtesy or friendship for granted and in due time he almost forgot that he had ever borrowed the money. Not only did he fail to repay the loan by the promised date, but he showed little intention of returning it at all. The lender was, naturally, furious and, after several failed attempts to collect the debt, he turned to local beggars for help.

Beggars, always glad to have business, acted quickly. The following is usually what happened next. It did not take long before the beggars detected the route that the debtor took in his daily transit and, one day on his way home, the debtor suddenly found himself surrounded by a group of filthy and fierce-looking beggars. In just a few seconds before he realized what was happening, he was pushed into a nearby "tiger stove," a common neighborhood store that sold hot water and served as a teahouse, where he was going to literally undergo a trial.[69] The beggars peeled off his clothes, tied him up with hemp ropes, and beat him. Now the man was only too eager to admit all his wrongdoings and moreover, if he had enough cash in his pockets, he was more than willing to pay off the debt at once. If he did not have the money handy he had to schedule a pay-off date right on the spot, a promise he would not dare break, otherwise he would be kidnapped in this fashion again. Only at this point was the man was released. In case he could not make the promised date, his second visit to the teahouse would be more costly. He then had to pay interest on the debt, treat the beggars to tea and snacks right in the teahouse, or sometimes pay a lump sum of cash to the beggars as a "toilsome fee" (*xinku fei*) for all the trouble he caused.

Most of the collected debts went to the beggar head and his fellow beggars who carried out the collection. The lender got just a little of his money back; sometimes he got no money back at all. The whole event was, as an insider put it, "fighting for releasing one's anger, not for money." This became a service known as "assured debt collecting" (*bao taozhai*).[70]

Beggars also served a similar purpose by being hired out to beat people up. If one wanted to physically assault a foe but was too weak or too timid to do so by oneself, one could hire beggars to act on one's behalf. The payment ranged from a few dozen copper coins to a couple of silver dollars, depending on how much the person wanted his enemy hurt. An experienced beggar could be rightly called a boxer, for he excelled at predicating what was needed to inflict any given level of pain and injury and was able to hit at the right place with the right force, a measure entirely based on what he had been paid. This "assured battering" (*bao daren*) was solely a business deal. If the victim wanted to seek revenge, it was not unusual for him to hire the very same beggars to beat up his opponent. As far as the beggars were concerned, it made no difference, so long as they were paid.[71]

CHAPTER 7

Men's Limbs and Women's Mouths

STATISTICS ON THE gender ratio of beggars in China are largely absent or little more than educated guesswork. According to the Shanghai beggar headman Zhao, Shanghai's beggars in the early 1930s were about evenly split between men and women.[1] However, the Jiang-Wu survey of Shanghai beggars conducted at the same time, a random sample of 700 beggars (502 males and 198 females), seemed to suggest that the larger portion of Shanghai beggars were male.[2] Another survey of Shanghai beggars, conducted in 1927, also indicated that most beggars (57 percent) were male.[3] Given the murky nature of mendicancy and lack of official statistics, the exact gender ratio among Chinese beggars may never be known. But regardless of the numbers, mendicancy was a profession for both sexes and moreover one in which gender differences were put to good use.

Coiling up a Snake

A central image of the street beggar was a ragged unfortunate stretching out a filthy hand pleading for alms. This image was so engrained in the public mind that it earned beggars a satiric nickname, the Great General of Stretching Out the Hands. When a beggar did have something in hand, it was usually a bamboo pole, a broken bowl, or a live pet (most commonly, a snake). A long bamboo stick was perhaps the most enduring symbol of Chinese beggars. We have already seen the role of the shaft in the hands of beggar headmen. In fact ordinary beggars also had a long bamboo pole in hand, known as a "dog beating pole." The name suggests the implement was used for self-protection, but in reality it was an all-purpose instrument and a symbol of beggars of both sexes. For example, the famous genre painting *Along the River during the Qingming Festival* is noted for portraying hundreds of characteristic individuals; all the beggars depicted in the scroll have a bamboo pole in hand (and, typically, they are stretching out the other hand for alms).[4] In one of his masterpieces, "New Year's Sacrifice," the writer Lu Xun depicted how a modestly well-off peasant woman known as Sister Xianglin underwent a great deal of personal misfortune caused mainly by society's discrimination against widows. Eventually, around the age of forty and after her only son was tragically eaten by a wolf on an early spring day, she became a beggar: "In one hand she carried an empty bamboo basket; a broken bowl lay inside it—empty. With the other hand she supported herself on a bamboo pole that was taller than she and starting to split at the bottom. It was obvious that she had become beggar, pure and simple."[5]

While a bamboo pole in hand was typical of both male and female beggars, snake charming was almost entirely a male craft. A beggar playing with a blue or green snake, known as a "water snake," on the street in order to attract spectators—and potential almsgivers—was among the most common begging scenes in China. Indeed the scene was so common that it had made "a beggar with a snake in hand" a paradigmatic image of mendicancy. Artists' impressions of mendicants, from the works of the early Ming artist Zhou Chen (who painted scenes from life in Suzhou), to the late eighteenth-century British artists William Alexander and George Henry Mason (who depicted life in Guangzhou), all included snake charming as a symbol of beggars.[6] All over China, snake charming was exclusively associated with beggars. Mason, who made an admirable effort to draw "documentary pictures" of everyday people and customs of China, observed on the streets of Guangzhou that the snake charmer "carries a live serpent coiled round his neck, the greatest part of which he will, for a very small reward, cram head foremost into his mouth, allowing any person to draw it out by the tail." As if this were too implausible for Mason's Western audience, he affirmed that "from his personal knowledge . . . this mode of begging, however extraordinary, is practiced without the smallest trick or deception."[7] (See Figure 18.)

Even in North China, where the cold and dry weather made serpents less common, beggars were invariably associated with snakes. Early twentieth-century Beijing residents often saw beggars carrying a bamboo cage with a couple of small blue snakes. These "snake beggars," as they were commonly called, captured snakes mainly to sell them, either for their meat or for other uses. Snakeskin was popular for making purses and covers for pens and snake gallbladders were believed to have antipyretic properties, as we shall discuss later. Snakes were also sold alive. On Buddhist holidays across the city, beggars sold small water snakes to pilgrims for a ritual known as "releasing lives" (*fangsheng*), in which people bought captive small animals, such as fish and

FIGURE 18. An artist's impression of a snake-charming beggar, on a street of Canton (Guangzhou) in 1799. Note the very short queue of the beggar, which indicates the deviant nature of mendicants, as at the time the customary, as well as the government-required, hairstyle for men was to have a long queue. The stick in his hand, known as a "dog-beating rod," is typical of beggars. But for a mendicant of this type it could also serve as a sort of stage prop for performing his craft. SOURCE: George Henry Mason, *The Costume of China* (1804).

birds, and set them free.[8] The practice was derived from the Buddhist belief in reincarnation and in saving lives as one of the most important ways to accumulate good karma. The practice also allowed benefactors to feel morally superior. As a Qing author explained, "the petty man catches and sells; the gentleman (*junzi*) buys and releases."[9] Beggars fit, of course, into the "petty man" category. But in early twentieth-century Beijing at least, the "gentlemen" who practiced the releasing lives ritual were mostly old ladies.[10] However, the beggars were indifferent as to who the ritual practitioners were as long as there were plenty of them, and, given the large number of temples in Beijing, this seemed to be the case. Susan Naquin has identified more than 2,500 temples that can be documented in Beijing between 1400 and 1900, and she has indicated that the actual number of temples during the period could have been greater by at least one third. Moreover, the number of temples increased quite rapidly early in the twentieth century. Surveys have identified more than 1,500 temples in Beijing after 1911.[11] At the time Beijing had at least fifty major, regularly scheduled temple fairs, some of which were held as frequently as almost every other day.[12] Even if only some of the temples and temple fairs held the "releasing lives" ritual, that would still have meant there were enough devotees to make this form of mendicancy a playing proposition.

Snakes were favorite animals for this ritual in part because of a folk belief that they were "little dragons." Among the twelve animals of the Chinese zodiac, the snake ranks next to the dragon, and the dragon in Chinese culture was an emblem of great power and great fortune, so much so that sometimes its depiction was reserved exclusively for the emperor's use.[13] Beggars, of course, cleverly took advantage of this belief. In Wuxi, Jiangsu Province, beggars wrapped snakes around their arms to resemble mighty dragons, and as they walked along the street they loudly and rhythmically announced: "The dragon has come, the dragon has come, making fortune all year round!" If people ignored this chant, which everyone understood was a call for alms, the beggars released the snakes to scare pedestrians and shoppers.[14]

Although snakes were popularly associated with dragons, they were also feared, making them an excellent means of extorting alms, especially from women, who were generally regarded as snake phobic. Stott discovered this when she visited the beggar's den in southern Zhejiang Province:

> As my eyes wandered over that filthy place, I happened to notice among the garbage several old baskets containing snakes, mostly of a non-poisonous species. "Ah," I remarked, "so you include the art of snake-charming in your program?" "Not necessarily," answered the president, "but some of our members find these snakes useful in collecting their flowery dues from greedy-hearted ones. To dwell upon the fierce love of money in men, and especially in women, weighs down the spirit. Often the tao-fan [beggar] has to throw a snake round a woman's neck before she will drop her grudging gift. The act invariably arouses in those who behold it so great a degree of terror that they quickly avoid similar inconvenience." He summoned a member of the *hui* [guild], and I was shown a most skillful demonstration of "snake lassoing." Some days later I actually chanced to see the method tried successfully upon a well-dressed Chinese woman who encountered the beggars in the street.[15]

Snake charming, however, was not always all fun for beggars; in fact, it could be deadly. In an incident reported in Sichuan, when a beggar was performing a "swallowing a snake" show on the street, such as the one de-scribed by Mason, a bystander touched a burning cigarette to the tail of the snake, which swiftly scurried into the beggar's stomach, causing his instant death. The prankster was described as an "evil man" (*e'ren*) but no lawsuit was mentioned in the report.[16]

A very similar kind of incident, which led to a lawsuit, was recorded in a Qing dynasty personal note. A man, whose name is unknown but was noted in a town in the Yangzi delta region for his upright character, one day saw a beggar attempt to break into a home. He shouted at the beggar and chased him away. A few days later, the man saw five or six beggars drinking on the roadside; among them was the beggar he had confronted the other day. The beggar, who was the ringleader of the group, also recognized him and thought it was a good chance to take revenge. On his orders, the beggars trussed the man up and pulled down his pants. Then, holding the head of a snake against the man's anus, the headman touched a fire to the tail of the snake, which, reportedly, quickly squeezed itself into the anus. As it disap-peared into the man's body, the beggars let him go. The man was in un-speakable pain but managed to walk back home. When he finally stepped across the threshold, he was in such agony that he could only disjointedly utter a single word: "snake . . . snake . . . snake." In the local Wu dialect "snake" is a homophone of "tea." Again, the sources say his wife thought he was terribly thirsty and wanted to have a cup of tea and, in a great hurry, brought one to him. Unable to explain anything, the man took a few sips of the tea and then died. The family thought this was an unfortunate sudden death and no one suspected that the man had been murdered. A few days af-ter the funeral, a young beggar knocked at the door and told the family the truth, saying he would be willing to serve as a witness in court. The motive for the street urchin was that he had recently been badly beaten by the head-man and therefore sought revenge by turning him in. The family was as-tonished and only then realized that the man's last words were in fact "snake," not "tea." The case was brought to the local yamen and, at the in-sistence of the victim's wife, the magistrate ordered an autopsy. As a snake was found in the man's intestines, the beggar was executed.[17]

Street crimes and maliciousness of this sort may not have been common, but they did happen, and tales like these entered the written record largely because of the "beggar and snake duo" that had caught the popular imagi-nation, making beggars' ingenuity with the little animal a common subject for centuries. Beggars were reputedly skillful snake catchers and households troubled by snakes often hired them to eliminate the pests. An eighteenth-century story about how a beggar caught a hidden poisonous snake in a mountain resort near Hangzhou and hence removed a public hazard remained a favorite tale in the early twentieth century. The Bell Tower of the Southern Screen Hill at Dawn (Nanping xiaozhong) was one of the ten most famous scenic spots of Hangzhou. One of its attractions was a pavilion where numerous ancient stone tablets were preserved. A flight of stepstones, on which climbers could sit and relax, led to the pavilion from both sides of the hill. In 1739, something weird happened on the stepstones on one side of the hill: the people who had sat on the stones often got infections on their thighs and legs; some of the infections were so severe that the inflamed legs rotted to the bone. The steps looked perfectly normal, but the frequent incidents made them seem cursed. A beggar, described as "dark skinned and with a heavy beard," and known to be a skillful snake catcher, was asked to go to the pavilion to see what was wrong. With just a glance at the trouble spot, the beggar diagnosed the problem. "There is a poisonous snake stuck underneath the steps and it can't get out," the man said with absolute certainty. "It can only breathe through the chink between the steps. If people happened to sit on the steps, they got poisoned by its breath." Sure enough, as the stones were pried up, a snake, which looked like a flat carp, slithered out. Apparently it had grown up in that flat crack and its body was shaped by the limited space. All people, especially residents in the area, cheered. The neighbors collected money to have a dinner party in honor of the snake beggar.[18]

Some beggars were not only professional snake catchers but also knowledgeable in the use of snakes to treat illnesses and herbal medicines to treat snakebites. In that regard, vagrancy or a life passed among the "rivers and lakes" could be an asset for collecting folk remedies or oral traditions of medical treatment and building up clinical experience. It was not uncommon for street beggars to be knowledgeable in folk medicine; some became what the Chinese called "rustic doctors" (*tu yisheng*) or "itinerant doctors" (*jianghu langzhong*, or "doctors of the rivers and lakes"). These expressions were akin to "quack" in English, but the people so referred to were regarded more as amateur medical practitioners than as fakes. Snakes were often the aspirin in the pharmacy of these itinerary physicians. Snake flesh was a delicacy in Chinese (in particular, Cantonese) cuisine and also a dish that embodied the "food as therapy" (*shiliao*) theory in the Chinese medical tradition.[19] Snake blood and gallbladder were believed to be effective in treating inflammation. For this purpose venomous vipers were more efficacious than nonpoisonous species. According to traditional Chinese medical thinking, venom, if properly used, could have some role in curing difficult-to-treat diseases.[20]

According to a nineteenth-century report, a wealthy family in Beijing by the name of Li had a married son in his early twenties. One day, on the middle finger of his right hand there suddenly sprouted a long and narrow polyp. By the time the polyp stopped growing, it was a purple-colored "flesh pipe" over three feet long, which frequently went into spasms that caused excruciating pain. The young man's father hired many doctors to treat the malady, but none was effective. One doctor had the polyp excised and the young Li bled severely, only to see the polyp grow again in few days to its full size. At that time, a skinny beggar knocked at the door and recommended himself for treating the problem. The desperate father treated the beggar with honor, saying that he would offer half of his family's property if his son could be cured. The beggar, who brought a snake with him, walked into the young Li's bedroom and called loudly: "Be quick, ask your wife to come!" When the wife came in, the beggar asked all other people to leave the room. He then told the wife to hold the snake inside her coat while squatting on the ground near the bed on which her sick husband was sitting. Uneasy inside the stuffy coat, the snake found a way to sneak out. Once its head was out, its mouth reached for the end of the polyp, which was hanging from Li's finger almost down to the ground, and started to suck on it. One could hear the snake breathing heavily while sucking on the polyp. The polyp visibly began to shrink, and when it eventually was entirely sucked up by the snake, the snake lay down on the ground and died, its body full of red stains underneath its skin as if it had died of internal bleeding. With no further treatment, the young man was cured. The overjoyed father rewarded the beggar generously, although not with "half of the family's property" he had promised.[21]

This story, published as a piece of social news in a leading late nineteenth-century newspaper supplement, might be groundless from the perspective of modern medicine, but it quite typically conveys an image of the magical power of beggars using snakes to cure unusual ailments. The report did not elaborate on why the snake was able to clean up the polyp—if indeed the incident happened as reported at all—but the underlying tone was the Chinese notion of using poison—in this case, the snake—as an antidote for poison (*yi du gong du*, or "combat poison with poison"), an essential concept of traditional Chinese medicine.[22] One may add that even if the snake was not poisonous, Chinese medical theory can still explain its efficacy. In yin-yang theory, ailments are caused by an imbalance of yin and yang. Since the snake belongs to the yin category, in this case it was called upon to counteract or overcome yang, the fire-like infection.[23] Moreover, having the wife hold the snake had to do with the notion that women were in the yin category and thus her presence would bring another weapon into this yin-yang battle.[24]

The association of the men who wandered about the "rivers and lakes" with the reptiles that haunted bushes and grasses lent a mysterious image to snake beggars. But beggars' ability to treat snakebites and use snakes to cure ailments was really not so mysterious. The writer Shen Congwen's foster father, as we have seen in Chapter 3, was a real "rustic doctor" and there were literally thousands of vagrants like him. As a scholar of Chinese medicine has pointed out, "It should not be forgotten that the medicine of the scholar physicians was that of a minority; the bulk of the population had no access to the theoretical foundations and clinical applications of the medicine of systematic correspondence."[25] Well into the twentieth century it was itinerant doctors—among whom were the snake beggars—that constituted the majority of healers for the general population.

One of the most famous of all "snake medicines" carried the name of its founder, Ji Desheng (1898–1981), a fifth-generation snake beggar who was born in a deserted temple in Suqian, a rural county in northern Jiangsu. When Ji was six his mother and younger brother died in poverty. His father, Ji Mingyang, brought him to wander along the Grand Canal down to the lower Yangzi River valley, begging and selling homemade snake medicine for a living. When Ji was twenty-five, the father and son wandered to Chahe, a rural town in Rudong County at the mouth of the Yangzi River. They were sheltered in a tiny village-god temple where, during the night in a bitterly cold snow storm, Ji Mingyang died of typhoid, leaving his son the formula for the "Ji family snake medicine," which was said to have been passed down from his great-grandfather. Ji Desheng, now totally alone in the world, continued to wander about the Yangzi delta region as a "snake beggar." The warm and wet environment of the area was ideal for snakes, and the wandering life enriched Ji's experience with the species. At the age of forty he was already quite well known in the region as a "beggar doctor" expert at treating snakebites. The reputation came at a price. Ji often used himself as the guinea pig, testing the effectiveness of herbal medicines by letting poisonous snakes bite his own hands, arms, and shoulders. Over the years he learned to identity over a hundred poisonous snakes. His specialty also included using snake gallbladders to cure coughs, infantile convulsions, rheumatoid arthritis, and some eye diseases. But the main recognition of his achievements came after 1956, when he presented the family's secret formula—a list of a few dozen types of herbs and their doses—to the now socialist state.

In August 1958, Ji was granted an audience with President Liu Shaoqi (1898–1969) and Premier Zhou Enlai (1898–1976), the highest honor a Chinese citizen could have received. And the drug named after him became a renowned medicine. Even during the radical Cultural Revolution (1966–76), when many traditions were condemned as "feudal" and "superstitious,"

Ji's skill was still acknowledged. In 1967, at the peak of the Cultural Revolution, he treated 123 patients who were severely wounded by snakebites and saved all of them. In 1980, a few months before his death, Ji proudly recalled that during his life he had treated thousands of patients and never failed once.[26] To this day Ji Desheng is still a household name in the Yangzi delta city of Nantong and its vicinity, where he had lived most of his life, and the snake pill named after him is still a popular over-the-counter medication.[27]

Beggars' Legs

About a quarter of the 700 beggars surveyed in Shanghai in the early 1930s were handicapped, mostly by blindness and lameness.[28] Although data were not available to verify if this percentage was representative of the entire nation, it is certain that many beggars were handicapped and that the public display of physical impairment was an archetypal technique for begging. Extremely disfigured beggars were not unusual in the streets. The *Dianshi Studio Pictorial* (published 1884–98) once carried a drawing of two extremely deformed beggars sitting by the side of the road east of Ningbo, Zhejiang. One had his legs crisscrossed on his shoulders: the right leg on top of his left shoulder and the left leg under his right armpit—permanently—so that his entire body was "like a wax gourd." Squatting next to him was a beggar who had no facial features at all. The only things on his face were two big holes, each about the size of a copper coin, in the middle, presumably his nostrils, by which he took food. Both carried a cotton cloth bag and begged in the town. According to the caption, some pedestrians gave alms out of sympathy, while others, horrified by the sight, ran by as quickly as they could.[29] Similar responses to beggars horribly disfigured by leprosy were also reported in Guangzhou.[30] In Chongqing, up into the 1980s, senior residents could vividly recall some unusually handicapped street characters of the Republican era. One beggar nicknamed Meat Ball (*roudan*), who was about thirty years old in the late 1940s, had a normal head and spoke clearly, but his limbs were extremely short and virtually boneless and his belly was swollen, making him look strikingly similar to a big frog. He begged only on rainy days, when he, nearly naked, literally rolled along muddy streets, making an exceedingly miserable scene. Once he got enough alms, he was carried away on a rickshaw by a mysterious companion to an unknown place.[31] Severely disfigured beggars also came before the lens of the American photographer Francis E. Stafford (1884–1938), who lived and traveled extensively in China from 1909 to 1915 and took more than a thousand pictures of everyday life. Some of the photographs he took of real lives on the streets captured figures similar to those portrayed in the *Dianshi Studio Pictorial*.[32]

These cases might be extraordinary, but deformed figures were certainly ordinary. One need only consider some beggars' jargon to get a sense of how common were beggars' handicaps, which may or may not have been genuine. "Three-legged toad" (*sanjiao hama*; also known as "deformed devils") referred to handicapped children, who might have been deliberately disfigured, exhibited to arouse pity. In "opening skylights" (*kai tianchuang*) beggars created a bloody scene, such as cutting the head or face, as a way of stimulating compassion, especially after a mild plea failed to obtain alms. Special techniques were usually applied to avoid real wounds. In "keeping silent" (*bu kaikou*, or "not opening the mouth") the beggar pretended to be deaf or dumb.[33]

That beggars exhibiting physical disabilities were often not truly handicapped was generally known even among foreigners. An American wrote about Shanghai's beggars in an unsympathetic and indeed disgusted tone, which evidently reflected her experience in the city: "Everywhere you were besieged by them. The professionals were cruel—in order to excite pity, or to make themselves so repulsive that anyone would pay quickly to lose sight of them, they would maim themselves, twist children's limbs to make them seem even more piteous, have women carry starving babies, who would be hired for the purpose."[34] Of all the physical disfigurement of Chinese beggars, the most common involved the legs. The term "three-legged toad," for instance, suggests that the legs were the centerpiece of the deception. Needless to say, if some part of the body is to be sacrificed to create a deformity, the legs are probably preferable since deformity is readily apparent and the risk of fatality is low. Late in the Qing dynasty, John Macgowan commented on an obnoxious beggar:

> The most offensive thing, however, about him is one of his legs; this he thrusts out most ostentatiously before the passers-by, very much as a shopkeeper displays his wares to induce people to buy. A huge sore has eaten away nearly all the flesh from the front part of it. It is raw and bleeding, and the man points to it as you come near and, in the professional whine, tries to excite your sympathies.
>
> It is a remarkable fact that with the Chinese beggar these diseases, which constitute his stock-in-trade, are always in the right place. They are never seen on the back of the legs, nor on other parts of the body that could not easily be exhibited to the public. They never seem to get either better or worse. In the summer days, when the great sun pours down his fierce rays, and bloated, vicious-looking flies swarm in clouds, it seems to make no difference to them. Again, when winter comes round and Nature tries her healing art to close the festering wounds she does so without any success. The cold north winds blow around him, but with no healing in their touch, and then he sits in some sheltered nook, shiv-

ering with cold, but, fortunately for him, the sore that brings him in the cash is as hideous as ever.[35]

Obviously, Macgowan had suspicions about the authenticity of the sore. The sinologist Chester Holcombe (1844–1912), who for fifteen years was an interpreter, secretary, and the acting minister of the United States legation at Beijing, found at least one case to justify Macgowan's doubts.

> I well remember one case among all the wretchedness and revolting sights found in the beggar class of Peking [Beijing] which moved my pity, and which, as a solitary exception to my rule, was for several months regularly relieved. It was an old man, ragged and shivering with cold, who sat every day by the side of the street. He was clothed in only a few rags, and thrust out in front of him were his feet, which were literally rotting off. They presented a sight too offensive for more detailed description. One day I missed the old man from his accustomed place, but walking rapidly homeward. I overtook him trudging along, and no signs of frozen feet and decomposition were visible.
>
> "Why," said I, walking along by his side, "how can you manage to walk with those wretched feet?"
>
> "Oh," said the old man, "they are in my bosom. It would spoil them to wear them home."
>
> Then, without hesitation or sign of shame, he thrust his hands into his bosom and drew out a pair of socks padded with cotton in order to represent his feet as swollen and out of shape. They were made of canvas, and so accurately painted into the resemblance of feet with toenails dropping off and the flesh a mass of putrefaction, that they had deceived me in broad sunlight and on many occasions.
>
> Naturally, I was furious, and I said: "I should think that an old man like you would be ashamed to swindle people in this way. Have you no trade, or are you too lazy to earn your rice in any honest fashion?"
>
> To which the venerable humbug replied as simply and frankly as though his recent deception had been quite respectable and praiseworthy: "Oh, yes, I am a shoemaker; and I have been thinking about giving up this line of business, for my feet are getting to be too well known, and it does not pay as well as it did. After all, it is hard work sitting there upon the ground all day and shouting out, 'Have pity!' I believe that I will go back to my old trade of mending shoes."
>
> In a day or two he appeared with his kit of tools and his bench, and asked permission to establish himself quite near the entrance of the Legation, by the side of the street, which was granted. There he cobbled shoes for nearly ten years, when he died; and his son, who "succeeded to the title and estates," asked assistance to bury the old man, basing his plea upon the close intimacy which had so long existed between us.[36]

Holcombe apparently offered this story as an interesting anecdote of his life in Beijing, but what he encountered was actually a common technique among Chinese beggars. In Guangzhou, more than one thousand miles south of the capital, the same trick, known to beggars as "pretending to be a dead dog," was frequently used in the late Qing and Republican period. The southern beggars seemed more creative (and food-oriented, as were most Cantonese), and instead of using cotton and canvas, they used beef. A few slices of thinly cut beef soaked in dirty water for a couple of days until the color turned to something between red and purple and the odor became overpowering, could be applied to the leg to simulate a putrescent and horribly painful sore. It was said that often the smell alone forced pedestrians into surrendering a coin in order to get rid of the beggar.[37] The methods for forging handicaps and diseases were kept secret and passed on by oral tradition, usually to the headmen only. An investigator of Sichuan's beggars reported that, based on some information released by insiders, the masquerades were quite complex. The investigator admitted that "one cannot help admiring beggars' knack for deception." In sum, beggars were able to use materials such as the viscera of pigs, oxen, and sheep, chicken blood, waxed or oiled paper, turmeric, crotons, rice powder, bean dregs, and so on to simulate broken arms or legs, burns, rotting sores and carbuncles, or even ascites (commonly known as "drum swelling" in China), symptomatic of advanced-stage liver disease (such as hepatitis). According to the report, the beggars' techniques followed "traditional formats passed down from the ancestors" and were so authentic in shape, color, and smell that they could fool even experienced doctors.[38]

Harold Rattenbury (1878–1961), the president of the British Methodist Conference and a long-time missionary in Republican-era China, noted that "blindness and all human deformities are exploited and even invented" by beggar guilds. In the central city of Hankou, Rattenbury reported that "I have known beggars refuse healing in a hospital on the ground that it would take their means of livelihood away."[39] While the public might rightfully have resented being exploited by beggars with invented deformities and diseases, it should be pointed out that only the desperate would want to maintain a true disease for the sake of pacifying an empty stomach.

The Subtlety of Womanhood

Was the public more sympathetic to female than to male beggars? Did gender play any role in almsgiving? The answer in general is yes. The Jiang-Wu survey conducted in Shanghai in the early 1930s found that female beggars tended to garner more alms than their male counterparts. On average, the daily alms obtained by a beggar were 360 cash (*wen*) for females and 330 for males. In certain types of begging, women garnered considerably more than men. The greatest difference was in "ground petitions," where men averaged 200 cash a day and women, 800 cash.[40] It was unclear if the gender of the almsgivers played any role in the disparity, since data on almsgivers are largely absent. Explanations of why female beggars were relatively success-ful were mainly based on conventional wisdom, that is, a woman who had lost the support of her family was more likely to engender sympathy than would a man and if children were at her side, the sympathy would be greater still (Figure 19). Moreover, a feminine appearance might also help. In Bei-jing, a popular song about soup kitchens contained a witty remark about fa-voritism for women:

> When the train whistle blows,
> the door of the soup kitchen opens.
> Little children are given a little;
> Old people are given the surface of congee;
> But pretty women are given full basins.[41]

The "pretty women" mentioned here were not necessarily beggars, but most of them were and clearly being young and female could be an ad-vantage in mendicancy. Gender sometimes was exploited in subtle ways in begging, and certain types of begging were exclusively female. In Beijing's temple fairs, for example, the service of dusting pilgrims was entirely pro-vided by women beggars. This requires some explanation. The beggars, who were not the typical ragged wretches, had a cotton cloth wrapped around their hair, almost like a chef's hat, and held a feather duster in one hand and a bunch of lit joss stick butts in the other. They helped dust down the shoul-ders and backs of pilgrims and lit their cigarettes. Because of Beijing's noto-rious gusting winds and swirling dust, when a well-off gentleman returned home, the first thing he did was have his servant dust him down. But since average Beijing residents did not have such luxury at home, the beggars' ser-vice at the temples was therefore a welcome encounter, especially for men, who generally were pleased with this personal and slightly intimate service and did not begrudge the beggars a reward.[42]

Except for snake charming or the use of other animals in begging, women beggars also played a major role in street performances. Lotus ballad singing (*lianhualao*), a form of entertainment for potential almsgivers, was mostly a women's show.[43] The more elaborate flower-drum opera (*huaguxi*) was usu-ally performed by a couple, but the woman always played the leading role, which led to the performers being simply known as "the Fengyang lady" (Fengyang, as we have seen, was well known for its beggars). The Jiang-Wu report gives a glimpse of a typical flower-drum opera street performance early in the twentieth century:

> The man held a stalk of sorghum and the woman shook the little flower drum in her hand. She wore an open-topped straw hat cocked at an angle. A few old red

FIGURE 19.   A beggar woman holds her child and an empty rice bowl outside the home of an affluent family. Photo taken by Francis E. Stafford around 1912. SOURCE: Courtesy of Ronald E. Anderson.

velvet flowers were untidily stuck along the edge of the hat. She had a hair knot that looked like a bundle of chicken feathers at the back. Her face was heavily powered and her lips were rouged. She was not pretty, and with such heavy makeup, she looked like a living demon. Rhythmically shaking the drum, she started to sing. She was slow at the beginning but increasingly became spirited and, all of a sudden, she started to dance. Following her posturing, the man waved his sorghum stalk to punctuate her performance. This was pretty funny, it is fair to say.[44]

Women beggars also adopted more aggressive and sexually seductive ways of begging. One of the ten major begging methods in Republican-era Shanghai was described by a contemporary as "a lonely girl walking after male pedestrians introducing herself as a refugee while glancing seductively."[45] In a city where the lowest class of prostitutes sold sex for only a few copper coins and plied their trade in brothels called "nail sheds" (*dingpeng*), implying that sexual intercourse there was as quick and straightforward as driving a nail, the boundary between mendicancy and prostitution could be very thin.[46] Although most female beggars were not streetwalkers, sex could still be intermingled with begging. For instance, in Quanzhou, Fujian, a group of slightly handicapped women beggars gathered in a shantytown called Dead Cat Alley, where they essentially sold sex to male paupers, at the rate of twenty cents per night. The fee sometimes included mending clothes for the customer.[47] The following story of an old beggar woman who trapped a young man into sex was recorded by a noted journalist-historian in 1916. It entered into his "unofficial history" of the late Qing perhaps because it was sensational, but nonetheless it provides an illustration of sex-based rackets that were inevitably a facet of the world of mendicancy but seldom made it into the written record.

There was a liner service between the lower Yangzi River valley cities of Hangzhou (the author's native town) and Fuyang, both in Zhejiang Province. The liner did good business, for it departed in the evening and covered a distance of about thirty miles along the Fuchun River overnight. The passengers slept during the trip and woke up in the morning at their destination.[48] Men and women were packed into the boat, with a movable board separating the sleeping berths. On one trip, among the passengers was a young man named Zhang, a native of Hangzhou, a fop who boasted of being a ladies' man and was known in town as a womanizer.

At the beginning of the trip he noted that the passenger in the next berth was a young woman. He peeked at her and it seemed that she smiled back at him as if, Zhang thought, she found him attractive. After midnight, when all the passengers were sound asleep and the cabin was in complete darkness, Zhang heard the board between his berth and the woman's being slowly opened. A hand stretched out and began to caress him. Overjoyed, the young man crawled over into the next berth and had his way with the woman. In the whole process the two did not exchange a word. When the roosters on the boat started to crow, Zhang knew dawn was near and wanted to creep back to his own berth. The woman, however, embraced him even more tightly and the rapturous Zhang stayed put.

As the dawn light finally came to the cabin and some passengers were getting up, Zhang suddenly found out that the woman he was sleeping with was a gray-haired old woman, not the one he had peeked at the day before. He was startled and wanted to leave at once. But the woman grasped him tightly and declared:

I'm a street beggar in my sixties. I have no husband, no children, and no rela- tives—no nothing. As I was worrying that I had no place to live, it was my good fortune that you, sir, showed love and affection to me last night. You know how the saying goes, "Making love one night brings love for hundreds of nights." So, now you, sir, are practically my husband. It won't cost you a penny in bride price [that is, betrothal gifts], because I'll willingly become your wife. If you have gruel, I'll eat gruel; if you have steamed rice, then steamed rice will be my meal. How about it?

Astonished and scared, Zhang yelled out for help. By then all the other pas- sengers had awaken and, having heard the story, they all jeered at the young man. A few passengers came out to mediate the dispute. In the end—and under the gaze of the other passengers—Zhang paid ten silver dollars to the beggar. Only then did the woman let him go.[49]

Ten silver dollars was a fortune at the time, equivalent to nearly an entire year's salary for an entry-level shop clerk.[50] Apparently, if the story is to be believed, the two women beggars had known of Zhang's reputation and had jointly plotted to blackmail him. It must have been unusual for an elderly woman to play such a role in a swindle, but in another begging tactic old women were commonly used as "stage property." In this ruse, a male beg- gar carried an elderly woman on his back and walked haltingly door-to- door in a neighborhood, begging: "My mother is very sick and I don't have money for medicine, please help!" In a culture where filial piety was the most respected virtue and a son's devotion to his mother was particularly es- teemed, people usually responded positively to such a plea.[51] In beggars' cant, this team play was known as "Piggybacking the Goddess of Mercy."[52]

Occasionally, women beggars directed their appeals at women only, as was seen in Lanzhou, the capital of Gansu Province, in northwest China. There seasonal woman beggars from Pingfan (today's Yongdeng County) acted as if they were pilgrims returning to Lanzhou from the Temple of the Peach Blossom Goddess on Mount Peach Blossom, about seventy miles from the capital city. These were all young or middle-aged women, travel- ing in groups of two to three, and were specially dressed: their hair was wrapped with a black handkerchief, and they wore long earrings, a double- breasted garment trimmed with lace, trousers, and shoes with pointed toes. The attire looked a bit too fine for beggars, but each of them held a pole, an unmistakable symbol of mendicants, and they were not shy about admitting that they were beggars. They had a clear objective: the women in the town. These beggars were highly sociable and glib. They would approach a house- hold and greet the housewife as "elder sister" (a respectful and affectionate way of addressing a woman) and then start to make conversation by saying they had made a vow to the Peach Blossom Goddess to be a mendicant in order to fulfill a vow. The purpose of their visit, they claimed, was to encourage the woman to make a wish—and to collect a contribution to the goddess. They would leave their donor with a red ribbon for her hair and promise they would return the next year to find out if the goddess had granted the woman's wish.[53]

The Crying Crones

In Guangzhou early in the last century there was a special job for women beggars known as "crying crones" (*hankoupo*), that is, crying and chanting at funerals. These were mostly elderly widows without children or other family to support them. They lived under the control of the beggar guild known as the Temple of Lord Guan, a name derived from the place where the guild was located. These women, without the normal means of support, must have considered themselves lucky to be hired out to perform an integral part of funerals.[54]

To begin with, the job was not a quick roadside performance, but involved at least a couple of weeks of work. Chinese funeral rituals and the mourning period could last more than three months, with highlights on the seventh, the twenty-first, the forty-ninth, and the hundredth day after the death.[55] Crying crones were hired for a part of or the entire period, depending on how extravagant a funeral a family wanted. During the period the women were on the payroll, so to speak, the mourning family provided them with room and board. The crying crones had to bring their own bedding, but they were entitled to have all the daily articles that the deceased had used and left in the room, such as clothing, bedclothes, mosquito nets, smoking pipes, lamps, and so on. These items were evenly divided among the crying women and servants from the funeral service or mortuary.

In most cases only wealthy families could afford the luxury of extravagant funerals and hiring crying crones, for the compensation for these women was quite handsome. In the early 1930s, the pay was $15 for the first week, $40 for a three-week period, and $60 for a seven-week period. In comparison, the monthly pay for an unskilled worker at that time was about $7–10 (and room and board were not provided).[56] In addition, gratuities to the crying crones, the amount of which depended on the generosity of the mourning family, were on the top of the pay. Although the beggar guild took at least 20 percent of the compensation as its commission, the income of these old women was still considerably higher than that of most other beggars.

But the services they were expected to provide were odd, to say the least. Before modern Western-style hospitals were common in China (that is, before the middle of the twentieth century), most Chinese died at home. The crying crone's first duty was to stay day and night in the room where the person had died and where the corpse remained before the funeral, a practice known as "accompanying the soul" (*peiling*). Duties also included taking care of the joss sticks and candles, burning incense, folding tinfoil paper imitations of silver ingots (to be burned as an offering to the dead), and other funeral-related chores. Her main duty, as the name clearly indicated, was to cry, on the behalf of the mourning family, as much as possible and with as much doleful wailing as possible. In China, the more mourners ululate, the better. Ululation was to show that the deceased was deeply beloved and the survivors (especially the offspring) were full of devotion and filial piety. Some folklore also had it that the sound of lament would accompany the dead to the nether world, where the King of Hell would judge the life of the newcomer by how much sadness the person has generated in his or her family and would assign him or her a position in the afterlife accordingly.

During this period when the soul was being accompanied to the netherworld, the hired women beggars were expected to dutifully wail with grief thrice a day, at the usual mealtimes—breakfast, lunch, and supper, in other words. Some families also requested a fourth cry, that is, a final weeping at bedtime. But the major performance was at the funeral procession down the street. As the coffin was being carried from the home to the cemetery, men followed the bier on foot while all female members of the family were shrouded in a slow-moving white mourning tent edged with blue lace. This was when the crying crones became stars, for they too were in the tent—mingled with the family women, indeed pretending to be part of them—howling. It was considered improper to present mourning women to public view; hence the tent. But while custom dictated they must be hidden, it also dictated that the sound be broadcast with utmost vigor. Spectators, of whom there were usually many on both sides of the road, could not see the female mourners but they could certainly hear their terrible wailing. Touched by the deep sorrow transmitted from the tent, they admired the great love and affection the deceased had had in the family, many of them quite unaware that much of the lament was just the noise made by the hired beggar women.

The ululation, nevertheless, was more than simple wailing. In their weeping, which had a certain rhythm and tempo, the crying crones were practically singing dirges. They were instructed beforehand by the family about what to say during the wailing, and the rest was up to them. A good crying woman was articulate in her speech and hysterical in her keening, as the Chinese saying put it, "lamenting to heaven and knocking one's head on earth" (*hutian qiangdi*). However, she was not to act demented; rather, her crying was to be intermittently broken with periods of softer moans and whimpers, by which the grief and heartbreak might be rendered more touching and her words could be clearly enunciated.

The last part was sometimes very important. It was usual that in a Chinese extended family married children and in-laws could not get along with each other. With several generations living under the same roof and sharing the same kitchen and a grandparent making all financial decisions, discord and conflict were almost inevitable.[57] When the real issues, of which the most prominent was the inheritance of family property, surfaced upon the death of a grandparent, the infighting often intensified. But Confucian ethics and rituals tended to prevent open wrangling, thus the crying crones were more often than not used as a secret weapon to attack one's enemies within the extended family. The old women might be hired by different relatives and therefore each was to cry on behalf of her employer. The mourning words were carefully thought out, like hidden bullets to be fired at each other. Years of accumulated complaints, disputes, and resentments were aired through the mouths of the crying crones, who engaged in a battle of words through their adroit keens. Those who got the upper hand and defeated their opponents were handsomely rewarded on top of their regular pay. Often, the dirty laundry of well-to-do families displayed during the mourning period became source material for local tabloids.

Hiring old beggar women to cry for the purpose of creating a grieving atmosphere was of course hypocritical, revealing the sham morality and vanity of the hosting families. The old women who literally sold their tears had to falsify their grief as well. Mint calms and peppers were used to stimulate tears and a homemade transparent liquid (probably made of thin rice pottage) was put into the nose as mucus. With these props the runny-nosed women sniveled and cried a mess of false tears. The women also swallowed a couple teaspoons of sesame oil on an empty stomach before the performance, which was believed to give the voice the proper timbre.[58]

This sort of ritualized mourning was not just a Cantonese custom but could be found elsewhere in China also. In the Northeast (Manchuria), for example, funeral weeping had developed into quavering, eight-note dirges and employed musical instruments such as *suona* horns, *dongxiao* vertical bamboo flutes, and *erhu* two-stringed violins as accompaniments.[59] The melody "On the Songhua River," arguably the most popular patriotic song in the wake of the Japan's sudden attack on Manchuria on September 18, 1931, and which has remained one of the best-known musical classics of twentieth-century China, has an obscure origin. According to the musician Zhang Hanhui, who composed both the music and the lyrics, the song was adapted from the funeral cries of old country grannies in his hometown,

Dingxian, a county seat in Hebei Province.[60] The original dirge did not survive, but the words of "On the Songhua River," if one can transfer its nationalistic and home-loving sentiment back to that for the death of a family member, may give us a glimpse of the format of the funeral dirges that were prevalent in North China:

> My home is on the Songhua River in the Northeast,
> where we have forests and coal mines
> and where the soybean and sorghum fields cover hill and dale.
> My home is on the Songhua River in the Northeast,
> where I have my countrymen and my aged and feeble parents.
>
> "Nine Eighteen!" "Nine Eighteen!" from that miserable moment on,
> "Nine Eighteen!" "Nine Eighteen!" from that miserable moment on,
> I lost my homeland, and abandoned its countless treasures,
> Roaming about! Roaming about!
> outside my homeland,
> Roaming about!
>
> When can I return to my homeland?
> When can I recover its countless treasures?
> Oh, my dear father and mother; Oh, my dear father and mother!
> When can we happily be together again?[61]

Not only was the custom of crying crones widespread, but it was also old. In his will, Wang Xiuzhi, a scholar-official active in the fifth century, avowed "it is a custom that people send servants and concubines to help cry at funerals. This is because the host of the funeral who should be crying is not genuinely sad, so he covers it up with lots of noise. If there is a soul in the afterlife, it would laugh at the insincerity of this kind of grieving."[62] No doubt sober-minded criticism like Wang's was rare; the custom was common even in his time. Specifically hiring beggar women to mourn at funerals might be a more recent practice, but the mentality that sustained this method of beggary had a very long history.

CHAPTER 8

Chairman Mao Picked on a Beggar

FOLLOWING AGE-OLD BEGGING methods was only part of how the mendicant way of life was sustained into modern times. More conceptual components of the culture on begging, such as accepting mendicancy as an avenue of social mobility, valuing adversity as a way of tempering oneself, taking inspiration from rags-to-riches stories, and so on, also served to sustain the mendicant way of life well into the twentieth century. The historian Philip Kuhn once analyzed a number of axes of social differentiation in China: the four traditional occupational statuses (scholars, farmers, artisans, and merchants), rulers and ruled, free and unfree, and rich and poor; and he noted that the last was "the most difficult to deal with in the Chinese case. That is because it is not entirely clear whether it really represents an axis in the Chinese scheme of classification."[1] As academic questions sometimes can be answered, imperfectly yet plainly to the point, by common sense, a simple Chinese metaphor about upward social mobility widely known among people of all walks of life for centuries might be cited here to explain the rich-and-poor axis in the Chinese mind: "Even a rock sitting at the bottom of a cesspit may flip over (*fanshen*) some day."[2]

We have seen a number of such "rocks sitting at the bottom of a cesspit" that turned over and made a great mark in history: Zhu Yuanzhang, Han Xin, Wu Zixu, and others. These ancient luminaries remained household names in modern times and their mendicant ordeal inspired millions. Yet the nineteenth and twentieth centuries also had their versions of beggar heroes. Unable to equal the previous giants yet faithful in imitating their spirit, beggar notables in modern times personified the continuity of the Chinese notions of poverty, morality, and individuality. For instance, one of the best-known musicians of twentieth-century China, Hua Yanjun (1893–1950, popularly known as Abing), was regarded as a beggar, although he seems to have always played his music on the street for alms instead of just "begging." Contracting an eye disease at the age of twenty-one and becoming totally blind at thirty-five, Blind Abing, as he was commonly called, learned to play various Chinese musical instruments (in particular, the *pipa* and the *erhu*) in a Taoist temple in his hometown, Wuxi. He not only masterfully played instruments and sang songs on the streets from childhood, but also he composed his own pieces, which were to become classics in China, such as *The Moon Reflected on the Second Spring* (*Er quan ying yue*), *Great Waves Washing the Sand* (*Da lang tao sha*), and *Listening to the Pines* (*Ting song*). Abing was also known as a man who stood firm against social injustice and political corruption, using his music as a way of spreading local and national news, defending the small and weak, and criticizing the powerful. Despite his fame, he remained on the streets until 1948, two years before his death.[3]

The textile industry tycoon Zhang Songjiao (b. 1870) was another type of modern-day beggar hero. Born into a poor family in a small town near Hanyang (today a part of Wuhan), Zhang lost his father at the age of three and begged on the streets of Hanyang with his mother until he was ten, by which time he had started to earn a living as a street peddler. He then worked as a shop assistant and salesman before he was hired as an assistant manager by a textile mill in Wuhan in 1902. For his diligence and efficiency, Zhang was steadily promoted and he gradually became the major player in the company. He started his own cotton mill in 1922, and by the early 1930s his firm had developed into a conglomerate, Yudahua, one of the biggest of its type in China. Though by then an extremely rich man, Zhang never forgot his childhood experience as a beggar. It was said he often wept when telling his children of his past and instructing them to keep a simple lifestyle despite the family's wealth. As a token of his personal philosophy, Zhang refused to ride in rickshaws and he asked his family to do likewise, declaring that "the most inhumane thing is to use a human as an animal." Deeply regretting his lack of a formal education, Zhang established and funded a school in his hometown—the first Western-style modern school there.[4]

However, among the beggar notables of modern times, the most celebrated was Wu Xun (1838–96), a poor village day laborer who could hardly make a living for himself but nevertheless dreamed of establishing charity schools to provide free education for children of the poor "all under heaven." To fulfill this dream, Wu endured the hardship of mendicancy for over thirty years, and happily did so. Ultimately, he entered into the pantheon of modern-day Chinese paladins, exemplifying individuals pursuing a noble purpose with an iron will, absolute determination, and a willingness to endure great sacrifice. Wu also signified the continuation of the Chinese fascination with beggar heroes, the flow of culture between rich and poor, and the unusual role played by mendicants in national politics. Paradoxically, this real and lifelong cadger did not become an icon among beggars themselves but for the entire twentieth century he was a role model in mainstream society and, moreover, caused tremendous controversy at the very top of the political heap, which was highlighted in a major ideological campaign launched by Mao Zedong.

The Story of Wu Xun

Wu Xun was born into a poor farmer's family on December 5, 1838, in Wujiazhuang (Wu Family Village), three miles from the Tangyi county seat in Shandong Province in North China.[5] At his birth, his illiterate parents were unable to choose a name for him with the kind of deliberation that is usually involved in naming a child in China. The newborn was simply called Wu Qi, meaning "Wu the Seventh," for he was the seventh child in the extended family (that is, the Wu family under Wu Xun's paternal grandfather). In fact, like many vagrants, Wu was best known in his hometown by his nickname: Bubbles Wu. Wu earned this nickname by having fainted several times in public, foaming at the mouth, probably caused by a kind of epilepsy. He was called Wu Xun only after he founded a benevolent school at the age of fifty-one. The bestowed name *Xun* literally means "teaching."

When Wu Xun was seven, his father, a tenant farmer, died and with his death the family lost its source of livelihood. Wu Xun's elder brothers left home to strike off on their own, leaving the desperate mother and Wu Xun wandering about on streets, destitute. But the little boy, even in such poverty, hoped to go to school. He often passed a local school and overheard students in the classroom reading aloud, and he dreamed of being part of them. His eagerness grew to the point that one day he plucked up his courage and walked into the classroom, asking the teacher if he would allow him to sit in. Having a beggar boy dare to interrupt his class made the teacher (as usual, a Confucian pedant) furious. He pulled out his ruler, the standard instrument for punishing undisciplined pupils in the classroom, and threatened to strike Wu Xun. The students took this as a welcome interlude and hounded Wu out of the classroom. The crying boy went back to his mother for comfort, only to learn that a poor child such as he should never think of going to school. The best he could hope for, his mother told him, was to have enough food to fill his stomach.

Wu thus grew up illiterate. From the age of fifteen on, he worked as a laborer in nearby villages. As if life were making practical jokes, particularly as regards his illiteracy, he was cheated several times by his employers. Often he thought he had worked according to the terms verbally offered by an employer, but at the end of the job he was swindled: the terms the employer insisted on differed from those in the written contract, which Wu could not read. His frustration and anger burst out one day in 1859, when he was twenty, after he was once again cheated on a contract, this time by a relative. This incident seemed to make Wu psychotic and as if in a torpor, he slept in a village temple for three entire days and nights. But on the fourth day he suddenly dashed out of his den and danced in the street, yelling like crazy: "I will build a charity school for the kids of the poor! I will build a charity school for the kids of the poor!"

People thought Wu Xun was insane: How could a day laborer, who could not even earn enough to feed himself, found a school? At a time when the great majority of Chinese peasants were illiterate and education was a sheer luxury for most of them, such a statement from a village laborer certainly sounded crazy. But Wu Xun was resolute and determined to carry out his plan. He reckoned that the only possible way to fulfill the dream was to raise money through begging. In his own words, uttered in one of many "begging ditties" that he later often offhandedly made up as he roamed about villages and towns:

> Laboring is worse off than begging:
> You are cheated while you are working;
> You are on your own while you are begging.

Nevertheless, whenever he had a chance Wu continued to work as a laborer, often doing the least desirable jobs such as cleaning up human and animal waste for households. But his main endeavor was begging and in the cause of saving money to build a school he endured much suffering and humiliation. For example, to satisfy perverse almsgivers, for a few pennies he would eat human excrement, drink urine, and swallow scorpions or pieces of tile. He ate whatever leftovers he could find and saved every penny begged. As his savings grew he managed to invest with two local men. One of them, named Yang Shufang, held the prestigious Presented Scholar (*jinshi*) degree and was known as a shrewd moneylender. One may wonder, given the huge social disparity between the two, how Wu got into this relationship. Again, according to Wu's biographers, it was Wu's persistence that helped him get his way. When Wu first went to the Yang residence asking to see the moneylender, the doorman treated him like a usual beggar by throwing a couple of copper coins to him. Wu declined the alms, but insisted on seeing Yang. For this simple request, he knelt several days and nights at the gateway until Yang finally gave in and received him.

"This beggar has a favor to ask your honor," Wu Xun said to Yang, still kneeling. "But I am going to say it only if your honor promises to help."

"Do you want money?"

"This beggar is not asking money from your honor, but wants to give money to your honor—in the hope of earning interest."

Yang finally agreed to be Wu's agent, apparently moved by Wu's sincerity and determination to open a charity school for the poor. Also the funds involved were not much by the standards of a wealthy man like Yang. Over the next ten years, whenever Wu Xun saved a full string of coins he would send the string to Yang. Gradually, his savings grew to thousands of strings and by 1886 he was able to purchase about forty acres (240 *mu*) of farmland, which was put under the management of Yang. Meanwhile, Wu himself continued to beg everywhere and lived an entirely beggarly life: he ate only coarse food and leftovers and slept in deserted temples.

His suffering and sacrifice finally paid off. By the fall of 1887, Wu Xun had saved 2,800 strings of copper coins and got a piece of land donated by two landowners, and with that he opened his first charity school, which was named Revering the Worthy (*Chongxian*), in Liulin (Willow Grove), a small town in western Shandong Province. The school, consisting of twenty rooms within a walled compound, had more than seventy students enrolled in the spring of 1888. Two years later, Wu Xun was able to cofound, with a local Buddhist temple, another charity school, in the neighboring county of Guantao. In 1896, a few months before his death, Wu founded a third school. In spite of many friendly entreaties that he get married and start a family, Wu Xun remained single all his life. He lived as a beggar right up to his death at the age of fifty-eight; his death was reportedly caused by having eaten some spoiled leftover food he had begged.[6]

The year Wu Xun founded the Liulin school, the governor of Shandong, Zhang Yao, received a report from the county magistrate about Wu Xun. Zhang was astounded to learn that a beggar had established a charity school. The governor later received Wu in person, donated 200 taels of silver to the school, and gave Wu a donation book stamped with the governor's official seal (so soliciting contributions would be easier). Furthermore, the governor reported Wu's deeds to Emperor Guangxu (reigned 1875–1908). With the sanction of the imperial court, a memorial arch was erected in the main street of the town of Liulin in honor of Wu Xun, with an inscription on the top of the arch reading "Benevolence and Charity" (*Le shan hao shi*), written by the emperor—the highest honor one could get during imperial times. Wu was also bestowed with a "Yellow Mandarin Jacket," the ceremonial attire granted by the imperial court to honor individuals of outstanding merit and high achievement.

By the early twentieth century, Wu Xun had become a national hero. The Qing official history includes his biography. Only the most important individuals during the 268 years of the Qing dynasty received such recognition. His name and his beggar's saga not only survived the Qing dynasty, which was overthrown by the Republican revolution of 1911, but also spread after the dynasty was gone. During the Republican period, the story of Wu Xun was put into the standard national textbooks as a role model for the young generation. Among those who praised Wu Xun in writing were the Republican president Chiang Kai-shek (1888–1975), the "Christian Warlord" Feng Yuxiang (1882–1948), the scholar-officials Liang Qichao (1873–1929) and Cai Yuanpei (1868–1940), the "modern educator" Tao Xingzhi (1891–1946), and celebrities of all sorts. Chiang Kai-shek's acknowledgment included an embellished horizontal wooden board inscribed with his calligraphy praising Wu as a "human teacher and role model" (*wei ren shi biao*) and a blank verse elegantly written in classic Chinese on an official letterhead bearing the words "Office of the Generalissimo":

> Exploiting the power of mendicancy,
> You have created an enterprise of promoting young talent with integrity;
> Sacrificing your own uneducated life,
> You have left a legacy of benefiting generations of youth.
> Oh, Sir! You are unique and without precedent.
> Your benevolence is conspicuous and your righteousness is remarkable.
> You personify the encomium "Utterly outstanding in profound
>   assiduousness."
> For those who live an easy life but are despicably self-serving:
> Should you not get off your bench and learn something?[7]

In 1937, a fund was raised for erecting a gigantic jade statue of Wu Xun on December 5, the centennial anniversary of his birthday; however, the project was interrupted by the outbreak of the Sino-Japanese war on July 7 of that year.[8]

But Wu's legacy continued to live on despite the wars and turmoil that rampaged across China. Numerous schools throughout the nation were named after Wu Xun. In Nantong, Jiangsu Province, a normal school even put his statue next to that of Confucius in the auditorium for daily worshipping. The famous Nantong community leader Zhang Jian (1853–1926) called Wu Xun "China and the world's brilliant and great beggar" and urged students "to constantly have in your minds and in your dreams a beggar named Wu Xun."[9] A number of Wu Xun Schools or Wu Xun Memorial Schools were established in Beijing and Shanghai in the late 1940s, after the Sino-Japanese War ended. Since China's poor public education system and low literacy rate were frequently blamed for the nation's backwardness, the spirit of Wu Xun was hailed as a way of promoting China's national salvation. As a prominent educator emotionally put it: "Although Wu Xun is dead, his spirit will live on for hundreds of thousands of years to come. If everyone in our country has Wu Xun's spirit, who would have to worry about the progress of our nation?" [10]

Mao Enters

Those who praised Wu Xun came from both the Nationalist and Communist camps. The two, of course, had been enemies in every arena since 1927, save for only a brief period of a reluctant and fragile coalition against the Japanese invasion. Chiang Kai-shek and many of his men, as we have seen, enthusiastically praised Wu. But praise also came from many Communist leaders and intellectuals, who were most acrimonious critics of Chiang but who were no less ardent about Wu Xun.

The popularity of Wu led to a movie entitled *The Life of Wu Xun (Wu Xun zhuan)*, directed by Sun Yu (1900–1990), a pro-Communist intellectual, and starring as Wu Xun, Zhao Dan (1915–80), one of the best-known movie actors in twentieth-century China and also a Communist sympathizer.[11] Sun started to direct the movie in 1948, but the film production was interrupted by the civil war between the Nationalists and the Communists. After the Communist victory in 1949, Sun was able to get support from the new regime to complete the movie, although in the process he had to significantly alter the script to fit the ideological straitjacket of Communism. The movie portrays Wu Xun as a person who fought against feudalism and social injustice and all his life remained devoted to the oppressed. First screened in the spring of 1951, the movie was a big success. Almost all top Communist leaders, including Premier Zhou Enlai (1898–1976) and the Red Army commander-in-chief Zhu De (1886–1976), saw the movie. After the screening they praised the film and came in person to congratulate Sun, a great honor for a movie director.

At this point no one could anticipate that this movie would become the fuse that set off the very first ideologically based political campaign in the history of the People's Republic. Like all these campaigns prior to 1976, Mao was the initiator and the architect. Perhaps from the rave praise of movie critics published in Shanghai newspapers Mao had foreseen that he might have a different view about the movie, which he did not watch in public with his colleagues as he usually did. According to Mao's wife, Jiang Qing (1914–91), Mao ordered the movie to be screened, with Jiang and a few staff members in attendance, in his private quarters in Zhongnanhai, the top government leaders' residential and office compound in the heart of Beijing.

As he watched the movie, Mao did not say a word but kept smoking cigarettes one after another, an ominous sign that he was deep in thought.

When the movie ended, Mao remained seated and, to the surprise of the others in the room, ordered the three-hour film to be rerun. Jiang and all the staff were puzzled. It was the spring of 1951: the Korean War was raging and, domestically, the Suppressing Anti-revolutionaries campaign was in full swing. Mao was incredibly busy at the time. How could he be in such an aesthetic mood as to watch a movie twice? But no one, including his wife, dared to question him, and the film was replayed. When the second run was over, Mao pondered for a while, then he said to Jiang Qing and the people in the room: "This movie is revisionist and it has to be criticized." And he immediately telephoned Zhou Enlai, instructing him to launch a nation-wide campaign criticizing the movie.[12]

Wu Xun, Mao said, was a "filial son of the feudal landlord class" who "donned a beggar's garment and crawled into the ranks of the exploiting class." The movie advocated "class compromise" instead of class struggle, the core of Marxism. The praise for the movie, Mao declared, indicated dangerous confusion and muddle-headedness in China concerning ideology and the political superstructure. This was the first case after 1949 where Mao critically differed in ideology from his Communist comrades.

Mao personally became involved in the campaign to criticize the movie. A *People's Daily* (*Renmin ribao*) editorial, anonymous as usual but this time in fact written by Mao himself, was published on May 20, calling for a national campaign to criticize the movie. In the political culture of the People's Republic, such an editorial has always functioned as a kind of supreme order of the state or a legislative document. In June, Mao sent Jiang Qing with a team of thirteen members to Wu Xun's hometown, Tangyi, and its vicinity to investigate Wu's story. Jiang Qing, using her pseudonym Li Jin and identified as a "cadre from the Ministry of Culture," was the key person in the team. It was also the first time that Mao had let Jiang Qing get involved in politics since their marriage in November 1939, a marriage that caused great controversy and much deliberation among the top Communist leaders.[13] Sending his wife to do the "fieldwork" indicates Mao attached great importance to this campaign. Again, the Korean War was being fought just across the border against a superpower and the new regime was waging a campaign against domestic "anti-revolutionaries," but Mao nonetheless took time in July 1951 to review the lengthy report written by the investigation group, which had conducted about four weeks of fieldwork in the areas where Wu had been active. A collection of Mao's manuscripts released in 1987 shows that he very heavy-handedly revised the report and even wrote fifteen new paragraphs for it. After finishing the report, Mao wrote a note to Hu Qiaomu (1912–92), then the head of *People's Daily*, asking him to take care of the proofreading and to be "extremely careful not to have typos."[14] The end result, "A Report on the History of Wu Xun," a document of 45,000 words, appeared in several installments in successive issues of *People's Daily* in July.[15]

The criticizing Wu Xun campaign lasted for a few months and numerous people, mostly intellectuals and cadres in charge of cultural affairs, were attacked, criticized, and subjected to "self-criticism." From May to October 1951, as part of the campaign more than 900 articles were published in over thirty newspapers and eighty periodicals nationwide.[16] This was the first campaign about "correct ideology" in the People's Republic and perhaps also the first of this kind in Chinese history.[17] Still, Mao was dissatisfied with the relatively mild nature of the criticism and self-criticism in this campaign. In a letter written in October 1954, he complained: "Although the movie *The Life of Wu Xun* was criticized, to this day no lessons have been learned."[18] To learn the lessons, Mao repeatedly launched political campaigns that all had a strong and clearly stated ideological agenda based on the theory of class and class struggle, aiming to achieve a kind of unified national ideological purification. The final episode of Mao's ideological fanaticism was the disastrous Cultural Revolution of 1966–76, but the basic idea behind the Cultural Revolution was fomented in the criticizing *The Life of Wu Xun* campaign of 1951.[19]

In fact the connection was not concealed. At the peak of the Cultural Revolution, in an unusual move *People's Daily* republished its 1951 editorial and for the first time revealed the identity of the author.[20] The editorial that had been published some sixteen years earlier now gained new prominence, for Mao's words by that time had become "supreme instructions," rather like revered imperial edicts and sacred biblical injunctions rolled into one. Wu Xun was forever banished from the ranks of the revered. As part of the renewed criticism of the "feudal landlord class's running dog in beggar's clothing," the movie was shown nationwide, free of charge, as a piece of "negative educational material" (*fanmian jiaocai*), that is, a politically incorrect sample that could serve as a lesson for the people. To apply a Maoist analogy, this was "turning poisoning weeds into fragrant flowers" (*hua ducao wei xianghua*). But quite paradoxically, the renewed criticism of the movie only helped spread the name of Wu Xun and made his story known to the entire Cultural Revolution generation.[21]

Mao's sensitivity about this film of course was not related to just Wu Xun, or we can say it was essentially not about the man per se, but about the "revisionism" that Mao believed the image of this beggar represented. The morals that others had derived from Wu's story and had tried to propagate—begging, compromising, selflessness, using education to promote national salvation, and so on—all contradicted Mao's convictions about class and class struggle. Mao called the movie "revisionist," a label that was to become a virtual death sentence under his reign.[22]

But besides Mao's obsession with ideology there is a possibility that his paranoia about this particular beggar (and the movie) was related, perhaps unconsciously, to an experience in his youth. Although only for a few weeks, Mao had been a beggar—and in a way like Wu Xun, a "voluntary beggar"—at the age of twenty-three.

Xiao Yu (Siao-Yu, b. 1894), Mao's classmate at the Changsha First Normal School and his sole companion in that mendicant adventure, recalled the vagrant episode, forty years later:

> The attraction of the beggar's life for me was the ability to overcome physical and psychological difficulties inherent in living outside the accepted pale of society. In China and in the East generally from time immemorial, begging has been considered a profession, rather than, as in the West, a mark of poverty or improvidence. It is fascinating to try travel about the country without a cent in one's pocket.[23]

Xiao no doubt overstated the positive view of mendicancy "in China and in the East." In most cases the Chinese did (and still do) regard begging as "a mark of poverty or improvidence." But the remark reflects the fascination with vagrancy among ambitious young people in the turbulent early Republic, a fascination that was often associated with revolutionary zeal. According to Xiao, in 1916, when he was a school teacher in Changsha, the capital of Hunan Province, he planned to spend his summer vacation as a tramp in order to toughen himself and learn how to overcome hardship. The idea fascinated Mao and the two went out together that summer, lived like true beggars and tramped through five counties in their home province of Hunan without spending a penny. By the end of that adventure, they had two dollars and forty cents left from the alms they got, which they divided evenly.[24]

The friendship, however, did not last long. Xiao later served in the Nationalist government and stayed overseas after the Communist victory in the mainland. In 1959 he published a book in English about his relations with Mao and gave the book a sensational title, *Mao Tse-Tung and I Were Beggars*. Xiao devoted sixteen chapters, or about one-third of the book, to the details of their lives as beggars in that summer. The book was quite self-serving, containing a considerable number of boastful statements and expressions of personal bias, but there is no doubt that Mao and Xiao indeed tramped together as beggars in the summer of 1916. In fact, Mao himself mentioned the adventure to a Westerner more than two decades before Xiao published his book. In 1936 in his cave dwelling in Yan'an, then the headquarters of the Communist revolution, Mao talked with the visiting American journalist Edgar Snow (1905–72) about his family, his youth, and the revolution. In his narrative Mao did not let pass the adventure with Xiao: apparently even in Mao's eventful life it was a memorable experience. Like Xiao, Mao's tone about living as a beggar was upbeat: "We walked through these five counties without using a single copper. The peasants fed us and gave us a place to sleep; wherever we went we were kindly treated and welcomed." [25]

Obviously, at least in his youth, Mao, like generations of people in China before him, considered vagrancy and mendicancy as a way to toughen one's willpower, temper one's strength, and gain experience with society. Unlike many other Chinese Communist leaders, who came from poor families, Mao grew up in a fairly wealthy farmer's home. But he was one of only two top Communist leaders who had experienced mendicancy. The other was Marshal Peng Dehuai (1898–1974), a Long March veteran and the commander and political commissar of the Chinese People's Volunteers army during the Korean War (1950–53). Peng served as China's minister of defense until 1959, when Mao purged him for voicing some mild criticisms of Mao's Great Leap Forward policy. If Mao was a "voluntary beggar" in his youth, then Peng was driven by sheer poverty to beg for food in his childhood. But he too looked back on the experience with some positive feelings.

Peng was born into a poor farmer's family in the province of Hunan, the county of Xiangtan (the same county where Mao was born). Life had been manageable for the family until Peng was eight, when his mother died and his father contracted a chronic illness and became unable to work in the field. When Peng reached the age of ten his family lost every bit of their livelihood. Peng recalled that they were too poor to have any real clothes: the whole family dressed in straw capes like, as Peng put it, "primitive people." On the Chinese New Year's day of 1909, there was absolutely not "a single grain of rice to put on the stove" at home, and Peng and his younger brother had to go out begging for food.

The brothers wandered among the neighboring villages at the time when many homes were setting off firecrackers and the New Year's celebration was in its peak. As they roamed to Teacher Chen's home in a place called Youmatan (Oil Crop Beach), Chen asked the brothers if they were the Fortune Boys, the legendary lads in Chinese folklore who were believed to bring good fortune to any family that encountered them (see Figure 14). Apparently, Chen just wanted to get the usual "yes" answer from the boys as an auspicious token on New Year's Day. But Peng was too honest or perhaps too devastated to have any sense of humor, for his answer was blunt: "No, we are just beggars." He thus got nothing. Seeing that his elder brother was artless, the younger one quickly made up for it: "Yes, we are the Fortune Boys!" He got a half bowl of steamed rice and a piece of pork.

The brothers begged for the whole day and by the time they went back home at dusk they had got about two liters of uncooked rice. Peng was so starved that when he stepped into the house he fainted. His grandmother made a vegetable soup to warm him up. The next day grandma went out begging with Peng's two younger brothers, as Peng recalled emotionally some half a century later: "It was snowing and a cold wind was blowing. She, an old woman in her seventies, gray hair, bound feet, hobbled along with a stick and two little boys (my younger brother was not yet four years old)." That day Peng went into the nearby mountains to cut brush (for firewood) to sell at the market. He earned ten cash, which enabled him to buy a small bag of salt. On his way home in a roadside copse he found a bunch of wild mushrooms. When grandmother brought home rice she had begged, mushroom soup and rice were the supper for the family that evening.[26]

Peng's biographer, Jürgen Domes, commented that Peng "may have exaggerated his own suffering between his seventh and twelfth years, but he correctly reflects the miseries of rural life in Hunan at that time, when he must undoubtedly have had a very hard life."[27] Mendicancy was part of that hard life, although it seems Peng's younger brothers had begged more than Peng did. His experience as a beggar must have had a profound influence on Peng's personality. In his memoir written during the Cultural Revolution in Mao's prison, Peng said: "The poverty I endured in my childhood was an experience that has toughened me. In my life I have often recalled my childhood and urged myself not to forget the lives of the poor and not to be corrupt."[28] Peng was generally regarded as the most upright of China's top Communist leaders. It would be hard to say to what extent his childhood begging experience influenced his personality, but what is revealed here is that a life of impoverishment—mendicancy is certainly the epitome of that—has always been seen in Chinese culture as having a toughening effect and being potentially meritorious.

Chairman Mao Would Not Be Amused

Despite Mao's hidden (or not so hidden) political agenda, his criticism of Wu Xun and the whole ardor for the panhandler may not have been entirely groundless.[29] Although he still lived in poverty and kept begging, Wu no doubt became a landowner and moneylender in his later years. But to the mainstream culture, such an attack on an apparently benevolent beggar was deemed to be a dissenting voice, which could prevail, as it did in Mao's time, only because Mao's regime was a dictatorship. With Mao's death in 1976 disappeared his radical thinking and despotism. The 1951 campaign has not been officially reassessed in China to this day, largely because, unlike most political campaigns under Mao, which involved large-scale persecutions, this campaign did not result in a serious purge (which is perhaps what Mao meant by "no lesson has been learned"). Therefore, from the official point of view, no formal rehabilitations were needed. But talk about the criticizing Wu Xun campaign being a wrongdoing of Mao started in the early 1980s, and by 1985 the campaign was openly dismissed by Hu Qiaomu (1912–92), a former personal secretary of Mao and then the top Communist leader in charge of "ideology," as "very lopsided, extreme, and harsh."[30] Hu's comments carried a particular weight since he was Mao's chief henchman during the campaign. Soon after, Wu Xun regained his positive image in China. In the 1990s, numerous books about the "righteous beggar" (*yigai*), as he was popularly called, both academic and popular, were published or reprinted, and the centennial of his death in 1997 was commemorated.

This reversal of the verdict was more a continuation of the age-honored Chinese principle of maintaining integrity in adversity than a setback for Maoism (which of course has been suffering reversals ever since Mao's death in 1976). In Chinese society not prey to Maoist revolution, mainly Taiwan, the virtue of Wu Xun has never been questioned and the Wu Xun type of spirit, that is, begging for the benefit of the others, is still extolled. For instance, a recent biography of Peng Baizheng, the head of Nantuo County in central Taiwan, was entitled *The Beggar County Magistrate*. The title has no derogatory meaning but is deliberately designed to signal approval for the magistrate who tirelessly worked for Nantuo County in the wake of Taiwan's great earthquake of September 21, 1999. The author states that Peng is a "beggar county magistrate" because he "begged" for help everywhere and in every way he could for the sake of his people and thus he is beloved in the county. The author even combines the metaphor "under the Cross" with the figurative word "beggar" to praise the magistrate.[31]

Describing Peng as a beggar is not an isolated metaphor but is integral to a culture that can every so often hold beggars in high regard. By the turn of the twenty-first century, taking a beggar as a role model or a type of social hero was still a practice very much alive. In 1999, one of Taiwan's Ten Outstanding Youths, the highest honor accorded young people below the age of forty in the island, was Lai Dongjin, a factory general manager who had been a beggar for nearly twenty years. In the Chinese community on both sides of the Taiwan Straits, Lai soon became a model of striving for success in the face of poverty and adversity.

Born in 1959 into a beggar's family in a temple in Taizhong that was used for holding corpses before burial, Lai had every reason to be caught in the trap of a "culture of poverty." His father had gone blind at the age of twenty-two and ever since had begged for a living. At the age of thirty-two, on a roadside in a village in Zhanghua in eastern Taiwan, the blind vagabond literally "picked up" a thirteen-year-old girl who had been abandoned under a tree due to her dementia. The girl became his wife and bore him twelve children. Lai Dongjin was the second child, having an elder sister and ten younger brothers and sisters. He started to beg when he was a toddler and for ten years slept in graveyards. The blind father was frequently violent and abusive and placed much of the burden of gaining a livelihood on the boy. (Still, Lai claims he deeply loves his father.) The father's proudest memory of his son, for example, was of "one day when Dongjin was just two years old." "We begged from Caotun to Puli," the father recounted, "and he walked 40 kilometers [twenty-five miles] in a single day!"[32]

As the oldest son, Lai Dongjin took care of the whole family from childhood, from feeding his baby brothers and sisters to regularly washing his mentally ill mother's menstruation clothes. (On one occasion, the bloody water flowing down the river scared a couple who lived on the lower reaches: "Have you killed someone?") One of his brothers was born with dementia, which made the task of taking care of the family even more of an ordeal. Often desperately hungry, the family stole leftover food people put outside the door for dogs and drank water from the gutter (Figure 20). When Lai was ten his ill-tempered father took the advice of some alms-givers about sending his oldest son to school, with the hope that one day the family could rise out of beggary. For that the family stopped wandering and settled in a deserted pigsty near Taizhong in central Taiwan. Meanwhile, Lai's thirteen-year-old sister was sent to an underground brothel and became the youngest prostitute there, receiving customers everyday no matter what her physical condition. Her sacrifice was in part to make her brother's education possible. For young Lai, that his beloved sister became a sex toy for strangers was his greatest agony, but he managed to transform the pain and anger to profound gratitude and determination to succeed in school. He did extremely well and by the sixth grade had won more than eighty awards. He practiced writing on a jumping pit in the school playground, using a twig as a pen and sand as the paper, for he could not afford stationery. For most of his teenage years he slept only three to four hours a day, for after school,

FIGURE 20. The artist Feng Zikai (1898–1975), who was famous for depicting daily life, left us a number of sketches of beggars drawn from real life. This cartoon shows a beggar grabbing the food left by a housewife outside the doorway for her dog. The caption reads "Scrambling for food." SOURCE: *Feng Zikai manhua quanji* (A complete collection of Feng Zikai's cartoons), 9: 4.

doffing his school uniform, he became a beggar boy again. Lai recalled his usual after-school activity:

> At the train station of Taizhong, in night markets, on bridges, main streets, back alleys—in short, wherever there was a crowd—Father and I would sit on the ground, begging. Father was playing the *yueqin* [Chinese-style guitar] or the *erhu* [Chinese-style violin] while singing. Sometimes he knelt on the ground, kowtowing. I was kneeling on the ground, doing my homework under the dim light of a street lamp. Every time there was a "dingdong"—that is, coins dropped into the small wash basin we placed in front of us—I would put down my pen and

raise my head to say: "Thank you! I wish you may make a great fortune! I wish you may have wonderful children and grandchildren!"[33]

The father and son typically begged until after midnight. Because of the extraordinary misery of this family, a local newspaper reported the story, with a photograph of the begging scene, long before Lai Dongjin became a national notable. Nevertheless, no government assistance ever reached the family. Basically, the father's singing and the son's "beg-study" order of the day supported the family of fourteen and allowed Lai to finish his education up to middle school. Although he earned the highest grade in every subject in his class, he could not afford to go on to high school. He entered a vocational school and found a part-time job, and thus gradually entered "normal" society, after having begged for seventeen years. His self-discipline and diligence paid off: By the age of thirty, Lai was the father of three, the head of a chemical factory with over fifty employees, and a homeowner.

In April 2000, he finished a memoir, entitled *Beggar Boy* (*Qigai jianzai*). It was published in Taiwan in May of that year, and became a national hit, setting a record on the island by selling half a million copies in four months. By October 2000, the book had already been reprinted fourteen times. Fifty-six celebrities from all walks of life, including Taiwan's president Chen Shui-bian (b. 1951), enthusiastically recommended the book, and many of them said they read it with tears in their eyes. Lai's story was taken as a moving and inspiring example of an individual fighting against extraordinary adversity while maintaining a sense of moral integrity and family responsibility.

Despite the decades of political separation and ideological hostility between Taiwan and the People's Republic, the new beggar model is something that is culturally accepted by the Chinese on both sides of the straits. It has been readily, indeed passionately, received on the mainland. After Lai won the Outstanding Youth award, he join a delegation of award winners on a visit to China, where they "exchanged views" with Chinese youth of similar status, and visited Mao's hometown, Shaoshan, a mecca in China (Figure 21). The mainland edition of *Beggar Boy* was published by the official Chinese Youth Press in March 2002. The message was clear: the beggar boy is a role model for Chinese youth. Praise for the book has come from prominent writers who have been moved by this real-life story that resembles, as one writer has put it, a "miracle of humanity" and a true story that reads like a "fairy tale."[34]

In an interview after the publication of the book, Lai was asked if he had a religious faith to sustain him in the extraordinary hardship. He replied that all he had was the plain faith that even a beggar might someday "rise head and shoulders above others" (*chu ren tou di*).[35] Lai recalled that on one occa-

FIGURE 21.   Lai Dongjin (in the middle, the second row) in Mao's hometown, Shaoshan. The group is holding a sign reading "Delegation of the 37 Outstanding Youth to the Mainland." The house in the background is where Mao was born and lived to the age of twenty. SOURCE: Lai Dongjin, *Qigai jianzai* (Beggar boy).

sion when the whole family was humiliated in the street, the father threw his stick heavily to the ground and swore: "Even a beggar may one day be an emperor!" Such a wild claim, which clearly came from the story of the first Ming emperor, impressed Lai deeply, as he mused on the day: "These were words I would forever remember. In tears I clenched my fists and ground my teeth: I shall strive! I shall bring honor to the family! I shall prove to heaven that a beggar may one day become an emperor!"[36]

This late twentieth-century beggar saga brings alive the spirit of Wu Zixu, Han Xin, Zhu Yuanzhang, Wu Xun, and others in China's long and variegated tradition of mendicancy. That the cheers for Lai's story are echoed in the mainland also indicates the common fundamental cultural roots of the Chinese on both sides of the straits despite decades of political separation. Time and space, war and revolution, ideology and foreign influence—none of these seems to have been penetrating enough to sever this culture on mendicancy. Mao certainly had the notion and the power to bring a beggar to trial in a national campaign for the purpose of carrying out his version of Communist purification, but he too failed. In the end, in a historical irony, a modern-day beggar hero happily visited Mao's home, and duly paid his respects, quite unaware of Mao's grudge against men of his type. With this pilgrim and the traditionalism he represents, "Chairman Mao would not be amused."[37] But Mao's dismay can only reveal that even a formidable revolution like his and the absolute power he, as the "great helmsman," once held were still too fragile and transient to uproot China's tenuous cultural tradition.

Conclusion

THE BEGGAR'S WORLD in China—its culture, its standing in public opinion, and its place in state policy making—was continuous from late imperial times through the first half of the twentieth century. If one thinks of beggars as the most vulnerable members of society, as conventional wisdom has it, then the methods, techniques, and organizations of beggars depicted in the foregoing chapters at times might seem excessive for an urban underclass. It should be emphasized, however, that this subaltern culture for the most part developed out of the fundamental human drive for sheer survival. Since the decline of the imperial order in the late eighteenth century, struggling for a bare living was the fate of millions of people in China. The commonality and persistence of beggars' culture was a direct result of this ubiquitous struggle for survival through the centuries.

The same also applied to the policies of the state with regard to beggars as well as to the public's attitudes toward the poor. In almsgiving, the general public was frequently caught up in an emotional and often contradictory mixture of sympathy, fear, and antipathy. While the Chinese state was equally ambiguous about beggars, ultimately it saw them more as social elements threatening to its rule than as simply poverty-stricken people who ought to be helped. Most of the time it was unable to act upon either of these views effectively.

This prolonged situation was to undergo a major change with the epoch-making victory of the Communists in 1949. The founding of the People's Republic of China (PRC) that year and the Soviet-model socialist system that was established across the mainland in the early 1950s signaled a major break from the past, which has been often melodramatically described by a Chinese metaphor as "turning heaven and earth upside down." As far as beggars are concerned, Mao's China seems to have been a unique phase in history. This book has not addressed the postrevolutionary era, but a few thoughts on beggars in the PRC perhaps could put the issues involved, especially those related to the tenacity of mendicant culture, in a more comprehensive historical perspective.[1]

Although mendicancy did not completely disappear in socialist China, it is undeniable that for more than three decades after 1949 beggars were a rare sight in Chinese cities. From the very beginning of the regime, the government was able to effectively control population mobility from rural to urban areas. To carry out its policy on mendicancy and vagrancy, in the early 1950s more than 600 detention centers were set up in cities across the nation to hold and then deport to the countryside what were officially called "wandering and begging persons."[2] Immediately after the Communist takeover of Shanghai in May 1949, for instance, 6,293 homeless vagrants were put in detention centers and then sent to a newly established reclamation farm in northern Jiangsu on the banks of the Huai River. By September, more than 400,000 wartime refugees in the city had been sent back to their native places.[3] No doubt the PRC's socialist program and rigid organizational control greatly contributed to the effectiveness of the policy. In the countryside, the Land Reform and the rural collectivization movement provided an institutional mechanism to absorb surplus labor and contain poverty in the villages. In the city, the urban household registration (*hukou*) system established in the mid-1950s and the decades of rationing of daily necessities made living in a city without a legal resident permit nearly impossible. Also, should any vagrants appear on the street, the neighborhood organizations that were set up in every city and town not only kept a watchful eye on them but functioned also as a virtual police force.[4]

As a result, the omnipresence of street beggars that had so strikingly characterized Chinese cities for centuries was largely ended in Mao's China. Even in the early 1960s, when Mao's Great Leap Forward resulted in a nationwide famine that caused an estimated thirty million premature deaths—predominantly in rural areas—swarms of beggars like those of old China did not reappear in the cities.[5] Indeed, eliminating social problems such as mendicancy, prostitution, and secret societies has often been cited as an achievement of the People's Republic. To Westerners who had lived in pre-1949 China, the disappearance of beggars from Chinese cities was impressive. On Edgar Snow's "good-bye" list to old Shanghai were "beggars on every downtown block and the scabby infants urinating or defecating on the curb while mendicant mothers absently scratched for lice."[6] Seymour Topping, a *New York Times* correspondent who lived in China during the civil war (1946–49), recorded that in his 1971 revisit, he took an evening stroll along familiar streets in downtown Guangzhou, and "with a start, I realized that the swarms of beggars had disappeared."[7] An American who revisited Beijing in 1977 noted that in the neighborhood where she and her husband had studied Chinese thirty years earlier, the "'hutungs,' small, winding streets, were similar to those we had walked, except that they were clean and there were no beggars."[8] It is probably no exaggeration to say that this was the first time since Jesuit missionaries arrived in China in the sixteenth century that foreign visitors had ever encountered beggar-free cities. Although Westerners were likely to be shown the best of Mao's China, these observations were not limited to foreign visitors. In general, Chinese residents in various cities seem to agree that up to the early 1980s beggars were uncommon.[9]

But beneath the "clean" surface of the cities, the problem of mendicancy lingered on. The exact situation of beggary in Mao's China is yet to be determined, largely because of insufficient information on the subject (government data, for example, are totally absent). Occasional reports, mainly from political dissidents who left China, indicate that beggars had far from completely disappeared. The army of professional beggars organized by spontaneous guilds like those in the pre-1949 era no longer existed, but beggars not only persisted in various parts of the country, but sometimes could amount to a crowd—they were just restrained to remote areas and peripheral towns.[10] Also, there were some similarities between these beggars and their counterparts in the pre-1949 era. As in the old days, the main cause of beggary in Mao's era was rural poverty. And, in impoverished districts, local authorities, now in the form of the people's commune, sometimes encouraged farmers to go out begging in richer areas and provided them with official letters of reference certifying that they were members of the people's commune and asking for assistance, a practice that in every detail echoed the Qing custom.[11]

If the Maoist regime had effectively reduced mendicancy to the minimum and to a great extent eliminated it in major cities, the post-Mao government was effective in bringing beggary back to the streets within merely a couple of years after the launching of economic reforms in 1979. In the last two decades of the twentieth century, the relatively moderate political control and the market economy adopted by the state worked together to create a vibrant yet indifferent social environment in which disadvantaged groups, chiefly peasants in less developed areas, were marginalized and neglected. When the slogan "getting rich is glorious" was officially promoted, poverty in fact spread. In particular, once the government softened its migration policy, the poverty that had previously been contained in rural areas stretched out and engulfed the cities. As the most recognizable symptom of the side effects of the reform, starting from the mid-1980s a large army of beggars reemerged in Chinese cities. No official statistics are available on the number of street beggars in China, but the China News Agency estimated in October 1993 that the total number had reached a quarter million, with over one-fifth in the four cities of Beijing, Shanghai, Guangzhou, and Shenzhen. It was reported that in 1991 police arrested 28,000 beggars in the single southern city of Guangzhou alone. These beggars, however, were only a few drops in the sea of the so-called floating population or the tide of laborers (*mingong chao*).[12] The floating population mostly consists of peasants who have left their villages in search of jobs or a better life in urban areas. By January 1994 their number had reached twenty million and was increasing rapidly.[13] The official Xinhua News Agency reported in July 1995 that domestic migrants had reached the alarming number of eighty million.[14]

The main body of the "peasants of yesterday" in China's cities consists of migratory workers who are, as Dorothy Solinger has demonstrated, "contesting citizenship in urban China" on an unequal base with those who have permanent urban residential status.[15] But there is a sizable portion of the floating population that has ended up begging in cities—unable even to "contest." These people, who have for various reasons chosen or been forced to choose begging on the street, are among the least capable of competing for urban jobs, but cling to the city for its wealth. In historical perspective, the resurgence of beggars on a large scale in recent years—and the trend is likely to continue—is making the Mao era more a passing interlude than a significant break in the history of Chinese mendicancy.

Given the sweeping changes brought by the Communist revolution and the dramatic development attendant on the current economic reforms, it would not be surprising to see certain differences between today's beggars and their counterparts in old China. And in general the level of poverty in China today is much less alarming than it was in the early twentieth century and during the time of Mao's famine. But behind often-told stories of change, the beggars' world in contemporary China seems to bear some fundamental similarities to its pre-1949 predecessor. Not only is the composition of beggars today very similar to that in the prerevolutionary period (that is, beggars are mostly former farmers), but the beggars' world is once again organized in much the same fashion as it was more than half a century ago. Virtually all begging methods that were practiced in Qing and Republican China have been resurrected, as have the gangs and the beggar barons, who were now, in the late 1980s, among the new elite known as the "ten thousand yuan" magnates.[16] Organized beggars once again exert their power by ritual sabotage and contamination. A beggar in Guangzhou (who came from rural Jiangxi) quite lordly told a reporter, "Store owners dare not offend us beggars. He who gives us a bad time will live to regret it." A story he told in 1999 bears a striking similarity to the beggars' "creating a scene" strategy in the Qing and Republican periods:

> Not long ago there was an opening of a new restaurant in our area. The owner was a snob who thought money talks and nobody can do anything to him. He simply looked down on us, so when we walked in on the grand opening day asking for "red envelopes," he just drove us out.
>
> The next day, however, the restaurant was crowded with beggars. They touched all the customers with their dirty hands asking for "wine money." Soon customers all left the restaurant and the place had no business at all for a week. The desperate owner now understood our power and sent us red envelopes. And we, seeing him surrounded, acted as the saying goes, "To forgive a person wherever it is forgivable," and let the matter end.[17]

Inside the beggars' world, monopolization of begging turf is once again the cornerstone of beggars' organization. Shen Zhengfu, a forty-eight-year-old lame beggar from a village in Heilongjiang, told of his experience in Beijing:

> At first because I had just entered the trade without knowing its rules, I was often beaten. Several times I was so badly beaten that I could not even stand up. . . . Later, after I had wandered for a long time I became experienced and knew the inside rules. Now nobody dares hit me because I have paid my tribute and have been recruited. It looks like beggars are scattered everywhere on the streets without order, but inside our world everything is clear-cut. Which area is ours, which area is yours, the lines that should never be crossed—all is iron-clad. One cannot be careless. At the beginning I had thought beggars could go anywhere to beg. But once I entered the circle, I found there were rules and regulations and also rankings. It is quite something![18]

Even in less restricted environments, the sense of begging turf remains strong. A sixty-five-year-old country woman in Shandong led twelve elderly women from her village (the oldest of her team was eighty-two and had a number of great-grandchildren) to beg on the beach of the famous resort of Qingdao, and she too had a clear idea about where to go and not to go, as she told a reporter: "We know the rules, and except in the beach area we never go to the town, which is other people's place. If we go there it means we are taking away other people's rice bowl [livelihood]. This will cause trouble—that we know for sure."[19]

Although most of the beggar groups are still local and small in scale, like the bond between the Uncle and his Little Users in old Shanghai, the modern transportation system is making nationwide communication among beggars appear a possibility. It was reported that if officials had not suppressed it, a beggars' national conference would have been held in Wuhan in central China in the fall of 1986. This conference was to have met at the resort of the famous historic site of the Pagoda of the Yellow Crane (Huanghelou) to elect beggars' national leaders.[20]

In response to the resurgence of beggars, public opinion is once again caught in the dilemma of sympathy versus antipathy. Most of the published sources on the subject suggest that antipathy has been on the rise in recent years. Many people seem to believe that, unlike beggars in the old days, today's beggars are not truly desperate for food and clothing in order to "keep warm and be fed" (*wenbao*), as traditional beggars were, but take up mendicancy as a way to earn money and ride on the current trend of seeking economic well-being. In the spring of 2004 an infamous case, in which an entire village became rich by begging, caught the attention of the media and, later, became the subject of a government investigation. Gongxiaocun, a village of 370 households or about 1,600 people near Fuyang in northwest Anhui Province, is known as the "Beggar Village," for since the early 1990s, the village's main source of income has been mendicancy. The trade started with a villager who was handicapped in a coal mining accident. He begged on the streets of the town of Fuyang and soon became quite affluent. This inspired his fellow villagers who, once they begged in town, were amazed to find that "the hearts of city folks are particularly kind." This is an area where peasants in the Qing period had the tradition of going out begging in famines and slack seasons. But this time it has become a true trade. When there were not enough disabled persons to go around, the villagers rented handicapped children, usually between the ages of three to ten, from other places. The business grew from a local endeavor to a national enterprise: handicapped children were rented from everywhere in the country and their begging spots ranged from local towns and provincial capitals to metropolitan cities such as Beijing, Shanghai, Tianjin, Guangzhou, and reached as far as Harbin on the border with Russia and the deep inland city of Chengdu. The profitability of the business is self-evident in the village: two-story blue-brick homes with white tiled walls have been built in abundance. They typically have two stone lion statues as door guards, the traditional emblem for residences of wealthy families. A new folk saying in the Beggars' Village does not shy away from revealing the situation there: "[Having] 50,000 yuan is not rich, 100,000 yuan is getting rich, 200,000 yuan is moderately rich."[21]

Reports from various cities often tell how nowadays beggars can be oddly affluent: sending home money to build multi-story houses, plunking down thousands of dollars on gambling tables, investing in businesses, accumulating substantial savings accounts, and so on. Reportedly, more than half of the beggars in the southern city of Shenzhen have cellular phones.[22] And in late 2003 the Sichuan provincial government issued regulations on vagrants' relief that particularly mentioned that beggars who have "cellular phones and pets" are not eligible for government assistance.[23] Beggars in Shanghai reportedly can earn 200 yuan a day and their monthly income amounts to the salary of a white-collar college graduate. Many of them have quite regular "working hours" too, from 9 a.m. to 7 p.m. on an average day.[24] Beggars in Guangzhou have been noted to take airplanes to visit home during Chinese New Year. It was observed on a Wuhan street that a foreigner giving money to a woman beggar and her six-year-old son was shouted at by a man. The man, who was dressed in a trim Western-style suit, yelled to the foreigner: "Don't give them money! Don't you know that these people are better-off than I?"[25] Beggars themselves sometimes also admit that begging is "addictive."[26]

In spite of the public suspicion of or grudge against beggars, sympathy for beggars must still be common enough to support the social milieu for mendicancy. Without it, thousands upon thousands of beggars would not have been able to resume mendicancy as a "trade." The media discussions on beggars in Guangzhou that generated keen public responses in early 2004 may well reflect the popular concerns about how to give alms to the "right persons." The public feeling was described as "if I give money [to beggars] I worry about being cheated; if I don't give money, I feel uneasy." The proposed solutions were diverse, including giving beggars food and clothes but not cash, licensing beggars, using the internet for identification, helping with child beggars, and so on.[27] The discussion was not much different in its nature from the debate about whether homeless people in contemporary America are "deserving or undeserving" of social welfare. The proposed solutions, such as licensing beggars and setting up identification dossiers, bear some striking similarities to the Qing *baojia* system and the eighteenth-century French institution of licensed beggars.

Like its predecessors, the Communist government ever since it came to power has considered mendicancy as a social disease and has held largely negative views of beggars. In theory, the Communist revolution is a proletarian revolution for the poor and oppressed, and beggars may fit perfectly well in the category of the "propertyless class" (*wuchan jieji*, the Chinese word for "proletariat") and thus ought to win sympathy from a government that claims to represent the interests of the mass of the poor. The reality, however, is that the regime established in 1949 has shared the view of previous governments that beggars are unrestrained or even criminal elements. Long before the Communist victory, Mao had penned two articles (written in 1926 and 1939) on social classes and the Chinese revolution that set the tone for the so-called lumpen proletariat, of which beggars and vagrants of all sorts were a part. The lumpen proletariat in China, according to Mao, is "made up of peasants who have lost their land and handicraftsmen who cannot get work. They lead the most precarious existence of all. In every part of the country they have their secret societies. . . . One of China's difficult problems is how to handle these people."[28] In the 1939 article Mao put beggars into the same category as robbers and gangsters and cautioned his people about their destructiveness. If one takes away the Marxist terminology from Mao's statements, his judgments on vagrants depart little from the traditional elite standpoint represented by the state that beggars jeopardize its rule and are potentially felonious. Once in power, Mao's thoughts regarding vagrants expressed in these documents became the foundation for government policy making.

According to the class categories commonly used in the cities after the revolution, beggars belong to the category of "urban poor" (*chengshi pinmin*), which is a part of the "working people" (*laodong renmin*) that was extolled in new China.[29] Mendicancy, however, was nevertheless regarded as "gaining without working" (*bulao er huo*), which, ironically, is a classic label usually applied to wealthy capitalists. The early 1950s policies of seizing and sending beggars back to their native villages or, for those who had no place to return to, employing them in urban work units, were based on the notion that beggars should become self-reliant and productive members of society. These policies were restated and carried out when beggars reappeared in large numbers in the early 1980s. For the two decades since then beggars have been subjected to detention and deportation back to their villages. Frequently, detained beggars are forced to labor at the centers in the name of earning enough money to cover their travel expenses back home.

As this study neared completion, there was a major development regarding government policy on beggars. On June 20, 2003, Prime Minister Wen Jiabao signed into law State Council Document No. 381, Regulations on Aiding and Managing Helpless Urban Vagrants and Beggars, to replace the Regulation on Detaining and Deporting Urban Vagrants and Beggars issued in May 1982. The new regulations have been seen as a major transition from "managing" to "service" and to protecting basic human rights. Beggars are eligible to receive some aid at the centers but are no longer being held and deported. In other words, the centers are supposed to become homeless shelters of some sort rather than police substations. In late June 2003, signboards of detention and deportation centers across the country were pulled down and replaced by new signboards indicating that these were now "relief centers."[30] By October, 777 relief centers had been established nationwide.[31]

This rather dramatic transition all started from an incident in a Guangzhou vagrant detention center where a twenty-seven-year-old man named Sun Zhigang was beaten to death in March 2003, only a few hours after he was detained for not carrying his identification card. Sun, a native of Huanggang, Hubei Province, was the only college graduate in his village. His education, however, came at a price: the family owed a huge debt that it would never be able to pay back without Sun finding a job outside his undeveloped hometown. Sun therefore went to Guangzhou, China's prosperous southern hub, in February and found a job in a garment factory. Although Sun was not begging at all, he might have looked like a suspicious "country bump-kin" to the police of Guangzhou. On March 17 he was arrested on the street for failing to produce his identification and sent to a detention center as a "three-without person," the official category for vagrants.[32] There Sun had a wrangle with either officers or other inmates, or both, which led to the physical confrontation that cost him his life.[33] The incident could have gone unnoticed had it not caught the attention of a journalist who reported the detention center's brutality in the *Southern Urban News* (*Nanfang dushi bao*). It was further reported, in more detail and in a more sympathetic tone, in *Beijing Youth News* (*Beijing qingnan bao*), and soon became a widely known scandal. The criticisms were not just about one man's death, but the general corruption of the detention centers: using beggars as unpaid laborers in the name of working off fines for vagrancy, squeezing "redemption fees" from inmates or their families, detaining undocumented peasants in the city for the purpose of extortion, and so on. Sun's story was eventually printed in *Internal Reference News* (*Neican*), the confidential briefing that is circulated strictly among high-ranking officials. Evidently, in April and May, Sun's death and the problems of detention centers it revealed were on the tables of the premier and other of Beijing's top leaders. The parallel of this event with the SARS epidemic at the time apparently added to the pressure on China's new leaders, who must be particularly concerned about the image of the government and the criticism of its social policy. By June, the new regulations were officially released.

This is certainly a positive move toward humane treatment of street people and, in the long run, a more civilized system of coping with urban poverty. But there are reasonable doubts about whether the new rules can effectively replace the old detention and deportation policy. Official data showed that by September, nationwide 76,000 people appealed for help at the relief centers, and 60,400 actually received help.[34] This was, of course, a small number in view of the size of China's vagrant population. Reports on the new system were mixed. Some cities reported beggars refusing to enter the relief centers, preferring to live in freedom on the streets, much like we have seen in Qing and Republican times; others reported beggars turning to relief centers as a "hotel" for the evening while begging during the day. The modest new policies have also caused an increase in the number of street beggars in some cities, and in many cities the relief centers have not been publicized enough to make them known in the vagrant community.

Even if the policy is implemented well, the best scenario is that the beggar centers will become a sort of government welfare, bearing some similarity to the Qing county poorhouses. But then the burden will be entirely on the local authorities, who in fact have few resources and have already started to make their own local policies to maneuver the interpretation of central government rules on mendicancy.[35] Organized social and civic assistance to the poor, suspended after the revolution, when the idea itself became quite a novelty, has been revived but has not yet returned to the pre-1949 level. Given the numbers of the "helpless urban vagrants and beggars" and the endless source of such people, the government alone cannot possibly afford or run effectively such a welfare institution. America's social policies toward the urban poor have been criticized for "losing ground."[36] In China, the government encounters a tougher job, for the ground has not yet been prepared, and the state is dealing with a new version of an old problem: the imbalance between the still-poor countryside and the increasingly better-off cities. As researchers on contemporary Chinese beggars have pointed out, before China can achieve comprehensive economic development across the nation, "people from the inland areas will continue to be attracted by the beggars' life."[37] The contours of begging may change in some way, but the essence is likely to continue. Ultimately, the three-decade-long suspension of the mendicants' world in urban China may only serve to prove the tenacity of a deeply rooted tradition. Much of the culture and many of the institutions of Chinese beggars depicted in this book may, sadly, serve as an introduction to understanding the revival of mendicancy in China.

But there are positive signs as well. The notion of *cishan* (charity), much criticized in Mao's time as the sham tenderheartedness of the feudal and bourgeois classes, has resumed its legitimacy as the due humanitarianism that a society needs.[38] An anecdote concerning the relief center of Chaoyang District of Beijing may signify the progress of China in both the concept and practice of humanity. Written on the screen wall facing the gate of the center are two big Chinese characters, *BO AI*, literally meaning "universal love," but the phase has almost exclusively been used as the standard translation for the French word, *fraternité*. Having such a sign at the entrance of a relief center may seem perfectly usual, but the words are a bit too elegant and old-fashioned to be conventional. According to Cao Lanshuo, the director of the center, having the words there as a sort of mission statement was merely a coincidence. The premises of the center formerly housed a boarding school and the characters had long been there. It was quite a rarity that they had survived the Cultural Revolution, perhaps because the place was located in an obscure rural spot about twenty miles from the center of the city, or perhaps no Red Guard at the time understood the French (therefore "bourgeois") connection of the phrase. Whatever the case, in late 2003, when this place was remodeled into a relief center, Cao and the staff members deliberately preserved the characters, for they thought, unanimously, that the phrase dovetailed with the philanthropic mission of this institution, and by preserving it they "*hope* to carry forward the spirit of these two words."[39]

The writer Lu Xun once said: "Hope isn't the kind of thing that you can say either exists or doesn't exist. It's like a path across the land—it's not there to begin with, but when lots of people go the same way, it comes into being."[40] To paraphrase these words, when most people in China, like those in the Beijing relief center, start to think along the lines of what can be called Bo Ai,[41] a true and lasting solution for the street criers may ultimately come into being.

Note: The Character List provides the Chinese characters for special terms and expressions. Names of people and places as well as the titles of works are generally not included. The transliterations are in the pinyin system. Capitalization and hyphenation follow the original text or source and may not be standard.

an tu zhong qian 安土重遷
ao 熬
ba 八
baishi 稗史
bang 幫
bao daren 包打人
bao taozhai 包討債
baobao 保保
baojia 保甲
bawangbian 霸王鞭
baxian 八仙
beifen 輩分
beishui chexin 杯水車薪
benbang 本幫
biede shengsi 癟的生絲
biesan 癟三
biji 筆記
Bo Ai 博愛
bu kaikou 不開口
buhaoyisi 不好意思
bulao er huo 不勞而獲
cai shen 財神
caishen dao 財神到
canglong wohu 藏龍臥虎
ceyin zhixin, renjie youzhi 惻隱之心，
　人皆有之

cheng'e yangshan 懲惡揚善
chenghuangmiao 城隍廟
chengshi pinmin 城市貧民
chi jiang cha 吃講茶
chongxian 崇賢
Chouanhui 籌安會
chu ren tou di 出人頭地
chuan tu bu chuan zi 傳徒不傳子
chusi wu dan'nan, taofan zai buqiong
　除死無大難，討飯再不窮
chuzhang 處長
cishan 慈善
cun 寸
da chusang 大出喪
da toumu 大頭目
daci dabei 大慈大悲
dagan 大杆
dagoubang 打狗棒
Dahang 大行
dan 石
dang ba gu 党八股
danmin 蜑民
dao 到
dao 倒
daotai (toutai) 道台
dibao 地保

dingpeng 釘棚
dongxiao 洞蕭
dou 斗
duomin 惰民
e'ren 惡人
erhu 二胡
fa 髮
fan 飯
fang 坊
fangsheng 放生
fanmian jiaocai 反面教材
fanshen 翻身
feigun 匪棍
Feng Xian 奉憲
fengshui 風水
fotiaoqiang 佛跳牆
gai 丐
gaichang 丐厂
gaifei 丐匪
gaihu 丐戶
gailun 丐論
gan 杆
gang 杠
gangfang 杠房
ganshang de 杆上的
gao dizhuang 告地狀
gaoyao 膏藥
Gelaohui 哥老會
gong xi fa cai 恭喜發財
gongren 工人
Guanyin 觀音
gugu yan 姑姑宴
gungai 棍丐
guokui 鍋魁
hangye shen 行業神
hankoupo 喊口婆
hanyanguan 旱煙管
hu 觳
hu luo pingyang bei quan qi, long you qianshui zao xia xi 虎落平陽被犬欺，龍游淺水遭蝦戲
hua ducao wei xianghua 化毒草為香花
huaben 話本
huaguxi 花鼓戲
huangdi 皇帝

huazi 化子（花子）
hui 會
hukou 戶口
huqin 胡琴
hutian qiangdi 呼天搶地
jianghu 江湖
jianghu langzhong 江湖郎中
jianmin 賤民
jiaohua 教化
jiaohua ji 叫化雞
jiaohuazi 叫化子（叫花子）
Jiaoyang yuan 教養院
jin 斤
jingshige 警世歌
jinshi 進士
jinzhao youjiu jinzhao zui 今朝有酒今朝醉
junzi 君子
junzi baochou, shinian buwan 君子報仇，十年不晚
juren 舉人
kai tianchuang 開天窗
kaitian pidi 開天闢地
kan 看
kejia 客家
laoda 老大
laodong renmin 勞動人民
laotouzi 老頭子
le shan hao shi 樂善好施
lianhualao 蓮花落
lianhuanao 蓮花鬧
Liexian zhuan 列仙傳
liugai 流丐
liumin 流民
luobo gongzi 落泊公子
mian you cai se 面有菜色
minghuang 明黃
mingong chao 民工潮
mingqu anlai 明去暗來
minyao 民謠
mu 畝
Nanping xiaozhong 南屏曉鐘
nian xige 念喜歌
nianhua 年畫
Nongpushe 農圃社

peiling 陪靈
pengmin 棚民
piaomu 漂母
pipa 琵琶
qigai 乞丐
qingtongyu 青筒魚
qiongren 窮人
qitao renyuan 乞討人員
ren 仁
ren qing wei tian 人情為田
ren shang ren 人上人
roudan 肉畾
sang jia zhi quan 喪家之犬
sanjiao hama 三腳蛤蟆
sanjiao jiuliu 三教九流
sanshi ding yiguo 三石頂一鍋
sheng 升
shengguan facai 升官發財
shenshou dajiangjun 伸手大將軍
shi 市
shihua 史話
shiliao 食療
shou huiqi 收晦气
Shuang cheng fu qi gai chu 雙城府乞
　丐處
shuxiang zhi jia 書香之家
suona 嗩吶
tao shenghuo 討生活
taofan 討飯
tao-fan-hui 討飯會
tian 天
tongxianghui 同鄉會
tu yisheng 土醫生
tuantou 團頭
tudi 徒弟
wang ba 王八
wanyuan hu 万元戶
wei ren shi biao 為人師表
wen (currency unit) 文
wen (literature) 文
wenbao 溫飽
wenshi bu fenjia 文史不分家
wenziyu 文字獄
wuchan jieji 無產階級
wushamao 烏紗帽

wuxia 武俠
xia jiuliu 下九流
xian 縣
xiao 孝
xiao toumu 小頭目
xiaokang zhi jia 小康之家
xiaopin bu xiaochang 笑貧不笑娼
xiaoren 小人
xiaoshuo 小說
xiaoyezhu 小業主
xiaoyong 小用
ximin 細民
xingshi ge 醒世歌
xinkufei 辛苦費
xishi 喜事
xiucai 秀才
xuewei 穴位
xusui 虛歲
yang 陽
yangji yuan (yang-chi yuan) 養濟院
yanyi 演義
yaopai 腰牌
yaoqianshu 搖錢樹
yasuiqian 壓歲錢
yeshi 野史
yeshu 爺叔
yi du gong du 以毒攻毒
yigai 義丐
yin 陰
yiren 异人
you 莠
youmin 莠民
youmin 游民
Youmin xiqinsuo 游民習勤所
yuan 元
yuehu 樂戶
yueqin 月琴
Yuhuating 雨花亭
zaju 雜劇
zayong 雜詠
zhanggu 掌故
Zhaocai tongzi 招財童子
zhen 鎮
zhengkai 正楷
zhengshi 正史

zhishang tan bing 紙上談兵

zhiyuan 職員

zhongdu 中都

zhou 州

zhutong fan 竹筒飯

zhuzhici 竹枝詞

zibenjia 資本家

zuofu 作福

zushiye 祖師爺

Appendix: The Sound of Mendicity

1. The music of "On the Songhua River," derived from a funeral dirge accompanying ritualized weeping and wailing in Ding County, North China, 1920s.

SOURCE: Music notes recorded and adapted by Frederic T. Lu.

2. An example of music for beggars' ballad singing known as "the over-lord's rattle stick" (*bawangbian*), similar to lotus ballad singing (*lianhualao*). SOURCE: Music notes recorded and adapted by Frederic T. Lu.

3. The music for the Fengyang flower-drum song, a popular beggars'
melody along the Huai River valley, early twentieth century.

SOURCE: Music notes recorded and adapted by Frederic T. Lu.

INTRODUCTION

1. Qu Yanbin, *Zhongguo qigai shi*, 6−7.

2. *Gujin tushu jicheng*, 815: 20.

3. See documentary evidence cited in Cen Dali, *Zhongguo qigai shi*, 2−3. Coincidentally, according to *Webster's Ninth New Collegiate Dictionary*, the English word "beggar" appeared roughly around the same time (the thirteenth century).

4. Schak, *A Chinese Beggars' Den*, 5.

5. For Skinner's model, see Skinner, "Marketing and Social Structure in Rural China," and Skinner (ed.), *The City in Late Imperial China*, 253−351.

6. Macgowan, *Men and Manners of Modern China*, 291.

7. The term "Chinese beggars" is used for the sake of convenience. It does not imply that beggars in China were a solidified group with a single unified outlook on life.

8. See Wilson, *The Truly Disadvantaged*.

9. The historian Gertrude Himmelfarb argues that modern Europe experienced a redefinition of poverty from moral philosophy to political economy due to the social and political changes brought by the Industrial Revolution. See Himmelfarb, *The Idea of Poverty*, especially pt. 1. For a discussion of the concept of the poor in Chinese history, see Liang Qizi, "'Pingqiong' yu 'qiongren' guannian."

10. For the theory of culture of poverty, see Lewis, *La Vida*, and Lewis, *A Study of Slum Culture*.

11. *Gujin tushu jicheng*, 488: 18.

12. In Chinese, *beishui chexin*. The expression comes from the Confucian classic, *Mencius*.

13. In Chinese, *zhishang tan bing*. The aphorism comes from Sima Qian's *Shiji*, *juan* 81.

14. Lao Tzu, *Tao Te Ching*, 57.

15. Calculated on the basis of the 1819 official figures, China had about 1,500 counties (*zhou* or *xian*, also translated as "district"). On average, counties had 250,000 inhabitants. See Hsiao, *Rural China*, 5.

16. Lobenstine and Warnshuis (eds.), *The China Mission Year Book 1919*, 38. In the post-Mao reform, the authorities came to believe that the government had for thirty years intervened too much in areas that should have been left to the people and to society. The Taoist saying "Govern a big nation like frying a small fish" was some-

times cited to justify a lessening of government control. See for example, Tang Zhenchang, *Zhongguo yinshi wenhua*, 9–10.

17. See *Liji* (*The Book of Rites*), chap. 4 *Tangongxia*; *Cihai*, 752.

18. Guanzi, *Guanzi*, 1: 52. The translation is modified based on the original text.

19. Kuhn, *Soulstealers*, 115.

20. Schak, *A Chinese Beggars' Den*, 45–64.

21. The government programs regarding beggars included building workhouses for healthy adults, an orphanage for destitute youth, a sanitarium for elderly people without families, and a hospital for injured and sick workers. See Stapleton, *Civilizing Chengdu*, 126–29, 150.

22. Wang, *Street Culture in Chengdu*, 144–47.

23. Lipkin, "Modern Dilemmas."

24. Bun, "Beggar Gangs in Modern Tianjin."

25. See Chapters 5 and 6 for details.

26. Beier, *Masterless Men*, 109–19.

27. Adams, *Bureaucrats and Beggars*, 42, 47, 137.

28. Piven and Cloward, *Regulating the Poor*, 109.

29. Guanzi, *Guanzi*, 2: 512; *Gujin tushu jicheng*, 815: 21.

30. On the reform in various Chinese cities, see Esherick (ed.), *Remaking the Chinese City*, especially chap. 1, "Modernity and Nation in the Chinese City" (by Joseph Esherick), and chap. 13, "New Chinese Cities" (by David Strand) on the tensions and contrasts between modernity and identity and the concept of "old" and "new" that stood behind the successes—and failures—of the reform.

31. Deng Yunte, *Zhongguo jiuhuang shi*, 40.

32. Kemp, *The Face of China*, 161; Ross, *The Changing Chinese*, 303; Stapleton, *Civilizing Chengdu*, 126.

33. Chen Lengseng, "Shanghai de youmin," 10; and Chen Lengseng, "Shanghai qigai wenti," 19.

34. Peters, *Shanghai Policeman*, 244.

35. Jiang Siyi and Wu Yuanshu, *Shanghai qibai ge qigai*, 237. Another investigation, in 1936, found there were about sixty charitable institutions in Shanghai but, in the words of the investigators, "except [for] one or two, we are ashamed to report that none of them admit beggars." See Liu, "Woman's Fight Against Beggary."

36. Buck, *Urban Change in China*, 37.

37. *Shanghaitan heimu*, vol. 2: 209–10.

CHAPTER I

1. *Er shi si shi*, 1 (*Shiji, juan* 129): 824.

2. To borrow the famous vow of General Douglas MacArthur (1880–1964), made in 1942, to return to the Philippines.

3. For another example, the Chinese character for "ocean" (*yang*) also means "foreign," and the character for "earth" (*tu*) also means "native" or "Chinese."

4. Legge, *The Four Books*, 50. The translation has been modified according to the original Chinese text.

5. Chen Yumen, "Jiefan qian Kaifeng," 163.

6. Ibid., 169. There were a few alternative definitions of the "lower nine." See Huang Junwu, "Bahe huiguan guanshi"; and Mao Zedong, *Report from Xunwu*, 104–5.

7. Both words have very old roots. *Qi* was seen in bronze vessel inscriptions and *gai* in the oracle bones dated to the Shang dynasty (ca. 1766–1123 B.C.). Also, both words contain a dichotomy: "to ask" and "to give." See Qu Yanbin, *Zhongguo qigai shi*, 6–7. A more formal but awkward term for "beggar" used in current Chinese official documents is "begging personnel" (*qitao renyuan*), which perhaps was created with an eye toward avoiding the rich connotations of the age-old word *qigai*.

8. Mallory, *China: Land of Famine*, 1.

9. Xie Zhaozhi, *Wu za zu*, 139; Xu Ke, *Qingbai leichao*, 40: 6. The coined word *jiaohuazi* (crying-converting-man) is an awkward combination of characters. The second character, *hua* (converting), was sometimes replaced by a homophone that means "flower" (*hua*), which made the term further diverge from its Buddhist origin. Mendicant monks, on the other hand, were called *huayuan heshang* ("wandering monks").

10. Qian Nairong, "Shili yangchang hua fangyan."

11. A common name (or sometimes a nickname) for the people of Subei (northern Jiangsu province), who were generally discriminated against, was Little Three (*xiao san zi*). See for example Honig, *Creating Chinese Ethnicity*, 52.

12. Qian Nairong, *Huyu pandian*, 192.

13. Wang Zhongxian, *Shanghai suyu tushuo*, 81–83.

14. Mao Tse-tung, *Selected Works of Mao Tse-tung*, vol. 3: 59.

15. Most of Mao's residences in Shanghai have survived to this day and some are carefully protected as relics, if not monuments, of the Communist revolution. See Yang Jiayou, *Shanghai fengwu*, 263–64. Also, in the summer of 1916, with the idea of learning how to overcome difficulties and getting to know grassroots society, Mao lived a beggar's life and tramped through five counties in his home province of Hunan without spending a penny. See Chapter 8 for details.

16. In Chinese, "Cushi wu da'nan, taofang zai buqiong." *Shehui ribao*, Aug. 8, 1936.

17. Interview with Liu Fumei and Zhang Deli, July 23, 1999, Nanjing.

18. Hsiao, *Rural China*, 457–59.

19. Kuhn, *Soulstealers*, 47. Wang Huizu (1731–1807), a magistrate of Ningyuan County, Hunan Province, recorded in his autobiographical chronicle how he had adopted drastic measures to drive out "beggar-bandits" from his jurisdiction. The bandits, numbering six or seven hundred and headed by a fifty-year-old vagrant from Guangxi nicknamed Flying Centipede and his wife, known as Flying Bitch, had regularly hounded the county's villagers for years before Wang came to office in 1787. Wang's success in cleaning up the beggar-bandits in the area earned him the reputation of being a capable and upright official. The Qing official history, *Qing shi gao*, also records this achievement in the section containing Wang's biography, which in a way suggests this problem was common. See Wang Huizu, *Wang Huizu xiansheng*, 150–53, 170–72.

20. Vermeer, *Chinese Local History*, 90–100. Ray Huang, a historian who served as a low-ranking officer in the Nationalist army for ten years, described being a pla-

toon leader in these words: "One half was similar to a beggar and the other half was like a bandit." Huang Renyu (Ray Huang), *Jindai Zhongguo*, 162.

21. Billingsley, *Bandits in Republican China*, 42.

22. Skinner, "Marketing and Social Structure in Rural China," pt. 1: 6–33.

23. That begging was mostly an urban phenomenon was noted both in contemporary records, such as missionary accounts and journalists' reports, and in more recent scholarly work. For example, Arthur Evans Moule (1836–1918), a British missionary who resided for more than three decades in Zhejiang and Shanghai in the late nineteenth century, observed that beggars only "occasionally haunt country towns and villages, but chiefly in the warm weather." In most seasons, whole tribes of beggars sojourned in the great cities. See Moule, *New China and Old*, 123–24. A number of scholarly works on Chinese cities have made brief reference to beggars. See David Buck on Ji'nan (*Urban Change in China*, 37), William Rowe on Hankou (*Hankow*, 236–37), and Emily Honig (*Creating Chinese Ethnicity*, 66–67) and Elizabeth Perry (*Shanghai on Strike*, 52) on Shanghai. Philip Kuhn's book on Chinese "soulstealers" in the mid-Qing discusses beggars mostly in relation to cities and towns, such as Suzhou (*Soulstealers*, 22–25).

24. These terms appeared in *Hanshu* (Book of Han), one of the twenty-four Chinese dynastic histories, which was compiled by the Han historian Ban Gu (A.D. 32–93). See *Er shi si shi*, 2: 294.

25. Youmin were a huge and diverse social group that was separated from the traditional "four peoples" (*si min*): scholars, farmers, artisans, and merchants. See Chen Baoliang, *Zhongguo liumang shi*, 21–22.

26. Faure, "The Rural Economy," 417.

27. Rowe, *Hankow*, 231.

28. Keyserling, *The Travel Diary*, vol. 1: 71.

29. Wang Gungwu, *The Chinese Overseas*, 43.

30. See Leong, *Migration and Ethnicity*, and Constable, *Guest People*.

31. Huntington, *The Characters of Races*, 167.

32. Adams, *Bureaucrats and Beggars*, 14.

33. Deng Yunte, *Zhongguo jiuhuang shi*, 51.

34. Hosie, "Droughts in China."

35. Zhonghua renmin gongheguo guojia tongjiju, *Zhongguo zaiqing baogao*, 20. The statistics are based on data contained in the official *Mingshi* (History of the Ming dynasty) and *Qing shi gao* (Draft history of the Qing dynasty). More statistics on famines and natural calamities in the Qing period can be found in Li Xiangjun, *Qingdai huangzheng yanjiu*, 113–236.

36. Ji Han, "Jiefang qian Tianjin."

37. Wang Ziguan, "Yi jiu si er nian da hanzai zhi Sishui," based on a 1943 government briefing on the drought. Famines and associated population loss such as this were not caused just by natural disasters but, as James Lee and Wang Feng have indicated, they were also "the products of political and organizational problems" (*One Quarter of Humanity*, 36).

38. Mallory, *China: Land of Famine*, 2.

39. Strand, *Rickshaw Beijing*, 29.

40. Huang, *The Peasant Economy*, 188–89.

41. Honig, *Creating Chinese Ethnicity*, 68.

42. Jiang Siyi and Wu Yuanshu, *Shanghai qibai ge qigai*, 63, and "Shanghai de qi-gai," 197; Macgowan, *Men and Manners of Modern China*, 291.

43. Gee, *A Class of Social Outcasts*, 3–4.

44. Typically, beggars and their families lived in squatters' areas located on the immediate outskirts of Chinese cities. In some ways these areas can be called the "home of the homeless." For an account of the living conditions in Shanghai's slums, see Lu, "Creating Urban Outcasts."

45. See Shen Ji, Dong Changqing, and Gan Zhenhu, *Zhongguo mimi shehui*, 186–87; Xu Yuanqing, "Diaocha Shanghai qigai zhi jieguo."

46. *North China Herald*, Oct. 4, 1856: 38.

47. Xu Ke, *Qingbai leichao*, 40: 21.

48. Billingsley, *Bandits in Republican China*, 46.

49. Yunyouke, *Jianghu congtan*.

50. Ho, "The Anti-Beggar Movement in Shanghai," 358.

51. These surveys were conducted in Shanghai in 1932–33 by Jiang Siyi and Wu Yuanshu, two female sociology students at Hujiang University, as part of their joint graduate thesis. In addition to library research (which frustrated them because of the paucity of written materials on this subject) and visiting charitable organizations and speaking with some sociologists, their research mostly involved visiting beggar' dens and interviewing beggars. They interviewed 700 beggars using a detailed, standardized questionnaire (see below). The result of this research was a two-part unpublished manuscript, *Shanghai qibai ge qigai de shehui diaocha* (A social investigation of 700 beggars in Shanghai), and a published journal article, "Shanghai de qigai" (The beggars of Shanghai). The manuscript is now in the Special Collections of the Shanghai Municipal Library. This is to my knowledge the most detailed and systematic social survey of beggars conducted in twentieth-century China. One may get a glimpse of the survey from the following questionnaire, which was used by the authors:

Questionnaire for Investigating Shanghai's Beggars

1. Name:
2. Age:
3. Gender: A. Male B. Female
4. Native Place: Province County
5. Family conditions:

This column lists 11 categories of family members in the following order: Father, Mother, Elder brothers, Younger brothers, Elder sisters, Younger sisters, Husband, Wife, Sons, Daughters, Others.

Seven questions were asked about each family member who was listed above:

1) Alive or deceased?
2) Age?
3) Your age at the time this person died?
4) Level of education?
5) Occupation?
6) Monthly income?
7) Did this member have a history of begging?

6. What is your ranking by seniority among your brothers and sisters? Are you married or single?

7. Education:
   A. No education
   B. Old-style private school (*sishu*)
   C. Elementary school
   D. Middle school
   E. Other

If you ever had schooling, indicate how many years you were in school and if you graduated.

8. What was your occupation prior to becoming a beggar?
   A. Monthly income: *yuan*   *jiao*   *copper*
   B. How did you lose that job [that is, the one prior to begging]?

9. Bad Habits
   A. Smoking: a. opium   b. cigarettes   c. other
   B. Alcohol: a. regular drinker   b. occasional drinker
   C. Gambling: a. *mahjongg*   b. *paijiu*   c. *huahui*
   D. Visiting prostitutes
   E. Other

10. Handicaps:
    A. Hands   B. Feet   C. Blind   D. Deaf   E. Dumb

11. Diseases

12. Reason for becoming a Beggar
    A. Unemployed
    B. Handicapped
    C. Bad habits
    D. Natural disaster
    E. Bankruptcy
    F. Influence of friends
    G. Influence of neighbors
    H. Other

13. Life as a Beggar
    A. How many years have you been in Shanghai?
    B. Why did you come to Shanghai?
    C. What was your occupation after you arrived in Shanghai?
    D. Where are you living now:
       a. rented house   b. temple   c. alley
       d. street   e. straw hut   f. other
    E. How many years have you been a beggar?
    F. Where is your begging spot(s)?
    G. What is your begging method(s)?
    H. Daily income: a. cash   b. clothing   c. food
    I. Have you received any relief: a. governmental   b. private
    J. Have you ever been arrested?
    K. Have you ever been expelled from your begging spot(s)?
    L. Do you want to be a beggar all your life?
    M. If you do not like begging, what kind of job would you like to do?

52. Jiang Siyi and Wu Yuanshu, *Shanghai qibai ge qigai*, 161.

53. Shanghai shehui kexueyuan, *Jiangnan zaochuanchang*, 237.

54. Jiang Siyi and Wu Yuanshu, "Shanghai de qigai," 193–94.

55. Xu Yuanqing, "Diaocha Shanghai qigai zhi jieguo."

56. Macgowan, *Men and Manners of Modern China*, 290–91.

57. Jiang Siyi and Wu Yuanshu, *Shanghai qibai ge qigai*, tables on p. 196 and p. 290, and Jiang Siyi and Wu Yuanshu, "Shanghai de qigai," 203–11. Of the 700 beggars, 233 did not report their daily income.

58. Jiang Siyi and Wu Yuanshu, *Shanghai qibai ge qigai*, 207.

59. Headland, *The Chinese Boy and Girl*, 106–7.

60. This truly happened in Guangzhou as a beggar head at the end of the Qing declined an offer from his brother-in-law to be a county superintendent in charge of food grain, saying he would rather "accompany the Buddha's Five Hundred Attendants [that is, beggars] than to bow down to five pecks of rice [that is, an official's salary]." See Shen Ji, Dong Changqing, and Gan Zhenhu, *Zhongguo mimi shehui*, 188. "To bow down to five pecks of rice" was a metaphor implying sacrificing one's freedom or dignity for the sake of making a living. It alludes to a classic story about Tao Yuanming (ca. 365–427), a scholar-official who resigned from office in the middle of his career in order to live a carefree and pastoral life in his home village in Xunyang (today known as Jiujiang, in Jiangxi Province). When he tendered his resignation, Tao, who was regarded as the greatest poet of his time, declared that he "would not bow down to five pecks of rice." That a beggar cited Tao's declaration is a small indication of the flow of culture between mendicants and the literati.

61. The most prominent contemporary author of knight-errant novels is Jin Yong (real name: Louis Cha Liang Yong, b. 1924), a Hong Kong–based journalist who from 1955 to 1972 published a dozen martial arts novels that remain immensely popular to this day. *Demi-Gods and Semi-Devils* (*Tian long ba bu*), which portrays heroes in beggar society, is regarded as one of his best works.

62. See Le Roy Ladurie, *The Beggar and the Professor*.

63. Pruitt, *A Daughter of Han*, 72–73.

64. Jiang Siyi and Wu Yuanshu, *Shanghai qibai ge qigai*, 225, 270.

65. Xu Chi et al., *Shanghai zhongsheng xiang*, 9. This interview was conducted in the early 1940s in an unusual manner. The interviewer, who was a journalist, disguised himself as a newly arrived poor peasant who desperately wanted to join a group of beggars at the Zhengjiamu Bridge, where many of the city's beggar dens were located. An experienced beggar instructed the interviewer as a complete novice without knowledge of his true identity.

66. Vale, "Beggar Life in Chentu."

67. Jiang Siyi and Wu Yuanshu, *Shanghai qibai ge qigai*, 223–25, and table 25.

68. Bredon, *Peking*, 446–47.

69. Ibid., 446.

70. Lu, *Hede zhuan*, 102–3.

71. *Biji xiaoshuo daguan*, vol. 14: 51.

72. Lin Shu, *Weilu xiaoping*, 8.

73. Elman, *A Cultural History*, 604–5, 608–25.

74. Chang, *The Chinese Gentry*, 4–5; Elman, *A Cultural History*, 140–42.

75. Sun Mo, "Nantong de 'chi ketuo fan.'"

CHAPTER 2

1. See Arthur Smith's very influential and much translated work, *Chinese Characteristics*, chap. 21. Many Chinese intellectuals highly recommended the book, regarding it as a mirror that accurately reflected the spiritual physiognomy of the Chinese people. Part of the book was translated into Chinese early in the twentieth century. Only a few days before his death in October 1936, Lu Xun, who first read the book in Japanese at the of age twenty-one and had had much sympathy for it all his life, urged that it be translated into Chinese. Enthusiasm for the book has recently revived. At least three full translations were published between 1995 and 2001 in mainland China (Lanzhou, 1995; Beijing, 1998; and Shanghai, 2001) and sold in the tens of thousands. For a scholarly discussion of Lu Xun, Arthur Smith, and China's "national character," see Liu, *Transnational Practice*, 51–60.

2. Legge, *The Four Books*, 861–62.

3. Soonthorndhammathada, *Compassion in Buddhism and Puranas*, iv.

4. The deeply rooted Chinese approach known as "no division between literature and history" (*wenshi bu fenjia*) has produced numerous works of literature that can be considered legitimate historical documents. In fact, many forms of traditional Chinese literature were first of all historical documents more than anything else. A mere listing of some of the names commonly used for the literature-history type of writings reveals the richness of this tradition: *biji* (notes), *xiaoshuo* (sundry narratives), *yeshi* ("uncultivated" histories), *baishi* ("barnyard grass" histories or unorthodox histories), *yanyi* (historical romances), *huaben* (story scripts), *zaju* (play scripts), *zhanggu* (anecdotes) and, more recently, *shihua* (historical narratives). Some unorthodox forms of poetry, such as *zayong* (sundry odes), *minyao* (folk rhymes), and *zhuzhici* (bamboo branch poems), are of unique value for the information they have preserved on local society and current affairs of a given time. These poems sometimes conjure up a vivid picture of a given locality—its scenery, customs, people's feelings, and the general mood of society—things that were rarely recorded in other sources. These types of literature, of course, are of uneven scholarly value; in using them for historical studies one must carefully scrutinize them and meticulously check them against other references. But the diversity of these writings is the most important remedy for the lack of information on the common people in official standard history (*zhengshi*).

5. Li Yu, *Li Liweng xiaoshuo shiwu zhong*, 34. For a comprehensive study of Li Yu and his work, see Chang and Chang, *Crisis and Transformation in Seventeenth-Century China*.

6. See *Er shi si shi*, 2 (*Hanshu*, *juan* 52): 610.

7. The "mean" category included various occupational groups in particular locations, such as "entertainer households" (*yuehu*) in Shanxi and Shaanxi, "indolent people" (*duomin*, who were mostly beggars and the like) in Shaoxing, Zhejiang and Suzhou, Jiangsu, "boat people" (*danmin*, fisherfolk, oyster gathers, water transportation workers) around the inner and coastal areas of Guangdong, Fujian, and Guangxi, and "small people" (*ximin*, who were hereditary servants) in the Huizhou and Nanjing areas. The designation of these groups as outcasts was mostly a result of political struggles during periods of dynastic transition. For instance, the "indolent

people" of Shaoxing had been loyal followers of General Chen Youliang (1320–63), the major rival of Zhu Yuanzhang (1328–98). After Zhu founded the Ming dynasty in 1368, Chen's fellows were banished as outcasts. During the Yongzheng period (1723–35), the "mean" categories were eliminated one after another and the mean peoples were emancipated. See Hansson, *Chinese Outcasts*, especially chap. 4; Jing Junjian, *Qingdai shehui de jianmin dengji*, 203–52; Zhang Kaiyuan (ed.), *Qing tongjian*, 2: Yongzheng period; Spence, *The Search for Modern China*, 94–95.

8. Even those in the "mean people" category in Shaoxing, Zhejiang Province known as "beggar households" (*gaihu*) were not necessarily beggars. See Cole, *Shaohsing*, 65.

9. Birch, *Stories from a Ming Collection*, 24. The translation has been modified according to the original Chinese text and the romanization of Chinese names has been changed to pinyin.

10. Li Yu, *Li Liweng xiaoshuo shiwu zhong*, 34–35.

11. *Shenbao*, Aug. 2, 1872.

12. See Stapleton, *Civilizing Chengdu*, especially chaps. 3–4.

13. Yang Du's dramatic and secret conversion to Communism—shortly before his death—through the guidance of Zhou Enlai (1898–1976) is an oft-told story in Chinese Communist history.

14. See Chapter 5 for details.

15. Xu Zhiyan, *Xinhua miji*, 392–94.

16. See Kuhn, *Soulstealers*, especially chaps. 1 and 6–8. A governor's complete list of soulstealing suspects arrested in Henan Province during the three-month sorcery scare shows that the alleged culprits were virtually all vagabonds and beggars. See *Soulstealers*, 231, 267–68n12.

17. Liu, "Woman's Fight Against Beggary," 100. The account was published in 1935; the author indicates that the phenomenon described started at least "15 years ago" and continued into the 1930s.

18. Zhongguo kexueyuan, *Wusi aiguo*, 507, 514–15. The beggar organizations in Shanghai will be discussed in Chapter 5.

19. Legge, *The Four Books*, 861–62.

20. *Gujin tushu jicheng, juan* 815: *qigaibu* (beggar section) *yiwen* (literature) 1.

21. Wen is a fairly common surname in China. For example, the maiden name of Mao Zedong's mother was Wen. See Snow, *Red Star Over China*, 130. The name is also included in *The Hundreds of Surnames* (*Baijiaxing*), the most popular booklet on the subject of surnames, which was widely used as an elementary textbook for literature in traditional Chinese schools. Having an alternative name (*hao*), which typically has an elegant meaning, was a common practice among educated Chinese prior to the middle of the twentieth century.

22. *Jinbao*, Nov. 21, 1922.

23. Yu Xiu, *Zhongguo qigai*, 201–2.

24. Cao Chen, *Yi huan bei chang ji*, 143.

25. Martin, *A Cycle of Cathay*, 77–78. For a biography of Martin, see Covell, *W. A. P. Martin*.

26. Ge Yuanxi, *Huyou zaji*, 141.

27. Xu Ke, *Qingbai leichao*, 40: 29.

28. *Shanghai zhoubao*, vol. 1, no. 9 (Jan. 26, 1933): 176.

29. Cui Xianchang, "Jiefang qian Sichuan qigai," 164.

30. Ibid.

31. Wang Zehua and Wang He, *Minguo shiqi*, 62, 94, 110.

32. Fritz, *China Journey*, 98.

33. Hu Xiang, "Wuhu jiu shehui de qigai bang."

34. Ibid.

35. Wang Xiyi and Lei Zihui, "Wenzhou de xiaceng shehui."

36. *Yuhai*, 2: 1465.

37. Hu Xiang, "Wuhu jiu shehui de qigai bang."

38. Eastman, *Seeds of Destruction*, 174.

39. Hu Xiang, "Wuhu jiu shehui de qigai bang."

40. Qi Ping, "You qigai yueli de hua."

41. Xu Ke, *Qingbai leichao*, 40: 29.

42. Li Cishan, "Shanghai laodong qingkuang"; Luo Zhiru, *Tongjibiao*, 74–76.

43. Weimin, "Suo heiqi."

44. Yuan Zheng, "Yi xi tan."

45. *Shehui ribao*, Aug. 8, 1936; Jiang Siyi and Wu Yuanshu, "Shanghai de qigai," 195–96; Yuan Zheng, "Yi xi tan"; Xu Yuanqing, "Diaocha Shanghai qigai zhi jieguo"; Chen Lengseng, "Shanghai qigai wenti de tantao."

46. *Shehui ribao*, Aug. 8, 1936.

47. Ribton-Turner, *A History of Vagrants and Vagrancy*, 660–61.

48. Jiang Siyi and Wu Yuanshu, *Shanghai qibai ge qigai*, 87; Chen Lengseng, "Shanghai qigai wenti de tantao."

49. Cao Chen, *Yi huan bei chang ji*, 43.

50. Lou Zikuang, *Shanghai xincun nianhua*, 180–81, and 119.

51. Yiren, "Qigai 'Huangdi.'"

52. Zhang Jiya, "Da jiangjun yan."

53. *Tongsu huabao* (Popular pictorial) (Chengdu), no. 6, 1909. See also Wang, *Street Culture in Chengdu*, 204.

CHAPTER 3

1. In Chinese, "huluo pingyang bei quan qi, long you qianshui zhao xia xi." The first half of the pair is the more popularly known and is in Smith, *Proverbs and Common Sayings from the Chinese*, 71. Dragons were believed to be the kings of the oceans.

2. See Li Qiao, *Zhongguo hangye shen*.

3. The story was recorded in *Kongzi jia yu* (The sayings of the Confucian school), a document compiled probably no earlier than the Western Han dynasty. See Zhang Tao, *Kongzi jia yu zhuye*. See also Legge, *Four Books*, 219–20.

4. For a Buddhist interpretation of the youth and mendicant experience of Sakyamuni (Siddhartha Gautama), see Sangharakshita, *Who Is the Buddha?* 32–34, 54–57.

5. Watson, *The Tso Chuan*, 40–49.

6. Cui Xianchang, "Jiefang qian Sichuan qigai."

7. Mao regarded Zhu as a leader of a peasant uprising, the highest possible praise in Maoism for great rebels of ancient China, and openly admired Zhu for his achievements. Mao disliked the way Zhu's biographer, Wu Han, wrote about his subject, which in part led to Wu becoming the very first victim of the Cultural Revolution. See Nie Yaodong, *Mao Zedong*, 199–200; Li Zhisui, *The Private Life of Chairman Mao*, 441–42.

8. Wu Han, *Zhu Yuanzhang zhuan*, 13–14, 285–299; Yang Jianyu, *Zhongguo lidai diwang lu*, 862–70.

9. In 1369, immediately after the new dynasty was founded, a grand tomb was built for Zhu's deceased parents, who had died in a pestilence and were hastily buried on land donated by a neighbor. Zhu initially intended to build a new tomb for his parents. However, according to fengshui, this donated land had led to such good fortune—it had contributed to making Zhu an emperor—that it was unwise to move the graves from it. Thus, the new tomb was built on the same site. In the same year, construction was started on a new imperial city (or palace), named Central Capital (Zhongdu). Construction continued for six years, but was left unfinished. By all accounts, magnificent structures were erected, but they were burned down in the riots that ended the dynasty in 1644 and all that remained were some vestiges visited by latter-day tourists.

10. Chen Guangzhong, *Liang Huai wenhua*, 350–51; Chen Guangzhong, *Huaihe zhuan*, 1.

11. Chen Guangzhong, *Huaihe zhuan*, 180–86; Pietz, *Engineering the State*, 10–12.

12. Yi Jihe, *Anhuisheng Fengtangxian zhilüe*, 28, 34.

13. Xu Ke, *Qingbai leichao*, 40: 8.

14. On the central capital in Fengyang, see *Er shi si shi*, 19: 266–67; Chen Guangzhong, *Huaihe zhuan*, 193–99. Remnants of the project, including a mile-long city wall and five stone foundations (each 3.7 square meters), can be found to this day.

15. Sima Qian, *Records of the Grand Historian: Han Dynasty I*, 163–64. The translation has been modified.

16. Ibid. The translation has been modified.

17. Lau, *Mencius*, 181.

18. See Sima Qian, *Records of the Historian*, 16–29, and *Records of the Grand Historian: Qin Dynasty*, 136–37.

19. Sima Qian, *Records of the Grand Historian: Qin Dynasty*, 136–37.

20. Sima Qian, *Records of the Historian*, 28–29.

21. In Chinese, "junzi baochuo, shinian buwan." See Zhong Minwen, *Suyan dachuan*, 403.

22. Ren Ping, *Qishi er hang*, 264–65. The historical facts were King Helü died in 496 B.C., and Wu Zixu did not get along with Helü's son, King Fucha, and committed suicide in 484 B.C. The state of Yue wiped out Wu in 473 B.C.

23. On the popular image of beggars as supernatural beings, see Schak, *A Chinese Beggars' Den*, 25–39, and Schak, "Images of Beggars in Chinese Culture."

24. Liu, "Woman's Fight Against Beggary," 99.

25. Giles, *A Gallery of Chinese Immortals*, 36.

26. Eberhard, *A Dictionary of Chinese Symbols*, 92.

27. For a recent study on the Eight Immortals, see Wang Hanmin, *Baxian yu Zhongguo wenhua*, a monograph based on the author's Ph.D. dissertation at Nanjing University (1999). See also Zhejiang wenyi chubanshe, *Baxian de gushi*, 24–27; Giles, *A Gallery of Chinese Immortals*, 122–27; and Werner, *Myths and Legends of China*, 288–304.

28. Based on Eberhard, *Folktales of China*, 134–35, 230–31, and Eberhard, *Chinese Fairy Tales and Folk Tales*, 139–40.

29. Eberhard, *Folktales of China*, 230–31.

30. The story of "the fisherman and the golden fish" was reworked by Alexander Pushkin (1799–1837) as a poem and now is regarded as a classic Russian folktale.

31. See Eberhard, *Chinese Fairy Tales and Folk Tales*, 141–43.

32. Schak, "Images of Beggars in Chinese Culture"; Eberhard, *A Dictionary of Chinese Symbols*, 165–66.

33. Yang Wenqi, *Zhongguo yinshi minsu xue*, 41–42.

34. Hu Juemin, "Lu Gaojian de yikuai bei."

35. Ibid.

36. A typical street scene in lower Yangzi cities in the late nineteenth century, such as depicted in the popular magazine *Dianshi Study Pictorial* (*Dianshizhai huabao*), included such a Lu Gaojian store.

37. *Shanghai zhinan*, 20.

38. Wang Zhongxian, *Shanghai suyu tushuo*, 5–6.

39. An overseas Shanghainese writing in 1994 in *Shijie ribao*, a New York–based Chinese newspaper, mentioned how she and her fellow Shanghainese missed Lu Gaojian and the stories related to it, and how she tried to make the Lu Gaojian type of dishes at her California home to entertain herself and her friends from Shanghai. See Qin Danhua, "Jiangzhurou he baiyejie."

40. Cui Xianchang, "Jiefang qian Sichuan qigai."

41. Variants on the dish were common. For a detailed recipe and cooking instructions, see Lo, *The Chinese Kitchen*, 166–75.

42. See Zhu Zhenfan, "Fo tiao qiang," for recipes of the dish and folktales surrounding it.

43. Zhang Zichen, *Zhongguo gudai chuanshuo*, 256.

44. Lu Yaodong, *Du da neng rong*, 66–67.

45. Recipe recorded at Wang Number Four's Restaurant, June 15, 1999.

46. Lu Yaodong, *Du da neng rong*, 66.

47. See Chapter 7 for details.

48. Anyang, an average rural town today, was the site of the capital of China's first historical dynasty, the Shang (ca. 1766–1123 B.C.). In the 1920s, a large quantity of examples of China's earliest writing, the so-called oracle bones, were found there.

49. Ren Ping, *Qishi er hang*, 180–85.

50. On the Yellow River Administration, see Pietz, *Engineering the State*, 24–26.

51. Dai Zhigong, Tang Zhenbei, and Shi Baozhen, "Tanglao Yizhengzhai yaodian jianshi."

52. Hsiao Ch'ien, *Traveller Without a Map*, 23.

53. On Xiao Qian's "anti-Christian" sentiment as reflected in his novels, see Lewis Robinson, *Double-edged Sword*.

54. Hu Pu'an, *Zhonghua quanguo fengsu zhi*, 2(3): 123–24.

55. Ibid., 2(5): 42–43.

56. Lu, *Beyond the Neon Lights*, 352.

57. These cases usually applied to boys, who were more valued in traditional Chinese society.

58. Cui Xianchang, "Jiefang qian Sichuan qigai," 208–9.

59. *Dianshizhai huabao*, vol. *Kui*: 77.

60. Cui Xianchang, "Jiefang qian Sichuan qigai," 208–9.

61. Chen Yundun, "Jiu Quanzhou de qigai."

62. Shen Congwen, "Teng Huisheng Tang jinxi." In his autobiography, Shen affectionately recalled how he used to consider his "godfather" a role model. See also Kinkley, *The Odyssey of Shen Congwen*, 23, 34–35.

63. Cui Xianchang, "Jiefang qian Sichuan qigai," 189–90.

64. Li Yuchuan, *Jianghu hangbang*, 237. The "bamboo stick" in this ditty refers to the symbol of beggar headmen or the heads of beggars' guilds. See Chapter 5 for details.

65. Cui Xianchang, "Jiefang qian Sichuan qigai," 161–62.

66. Feng Yinlou, "Gu Bian qigai shengya."

67. Ren Ping, *Qishi er hang*, 244–46.

68. *Er shi si shi*, 3: 696–97.

69. Especially in the type of beggars' singing known as "lotus ballad singing." See Chapter 7.

70. Feng Yinlou, "Gu Bian qigai shengya."

CHAPTER 4

1. Xu Dong and Ding Richang, *Baojiashu jiyao*, 32–33.

2. Ibid., 101–2.

3. Ibid., 105–6.

4. Kuhn, *Rebellion and Its Enemies*, 29.

5. Rowe, *Saving the World*, 388–89.

6. By the Republican period, some beggar headmen still bore the official title of *baozhang* (neighborhood chief in the baojia system).

7. In this regard, Philip Kuhn has noted the similarity of the bureaucratic attitude toward wandering beggars in the Qing to the attitude in present-day China. See Kuhn, *Soulstealers*, 44, 241n42.

8. *Gujin tushu jicheng, juan* 815: Beggar section (*qigaibu*). In her study on charities in late imperial China, Liang Qizi (A. K. C. Leung), consulted 2,615 local gazetteers to construct four lists of various types of official and privately sponsored charitable institutions, although most of them were not specifically established for beggars. See Liang, *Shishan yu jiaohua*, appendixes.

9. Huang Liu-hung, *A Complete Book*, 553–54.

10. Xiao Qian (ed.), *Shehui baixiang*, 62.

11. Elman, *A Cultural History*, 227–28, 233–34.

12. The annual budget for food before 1737 was 144.72 taels, and after 1737, 241.2 taels (an increase of 96.48 taels). The food budget for leap (intercalary) years

was 261.3 taels (an additional 20.1 taels). The annual budget for winter cotton clothing before 1741 was 13.4 taels; after 1741, 18.64 taels. See Ningjin xian zhi bianweihui, "Qiong jia hang," based on the 1900 Ningjin county gazetteer.

13. Some population figures of Ningjin from 1588 to 1949: 1588: 38,126; 1674: 34,032; 1898: 233,925; 1908: 290,674; 1931: 318,341; 1949: 301,645. See Shandongsheng, *Ningjin xian zhi*, 103.

14. Ma Wenhan, "Pingxuan liuyangju."

15. Pingquan xian zhi, *Pingquan xian zhi*, 150, 757.

16. Chen Que, *Chen Que ji*, 67–68; Will and Wong, *Nourish the People*, 241–42.

17. Guilinshi, *Guilin shi zhi*, vol. 1: 951.

18. Xiao Qian (ed.), *Shehui baixiang*, 61–62.

19. Guilinshi, *Guilin shi zhi*, vol. 1: 234–35.

20. Ibid., 952.

21. Huang Liu-hung, *A Complete Book*, 553–54.

22. Gray, *China*, 55–56.

23. Li Jiarui, *Beiping fengsu*, vol. 2: 416.

24. A seventeenth-century document outlined the operation of soup kitchens: "The magistrate should find out the budget provisions for rations of food, clothing and cotton wool and also the number of destitute persons on relief, to see how much can be granted to each recipient. On the first day of each month, the food rations should be distributed in the main hall of the yamen to the recipients themselves" (Huang Liu-hung, *A Complete Book*, 553). For a detailed discussion of government-sponsored "vagrant centers" in eighteenth-century China, see Will, *Bureaucracy and Famine*, 226–40.

25. Li Jiarui, *Beiping fengsu*, vol. 2: 404.

26. Gamble, *Peking: A Social Survey*, 277.

27. Strand, *Rickshaw Beijing*, 205.

28. Gamble, *Peking: A Social Survey*, 278.

29. Average monthly distribution of meals of hot porridge by twelve soup kitchens in Beijing, 1911–21:

Seven police-run soup kitchens: 350,000 to 400,000 meals
Three military guard–run soup kitchens: 120,000 to 150,000 meals
Two Ching Chao Ying [Jing zhao yin] (Beijing Municipal Government)–run soup
　　kitchens: 80,000 to 90,000 meals
Monthly total: 550,000–640,000 meals
Daily total: 18,333–21,333 meals
SOURCE: Gamble, *Peking: A Social Survey*, 278.

In the mid-1920s, the police estimated that soup kitchens were feeding 30,000 people each day. See Strand, *Rickshaw Beijing*, 205.

30. Hsiao Ch'ien, *Traveller Without a Map*, 10–11.

31. Wu, *Bitter Winds*, 1. For a glimpse of such a street scene, see pictures taken by the *Life* magazine photographer Jack Birns (b. 1919), in December 1947. Birns, *Assignment Shanghai*, 38–39.

32. Zhou Pei, "Hengyangshi de gaibang."

33. Chi Zihua, *Zhongguo jindai liumin*, 116; Qu Yanbin, *Zhongguo qigai shi*, 220.

The ditty was popular first among the beggars of Ji'nan, Shandong Province. See Cheng Gang, *Zhongguo qigai da jiemi*, 172.

34. Ningjin xian zhi bianweihui, "Qiong jia hang."

35. In the Republican period a few journalists, sociologists, and others tried to get into the beggars' world in a variety of locations, but often faced great difficulties. Some took great pains to disguise themselves as street beggars in order to approach a real beggar, and some tried to bribe beggars for information or find connections with the beggar head. For instance, the journalist Liu Yingyuan reported that in 1945 he spent a great deal of time trying to approach beggars in the streets of Baotou. As a customary courtesy (in particular, to strike up a conversation with strangers on a social occasion), he kept offering cigarettes to the beggars he met. "Although I let the beggars smoke packs of my cigarettes, as I asked for information about their guild they kept their months firmly shut," Liu wrote in a helpless tone. Only when he managed to make the acquaintance of the Baotou police chief the next spring was Liu able to get what he wanted. See Liu Yingyuan, "Baotou liumang diceng."

36. Birch, *Stories from a Ming Collection*, 23. The romanization of Chinese names has been altered to the pinyin.

37. Qu Yanbin, *Zhongguo qigai shi*, 78; Cen Dali, *Zhongguo qigai shi*, 100.

38. To nickname a person according to a physical defect, such as "Deaf Zhang," "Pockmarks Chen," or "Cripple Li," was sometimes regarded as evidence of a lack of compassion in Chinese culture (see for example, Arthur H. Smith, *Chinese Characteristics*, chap. 21). But this habit may not have been as offensive in China as it is in the West. This was particularly true among working-class people, who often apply such appellations to friends and acquaintances in an amiable, humorous, and good-natured way.

39. *Tianchang xian zhi, juan* 3: 30.

40. Xu Ke, *Qingbai leichao*, 40: 10.

41. Pineau, ed., *The Personal Journal*, 124–25.

42. Gray, *China*, 60–61.

43. Holcombe, *The Real Chinaman*, 324–27.

44. Li Jiarui, *Beiping fengsu leizheng*, 2: 405.

45. Holcombe, *The Real Chinaman*, 324–27.

46. Vale, "Beggar Life in Chentu."

47. Cui Xianchang, "Jiefang qian Sichuan qigai."

48. Stott, "Chinese Knights of the Open Palm," 830.

49. Ibid., 830–31.

50. Ibid., 831.

CHAPTER 5

1. Conger, *Letters from China*, 68–69.

2. China became a big cigarette market at the end of the nineteenth century. See Cochran, *Big Business in China*, 10–11, 27.

3. Xu Ke, *Qingbai leichao*, 40: 3.

4. See ibid., 40: 2; Yin Dengguo, *Tu shuo 360 hang*, vol. 1: 183–84; Chi Zihua, *Zhongguo jindai liumin*, 117.

5. Zhang Runqing, "Qingmo yilai."

6. *The Water Margin* had a tremendous impact on the mentality of Chinese vagrants and members of secret societies. The heroes of Mount Liang depicted in this novel were seen as exemplars of righteous rebels fighting social injustice. Many secret societies imitated the organization of Mount Liang and named themselves after it (or called themselves some sort of "mountain"). For a detailed discussion of the influence of Chinese popular literature on secret societies, see Wang Xuetai, *Youmin wenhua*, especially chap. 6, and Wang Xuetai, *Zhongguo liumin*, especially chap. 2.

7. Liu Yingyuan, "Baotou liumang diceng."

8. Ibid.

9. Jiang Siyi and Wu Yuanshu, *Shanghai qibai ge qigai*, 78–79.

10. Ibid., 37–38.

11. The house and the gaily-painted boat have been sacred sites in China since the Communist victory and are often portrayed with sun-like golden rays beaming from them, not unlike images used in religious traditions, such as portraits of the Trinity or the Virgin Mary.

12. Although the fact that the meeting was interrupted by a plainclothes policeman is well known, the man's identity remained unknown until 1990, when Xue Gengshen, a former police superintendent and Cheng's colleague in the department, released the information in an interview. See Ye Yonglie, *Hongse de qidian*, 270–73, 393. See also Xue Gengshen, "Wo jiechu guo de Shanghai banghui renwu," and Tian Hua, "Kaifu yihuo Shanghai."

13. Mao used the expression *kaitian pidi* to describe the significance of the founding of the CCP in his essay "The Bankruptcy of the Idealist Conception of History," written on September 16, 1949. The metaphor has since been frequently quoted.

14. Jiang Siyi and Wu Yuanshu, *Shanghai qibai ge qigai*, 61, 78.

15. *Shanghaitan heimu*, vol. 2: 201–2; Bao Ying, Zhang Shijie, and Hu Zhenya, *Qing Hong bang*, 242–44.

16. Jiang Siyi and Wu Yuanshu, *Shanghai qibai ge qigai*, 85.

17. Xu Chi et al., *Shanghai zhongsheng xiang*, 4.

18. Jiang Siyi and Wu Yuanshu, *Shanghai qibai ge qigai*, 82.

19. Ibid., 84; Shen Ji, Dong Changqing, and Gan Zhenhu, *Zhongguo mimi shehui*, 166.

20. Jiang Siyi and Wu Yuanshu, *Shanghai qibai ge qigai*, 50.

21. Hauser, *Shanghai*, 241. In later years, some old Shanghailanders verified the accuracy of Hauser's report. In an interview with three old Shanghai residents conducted by this author on August 20, 1996, one recounted an experience of recovering a camera lost in a public rickshaw through the help of a local beggar.

22. Jiang Siyi and Wu Yuanshu, *Shanghai qibai ge qigai*, 207.

23. Holcombe, *The Real Chinaman*, 324–27.

24. Cui Xianchang, "Jiefang qian Sichuan qigai," 163.

25. Ibid., 165.

26. Zheng Yuanchuan, "Laohekou de qigai."

27. Jiang Siyi and Wu Yuanshu, *Shanghai qibai ge qigai*, 83–84.

28. Williams, *The Middle Kingdom*, vol. 1: 742.

29. Macgowan, *Men and Manners of Modern China*, 293.

30. Giles, *Historical China and Other Sketches*, 187.

31. Gray, *China*, 60.

32. Li Song'an, "Jiefang qian Guangzhou," 231; Wang Chufu, "Guangzhou qigai jituan."

33. Doolittle, *Social Life of the Chinese*, 261. Emphasis in the original.

34. Moule, *New China and Old*, 124.

35. Gee, *A Class of Social Outcasts*, 21, 24.

36. Foster, *In the Valley of the Yangtze*, 13.

37. *Shanghaitan heimu*, vol. 2: 201–2.

38. Ibid., 202–4.

39. Gamble, *Peking: A Social Survey*, 274.

40. Jiang Siyi and Wu Yuanshu, *Shanghai qibai ge qigai*, 81–83.

41. Doolittle, *Social Life of the Chinese*, 261.

42. In one case, a group of five or six vagrants led by a headman by the name of Liu began to beg in a town that was protected by a local beggars' guild. A warning from the guild headman Zhang to the intruders seemed ineffective. Early the next morning, however, residents of the town woke up to the news that during the night the invading beggars had all been buried alive by the guild. More than a score of the guild members participated in this gruesome action. The incident was reported in a teahouse by headman Zhang as sensational news. The local constable knew of the incident, but took no action. See *Shanghaitan heimu*, vol. 2: 207–8.

43. Ch'ü, *Local Government*, 194–95.

44. *Shanghaitan heimu*, vol. 2: 205.

45. *Dianshizhai huabao*, vol. Yi: 30.

46. Ch'ü, *Local Government*, 25–27.

CHAPTER 6

1. Doolittle, *Social Life of the Chinese*, 259–60.

2. Hu Pu'an, *Zhonghua quanguo fengsu*, 2(1): 23.

3. Qu Yanbin, *Zhongguo qigai shi*, 207; Yin Dengguo, *Tu shuo 360 hang*, vol 1: 187.

4. Huang Qiang, "Huashen wei 'qigai' de laifangshen"; Jiang Siyi and Wu Yuanshu, "Shanghai de qigai," 200; Hu Pu'an, *Zhonghua quanguo fengsu*, 2(6): 23, 2(1): 25.

5. Huang Qiang, "Huashen wei 'qigai' de laifangshen."

6. Virtually every province in the empire had similar customs. See Lou Zikuang, *Xinnian fengsu zhi*, and Hu Pu'an, *Zhonghua quanguo fengsu*.

7. Lou Zikuang, *Xinnian fengsu zhi*, 49.

8. Chen Yundun, "Jiu Quanzhou de qigai."

9. Chen Yumen, "Kaifeng chunjie guoshen," 170–71.

10. Guan Shijie, "Jiu shehui Fuyu de huazifang."

11. Song Rulin, *Songjiang fu zhi*, 5: 10.

12. Eberhard, *A Dictionary of Chinese Symbols*, 325–26.

13. Jiang Siyi and Wu Yuanshu, "Shanghai de qigai," 200–201.

14. Yin Dengguo, *Tu shuo 360 hang*, vol. 1: 187–88. *Sheng, dou, hu,* and *dan* were units of dry measure for grain used mainly before the 1950s. The actual values varied by time and location. Conventional values were: 1 sheng = 1 liter, 1 dou = 1 decaliter, 1 hu = 10 (or 5) decaliters, 1 dan = 1 hectoliter.

15. Lou Zikuang, *Xinnian fengsu zhi*, 49–52.

16. Qu Yanbin, *Zhongguo qigai shi*, 208. Anthropological studies of contemporary Taiwan have noted very similar phenomena. Arthur Wolf's pioneering research on Taiwan folk religions found that beggars and bandits were sometimes treated like ghosts, and that the social identities of the three often overlapped. See Wolf, "Gods, Ghosts and Ancestors," 170–72. Donald DeGlopper reported that in Lukang, an old seaport on the west coast of Taiwan, the first day of the eighth lunar month was reserved for the beggars' festival, and in the seventh lunar month, when traditional offerings were made to ghosts, "it was their [the beggars'] habit to take the food set out for the hungry ghosts, who in some ways could be considered the supernatural analogues for the beggars." See DeGlopper, *Lukang*, 152.

17. Macgowan, *Men and Manners of Modern China*, 295.

18. Chen Yundun, "Jiu Quanzhou de qigai."

19. Yi Liyuan, "Qingmo keju tongzishi de xingxing sese."

20. Hu Xiang, "Wuhu jiu shehui de qigai bang."

21. Ibid.

22. Xiao Qian (ed.), *Shehui baixiang*, 115–17.

23. Ou Yangping, "Jiu Chongqing de gaibang."

24. Ibid.

25. For a typical scenario of harassment of this sort, see Macgowan, *Men and Manners of Modern China*, 295–97.

26. Hengshe lüTai tongren, *Du Yuesheng xiansheng jinian ji*, 37.

27. *Pudong difang zhilüe*, 25.

28. Jiang Siyi and Wu Yuanshu, *Shanghai qibai ge qigai*, 84.

29. Yin Dengguo, *Tushuo 360 hang*, vol. 1: 170. Here the measure "inch" refers to the *cun*, which is about one third of a decimeter. Bound feet were regarded as beautiful and associated with social status in late imperial China. Typical bound feet were described as a pair of "three-inch golden lilies," a standard size for women's feet before the bound-foot custom was gradually eliminated early in the twentieth century. Hence "eight-inch long" feet were considered ugly and disgraceful. For a history of foot binding, see Levy, *Chinese Footbinding*.

30. Kuhn, *Soulstealers*, 117.

31. Shen Ji, Dong Changqing, and Gan Zhenhu, *Zhongguo mimi shehui*, 176–80; Weimin, "Suo heiqi"; Yin Dengguo, *Tushuo 360 hang*, vol. 1: 190–92.

32. Zhang Guanding, "Jiefang qian Beijing," 224–25.

33. Smith, *Village Life in China*, 193.

34. Li Song'an, "Jiefang qian Guangzhou."

35. Chen Lengseng, "Shanghai qigai wenti de tantao."

36. By the late 1940s, modern funeral homes had gradually become the mainstream, especially for the treatment of corpses. See, Tu Shipin, *Shanghai chunqiu*, pt. 3: 95.

37. Stott, "Chinese Knights of the Open Palm."

38. In smaller cities, the practice seemed never to have been challenged. In Nantong, for instance, wealthy families prior to the Communist revolution typically hired sixteen men to carry the bride's sedan chair, virtually all of whom were hired from the ranks of beggars. Not only were the beggars well paid for that service, but also according to custom they were to be treated as honored guests at the wedding.

For instance, the banquet tables set for them contained eight more dishes—four main courses and four side dishes—than the tables for average guests. See Jin Feng, "Nantong jiu hunsu sheling."

39. Chen Lengseng, "Shanghai qigai wenti de tantao," 14. This was, of course, a figure of speech to emphasize the begging opportunities in the city. With thousands of corpses found on Shanghai's streets some years in the Republican period, such a metaphor can easily run the risk of being criticized as an exaggeration from an unsympathetic elite. On the other hand, one should also note that the corpses found on the streets of Shanghai were mostly victims of rural famine (many were abandoned infants of the refugees) rather than the city's regular beggars. The increasing number of street corpses in Shanghai in 1930, for instance, was a direct result of the North China famine of 1928–30. See Wakeman, *Policing Shanghai*, 84. More than 34,000 of the 36,000 corpses picked up in Shanghai that year were infants, many of whom had been killed by their desperate parents. See Isaacs, *Five Years of Kuomintang Reaction*, 63.

40. On various begging techniques, see also Chapter 7.

41. Zou Yiren, *Jiu Shanghai renkou*, 21–22, 97; Hu Huanyong (ed.), *Zhongguo renkou*, 172–74.

42. Yuan Zheng, "Yi xi tan," 70.

43. Qi Ping, "You qigai yueli de hua."

44. Hauser, *Shanghai*, 240.

45. *Da wanbao*, Feb. 20, 1931.

46. Xu Yuanqing, "Diaocha Shanghai qigai zhi jieguo," 22; Shen Ji, Dong Changqing, and Gan Zhenhu, *Zhongguo mimi shehui*, 174–75.

47. Tu Shipin, *Shanghai chunqiu*, pt. 3: 84.

48. For an English translation of the Ah Q story, see Lu Xun, *Diary of a Madman and Other Stories*, 101–72.

49. Tao Juyin, *Tianliang qian de gudao*, 166.

50. Yuan, *Sidelights of Shanghai*, 76–77.

51. Based on Zou Yiren, *Jiu Shanghai renkou*, tables 56 and 57.

52. Tao Juyin, *Tianliang qian de gudao*, 166; Shen Nianxian, "Jiu Shanghai tan."

53. Cui Xianchang, "Jiefang qian Sichuan qigai."

54. Lu Xun, *Dairy of a Madman*, 42–48.

55. The Slim Western Lake (Shou xihu) is a scenic resort comparable to China's more famous West Lake in Hangzhou, hence the name.

56. Ye Lingfeng, *Nen bu yi Jiangnan*, 17.

57. For more examples of remunerative tactics, see Schak, *A Chinese Beggars' Den*, 49–55.

58. Yang Jiayou and He Mingyun, *Ta qiao gujin tan*, 106–14.

59. *Shehui ribao*, May 5, 1936.

60. Shen Ji, Dong Changqing, and Gan Zhenhu, *Zhongguo mimi shehui*, 140, 175; Tu Shipin, *Shanghai chunqiu*, pt. 3: 84.

61. Most Chinese knew the stories of these historical figures through the *Romance of the Three Kingdoms*, a fourteenth-century historical novel that was among the four most popular classics in Chinese popular culture. For a recent English version of the novel, see Lo Kuan-Chung (Lou Guangzhong), *Romance of the Three Kingdoms*.

62. *Shanghaitan heimu*, vol. 2: 113–14.

63. Baum, *Shanghai '37*, 389–90.

64. Shanghai Jianshe bianji bu, *Shanghai jianshe*, 112.

65. On the sanitary system of Shanghai's average homes, see Lu, *Beyond the Neon Lights*, 189–98.

66. Xu Chi et al., *Shanghai zhongsheng xiang*, 7–8; Shen Ji, Dong Changqing, and Gan Zhenhu, *Zhongguo mimi shehui*, 168.

67. See for example *Renhaichao* (The tide of the human ocean), a popular novel published in 1926 that describes a great variety of social classes and life in Shanghai. One of its stories is of a hooligan who engaged in blackmail in a public toilet by "squatting over a ditch." See Wei Shaochang and Wu Chenghui, *Yuanyang hudie pai yanjiu ziliao*, vol. 2: 793.

68. Xu Chi et al., *Shanghai zhongsheng xiang*, 7–8.

69. For a detailed account on the "tiger stoves," see Lu, "Away from Nanking Road."

70. *Shanghaitan heimu*, vol. 3: 113.

71. Ibid., 118–21.

CHAPTER 7

1. Zhao placed the number of professional beggars in Shanghai at 8,000 men, 8,000 women, and 600 children. See Jiang Siyi and Wu Yuanshu, *Shanghai qibai ge gigai*, 50.

2. Ibid., 203.

3. The survey randomly selected 111 beggars (63 male and 48 female). See Xu Yuanqing, "Diaocha Shanghai qigai zhi jieguo."

4. Based on the Qing court version of the painting dated 1736. At least eight beggars are depicted in four different spots in this 1,153 centimeter (38 feet) long handscroll now preserved in the National Palace Museum, Taipei. The original painting was the work of the twelfth-century artist Zhang Zeduan and depicts a street scene from the Song capital, Kaifeng. The Qing court version is generally regarded as a work reflecting the street life in seventeenth-century Beijing. See Na Zhiliang, *Qingming shanghe tu*, 1–2.

5. Lu Xun, *Diary of a Madman*, 222.

6. Zhou Chen's famous "Beggars and Street Characters," which portrays life in Suzhou, was painted in 1516. For a reproduction of the painting, see Cahill, *Parting at the Shore*, 191, and plates 88–99 and color plate 12. Another Ming-dynasty scroll, "The Floating People" (by Yanshan Shiting, a pseudonym; dated 1588, with a postscript poem dated 1641), provides an extraordinary view of dozens of street people in an unknown location. The painting is in the Shaanxi Provincial Museum in Xi'an.

7. Alexander and Mason, *Views of 18th Century China*, 94.

8. On the ceremony of "releasing sentient beings" in Beijing during the Ming-Qing period, see Naquin, *Peking*, 196, 220, 422.

9. See Smith, "Liberating Animals," 77.

10. Li Jiarui, *Beiping fengsu leizheng*, 409.

11. Naquin, *Peking*, 19–20, and appendix 1. A "temple" in Naquin's data is defined as "a building dedicated to housing a representation of a supernatural spirit (a 'god') before which offering and prayer were made." Most such buildings were Buddhist or Taoist temples.

12. For a list of major temple fairs in old Beijing, including their religious affiliations, locations, dates, and major events, see Chang Renchun, *Lao Beijing*, 6–11.

13. There was a hierarchy of dragons based on the number of their claws: dragons with five claws on each foot were the symbol of the throne; four-clawed dragons signified the status of a prince; court officials were allowed only three claws for the dragons embroidered on their robes and other possessions. See Cotterell and Storm, *The Ultimate Encyclopedia of Mythology*, 468–69.

14. Zhang Danian and Gong Jiang, "Wuxi de qigai yu jiaohua jiatou."

15. Stott, "Chinese Knights of the Open Palm."

16. Cui Xianchang, "Jiefang qian Sichuan qigai."

17. Cen Dali, *Zhongguo qigai shi*, 146–47.

18. Xu Ke, *Qingbai leichao*, 40: 16.

19. On Chinese food cures, see Lu, *Chinese Natural Cures*, 290–97.

20. Li Shizhen, *Bencao gangmu*, vol. 2: 1583–94.

21. *Dianshizhai huabao*, vol. Le: 57.

22. See Obringer, "A Song Innovation."

23. This is good logic since the earthbound reptile is commonly associated with other yin categories: earth, dampness, darkness, coolness, and so on.

24. Traditional Chinese medicine recognizes four types of imbalance based on yin-yang theory. These may be characterized as follows: Yang impaired by a preponderance of yin; yin consumed by a preponderance of yang; an overabundance of yang caused by deficiency of yin; and an overabundance of yin resulting from a deficiency of yang. See Liu, *The Essential Book of Traditional Chinese Medicine*, 42.

25. Unschuld, *Medicine in China*, 73.

26. Ji Desheng, *Zuchuan sheyao jinxi tan.*

27. Interviews with local residents and pharmacists in Nantong, June 1999.

28. Jiang Siyi and Wu Yuanshu, "Shanghai de qigai," 186.

29. *Dianshizhai huabao*, vol. Ji: 40.

30. Xu Ke, *Qingbai leichao*, 40: 8–9.

31. Ou Yangping, "Jiu Chongqing de gaibang."

32. See Shanghaishi lishi bowuguan, *The Origin of Modern China*, 39–43.

33. Jiang Siyi and Wu Yuanshu, "Shanghai de qigai."

34. Candlin, *The Breach in the Wall*, 54.

35. Macgowan, *Men and Manners of Modern China*, 292–93.

36. Holcombe, *The Real Chinaman*, 328–29.

37. Wang Chufu, "Guangzhou qigai jituan."

38. Cui Xianchang, "Jiefang qian Sichuan qigai."

39. Rattenbury, *China*, 116.

40. Jiang Siyi and Wu Yuanshu, *Shanghai qibai ge qigai*, 206–8.

41. Johnson, *Folksongs and Children-Songs from Peiping*, 47–48. The translation has been modified based on the original Chinese text.

42. Tang Youshi, "Qigai," 405.

43. Lotus ballad singing probably originated in the Buddhist "Songs for awakening this mortal world" (*xingshi ge*) of the tenth century.

44. Jiang Siyi and Wu Yuanshu, *Shanghai qibai ge qigai*, 70.

45. Tao Juyin, *Tianliang qian de gudao*, 166.

46. Wakeman, *Policing Shanghai*, 113. For information on lower-class prostitutes in Shanghai, see Hershatter, *Dangerous Pleasures*, 49−50, and Henriot, *Prostitution and Sexuality in Shanghai*, 85−88.

47. Chen Yundun, "Jiu Quanzhou de qigai."

48. Liner services like this were called *ye hangchuan* (evening liners) and had been popular in the area since as early as the sixteenth century. At least three anthologies written in the Qing period were titled *Ye hangchuan*. The *Ye hangchuan* of the famous scholar Zhang Dai (1597−1679) is a virtual encyclopedia, with more than four thousand entries. Zhang, who was born in Shaoxing and lived most of his life in Hangzhou (both in Zhejiang Province), claims the book was written for the purpose of preserving the wisdom that had been generated in the packing mini-society of the evening liners. See Zhang Dai, *Ye hangchuan*, 1−2.

49. Xu Ke, *Qingbai leichao*, 40: 100.

50. In 1914, monthly pay in an average Shanghai silk shop was:

Apprentice: $0.2
Entry-level shop clerk after three years' apprenticeship: $1
Average clerk: $4−6
Senior manager: $8
SOURCE: Chen Chengren, *Yinyuan shidai*, 6−7.

51. An example of the great esteem for motherhood in Chinese culture is the *Twenty-four Stories of Filial Piety*, China's best-known and most-read enchiridion and textbook on filial piety (*xiao*), compiled by Guo Jujing of the Yuan dynasty (1279−1368). Most of the twenty-four moral examples of filial piety, cited from three thousand years of history and legends, were of devotion to mothers (seven to both parents, four to fathers, and thirteen to mothers).

52. Sun Jikang, "Jiushi Yunnan de qigai." This was particularly common in the city of Kunming.

53. Fan Zongxiang, "Minguo shiqi Lanzhou de qigai."

54. For an ethnographic account of funeral rituals in South China, see Watson, "Funeral Specialists in Cantonese Society."

55. For a detailed account of Chinese funeral rituals early in the twentieth century, chiefly in Beijing but also in other parts of China, see Cormack, *Chinese Birthday*, 91−117.

56. Chen Da, *Woguo kangRi zhanzheng*, 286.

57. There are a few classics in Chinese literature on this subject. The most prominent is *Dream of the Red Chamber* (*Honglou meng*) for premodern times, and for the early twentieth century, *Family* (*Jia*) by Ba Jin (Pa Chin). For an academic work, see Wakefield, *Fenjia*.

58. Li Song'an, "Jiefang qian Guangzhou."

59. For an introduction to these instruments, see Gunde, *Culture and Customs of China*, 92−96.

60. Liu Ji, "Zhang Hanhui he ta de 'Songhua jiang shang.'" For a field report on funeral customs of Ding County in the early twentieth century, see Gamble, *Ting Hsien*, 386–93.

61. Meng Xin and Feng Xuemin, *Tong yi shou ge*, vol. 1: 13. For the music of this song, see Appendix.

62. Zhao Yi, *Gaiyu congkao*, 555.

CHAPTER 8

1. Kuhn, "Chinese Views of Social Classification," 235.

2. *Yuhai*, 1: 1034. *Fanshen* literally means "to turn the body" or "to turn over." The word was one of the most powerful and commonly used expressions during the Communist revolution, particularly in the late 1940s and early 1950s, to indicate that the exploited and repressed proletarians and poor peasants had "turned over" and stood up against the exploiting classes. See William Hinton's classic *Fanshen*, xii. But the word itself has a long history in the Chinese vocabulary and is not, as Hinton suggested, a creation of the revolution.

3. Stock, *Musical Creativity*, 35–55; Sun Yunnian, *Jiangnan ganjiu lu*, 188–90.

4. Zheng Huanwu, "Cong Qier dao baiwan fuweng."

5. It was common in rural China for villages to be named after the surname of a major lineage of the village.

6. Based on Zhang Ming, *Wu Xun yanjiu ziliao daquan*, pt. 1; Li Shizhao and Sun Zhijun, *Wu Xun huazhuan*; Zhang Mosheng, *Yixing zhuan*, 143–51.

7. Yuan Xi, *Wu Xun zhuan pipan jishi*, 26–27.

8. Here the centennial birthday was reckoned by the so-called nominal age (*xusui*), the common way of reckoning age in China, that is, considering a person one year old at birth and adding a year each lunar New Year.

9. Zhang Ming, *Wu Xun yanjiu ziliao daquan*, 87–88.

10. Yuan Xi, *Wu Xun zhuan pipan jishi*, 34.

11. In 1935, Zhao Dan costarred with Mao's wife, Jiang Qing, then a twenty-one-year-old actress, in *A Doll's House* (*Et Dukkehjem*), an 1879 drama by the Norwegian playwright Henrik Johan Ibsen (1828–1906). The partnership, however, only brought Zhao misfortune during the Cultural Revolution, when Jiang Qing persecuted anyone who knew the details of her acting career in old Shanghai.

12. Yuan Xi, *Wu Xun zhuan pipan jishi*, 88–89.

13. Although they are unable to fully document it, most of Jiang Qing's biographers believe the Communist leaders in Yan'an had passed a resolution prior to Mao's marriage to Jiang, defining her role as "taking care of the day-to-day life and health of Comrade Mao Zedong" and banning her from assuming any position in the party or any involvement in politics for the next twenty years (see Ye Yonglie, *Jiang Qing Zhuang*, 161–63). Jiang's participation in the Wu Xun investigation was the first time this rule had been violated.

14. Mao Zedong, *Jianguo yilai Mao Zedong wengao*, vol. 2: 403.

15. *Renmin ribao*, July 23–28, 1951.

16. Yuan Xi, *Wu Xun zhuan pipan jishi*, 128.

17. There were of course a number of "literary inquisitions" (*wenziyu*) in Chi-

nese history in which authors were imprisoned or executed for their writings that the imperial court considered offensive. But Mao's campaign, by using modern media and party organs, effectively outdid traditional literary inquisitions.

18. Yuan Xi, *Wu Xun zhuan pipan jishi*, 176.

19. The criticizing *Wu Xun zhuan* campaign was the first of numerous political campaigns in the PRC that targeted the "ideological correctness" of a film or a play. Fifteen years later, the Cultural Revolution was ignited by a national campaign to criticize the drama *Hai Rui Dismissed from Office*, which was portrayed as having the "evil intent" of criticizing Mao's dismissal of Peng Dehuai, the minister of defense, in 1959.

20. *Renmin ribao*, May 26, 1967.

21. Yuan Xi, *Wu Xun zhuan pipan jishi*, 270.

22. A prominent example of numerous leaders purged under this pretext was Liu Shaoqi (1898–1969), the chairman of the People's Republic and Mao's chief rival within the Communist Party. Liu was called by Mao a "revisionist" and, so condemned, he was persecuted to death during the Cultural Revolution.

23. Siao-Yu, *Mao Tse-Tung and I Were Beggars*, 76.

24. Ibid., 76–155.

25. Edgar Snow, *Red Star Over China*, 146. Snow dismissed Siao-Yu's book as an "amusing apocrypha." Siao's book was translated into Chinese in 1989 (Beijing: Kunlun) under the title *Wo he Mao Zedong de yiduan quzhe jingli* (Mao Zedong and I and our tortuous experience) and sold about 100,000 copies.

26. Xiao Xinli (comp.), *Wo de xuanze*, 470–71.

27. Domes, *Peng Te-huai*, 11.

28. Xiao Xinli (comp.), *Wo de xuanze*, 473. For information regarding Peng's family background and early life, see *Hunan wenshi ziliao* (Cultural and historical materials of Hunan Province), vol. 31 (1988), especially pp. 1–11, 15–47, and 194–98.

29. For the major documents criticizing Wu Xun from a Maoist point of view, see Zhang Ming, *Wu Xun yanjiu ziliao daquan*, 611–768.

30. *Renmin ribao*, Sept. 6, 1985.

31. Lai Shuming, *Qigai xianzhang*, 5.

32. Lai Dongjin, *Qigai jianzai*.

33. Ibid., 37.

34. Lai Dongjin, *Qigai jianzai* (mainland edition), 3. A cartoon book for children has also been published.

35. Ibid., 193–95.

36. Ibid., 64–65.

37. To borrow the title of the volume edited by Howard Goldblatt, *Chairman Mao Would Not Be Amused*.

CONCLUSION

1. Although the Communist takeover was a major turning point in Chinese history, recent scholarship in the West is seeking to cross the 1949 dividing line, or as Paul Cohen has put it, "to break through the '1949' barrier" (Cohen, "The Post-Mao Reforms"). See, for example, Philip Huang's work on the rural Yangzi delta

(*The Peasant Family and Rural Development*), Gail Hershatter's study of prostitution in Shanghai (*Dangerous Pleasures*), and Jeffrey Wasserstrom's research on student movements (*Student Protests in Twentieth-Century China*). Research on Qing and Republican history has also found the roots of some Communist programs in unexpected places. Kathryn Bernhardt, for example, suggests that the concept and practice of the Communist Land Reform can be traced back to the seventeenth century (*Rent, Taxes, and Peasant Resistance*). James Gao's recent book, *The Communist Take Over of Hangzhou*, also seeks to reexamine the 1949 divide. It seems there is a general consensus in the field that, as Joseph Esherick has put it, "1949 was a watershed, not an unbridgeable chasm" (Esherick, "Ten Theses on the Chinese Revolution"), although the details of continuity pre- and post-1949 China in many areas still need to be fleshed out. For a recent essay on this issue, see Paul Cohen, "Reflections on a Watershed Date."

2. Liu Hantai, *Zhongguo de qigai qunluo*, 231.

3. Jiefang ribao she, *Shanghai jiefang yinian*, 12–13.

4. Schurmann, *Ideology and Organization in Communist China*, 376–77; Whyte and Parish, *Urban Life in Contemporary China*, 243–44.

5. There are different estimates of the number of deaths caused by the famine; the figure quoted here is from Becker, *Hungry Ghosts*.

6. Snow, *Red China Today*, 503.

7. Topping, *Journey Between Two Chinas*, 220.

8. Foster, *In Pursuit of Justice*, 141.

9. Sixteen senior residents of Suzhou, Nantong, Guangzhou, Xi'an, and Wuhan interviewed by the author in June and July 2000 gave consistent responses that beggars were "rare," "very rare," or "only occasionally seen" in those cities during Mao's time.

10. See for example the "eyewitness accounts" given by Wei Jingsheng, the well-known political dissident, and Zhai Yugui, a mainland refugee in Hong Kong. Both are cited in Fernandez-Stembridge and Madsen, "Beggars in the Socialist Market Economy."

11. Liu Hantai, *Zhongguo de qigai qunluo*, 211. Historian Xin Ping (b. 1954) recalled that in the late 1970s, when he was the head of a brigade (a village under the people's communes) in Laian County, Anhui Province, in the off season between winter and spring some farmers in his brigade ran out of food and went out begging. On behalf of the brigade, he wrote letters of reference for them every year, in the following format:

> To whom it may concern:
> This is to verify that _____ [name] is a poor or lower-middle peasant in our brigade. Due to life's hardships, he (or she) is going out to look for work. We hope everyone along the way will provide some assistance. For that purpose this certificate has been issued. /Signed and sealed./

Xin said that in retrospect he felt it was "absurd" to issue such letters, but at the time this was a way to ease the burden on the brigade, which had little means to help the needy, and also to protect the village's beggars from being considered vagrants and thus subject to arrest. See Xin Ping, *Cong Shanghai faxian*, 575.

12. See Dorothy Solinger's *Contesting Citizenship in Urban China*, the most comprehensive treatment to date of the current Chinese floating population.

13. *Shijie ribao*, Mar. 3, 1992; Oct. 7, 1993; Mar. 22, 1993; Jan. 26, 1994. For two substantial reports on beggars in present-day China, see Liu Hantai, *Zhongguo de qigai qunluo*, a 257-page record of actual events dedicated to the United Nations' homeless year, and Yu Xiu, *Zhongguo qigai diaocha*, a journalistic account of the lives of dozens of beggars in various cities based on the author's fieldwork conducted in the late 1990s.

14. For statistics on the floating population in 1993–95, see Solinger, *Contesting Citizenship*, 19–21.

15. Ibid., 3–7.

16. Ten thousand yuan amounted to a fortune in the early 1980s, when the average urban household income was about a hundred yuan per month. Since then the yuan has been significantly devalued due both to inflation and to the increase in living standards, but the expression "ten thousand yuan household" (*wanyuanhu*) remains a figure of speech, roughly equivalent to "upstart" in the English language.

17. From Yu Xiu, *Zhongguo qigai diaocha*, 184.

18. Ibid., 87.

19. Ibid., 196.

20. Liu Hantai, *Zhonghuo de qigai qunluo*, 21, 230; Qu Yanbin, *Zhongguo qigai shi*, 108.

21. *Shijie zhoukan (Supplement to World Journal)*, no. 1048 (Aril 18–24, 2004): 52.

22. *Yangzi wanbao*, Nov. 24, 2001.

23. *Chengdu wanbao*, Nov. 4, 2003. The commonality of cellular phone carriers among vagrants may be in part because of the existence of beggars' organizations. Few devices could be a more effective organizational tool for street people than the cellular phone.

24. *Shijie ribao*, July 3, 2003: p. A7.

25. *Shijie ribao*, Mar. 3, 1992.

26. A beggar in Beijing, who was originally a school teacher in his home village in Shaanxi Province, told a reporter that after a trip back to his village to bury his wife and marry out his only daughter, "I came back to Beijing to resume the old business [of begging]. I felt so comfortable and relaxed. After having been a beggar for a while, one will feel a sort of loss if one does not do it." In another case a peasant brought his wife from their tea farm in Jiangxi to beg in Guangzhou. Later, as he had saved enough money, he wanted his wife to quit begging. "To my surprise she didn't listen and several times she even blamed me for not bringing her to the city to beg earlier," the man exclaimed. "The trade of begging is indeed addictive." See Yu Xiu, *Zhongguo qigai daocha*, 40, 183.

27. *Xingxi shibao*, Jan. 12, 2004.

28. The two articles are "Analysis of the Classes in Chinese Society" and "The Chinese Revolution and the Chinese Communist Party," in Mao Tse-tung, *Selected Works of Mao Tse-tung*, vol. 1: 13–19, and 2: 305–31.

29. Prior to the 1980s there were five major class categories commonly used to classify urban residents based on their occupations and economic status before 1949: workers (*gongren*, mainly laborers and industrial workers), staff members (*zhiyuan*, including office workers, school teachers, shop clerks, etc.), urban poor (*chengshi pin-*

min, including peddlers, street entertainers, apprentices, unemployed, vagrants, etc.), small-business owners (*xiaoyezhu*), and capitalists (*zibenjia*). People born after 1949 were assigned their families' class categorization, which was based on the father's occupation and economic status before 1949.

30. *MeiZhong baodao*, Aug. 8, 2003.

31. www.sina.com.cn, Oct. 9, 2004.

32. The category of "three-without" refers to people in the city without a legal identification document, without a normal residence, or without a proper means of livelihood.

33. Although a total of twelve people were found guilty of beating Sun to death and received the death penalty or terms of imprisonment ranging from three years to life, the details of the case seem never to have been made entirely clear. On the trial and verdict, see *China Daily*, June 10, 2003.

34. www.sina.com.cn, Oct. 9, 2004.

35. For example, Changsha, Hunan Province, and Nanjing and Suzhou, Jiangsu Province, issued their own municipal rules about begging and relief in the name of implementing the central government rules, but they in fact tend to be much stricter than the latter. See *Changsha wanbao*, Jan. 7, 2004; *Jiangnan shibao*, Oct. 24, 2003; and *Xin jingbao*, Dec. 20, 2003.

36. Hence the title of Charles Murray's book, *Losing Ground: American Social Policy, 1950–1980*.

37. Fernandez-Stembridge and Madsen, "Beggars in the Socialist Market Economy," 228.

38. More than 1,200 charitable organizations are active in China today. On March 19, 2004, the State Council promulgated regulations—which became effective on June 1, 2004—on the administration of charitable foundations, a move that signifies that philanthropy is once again fully legitimate in Chinese society.

39. *Zhongguo qingnian bao*, Oct. 20, 2003.

40. Lu Xun, *Diary of a Madman*, 100.

41. A sixty-one-year-old beggar, Yao Fuhua, from Rongchang, Sichuan Province, exemplifies the notion of fraternity among beggars. Yao refused to accept more than one jiao (ten cents) when he begged on the street, telling well-wishers any extra should go to other needy people. He gave change to anyone who offered more than one jiao. If he had no change, he would simply decline the donation. *South China Morning Post*, Mar. 2, 2004.

Bibliography

Adams, Thomas McStay. *Bureaucrats and Beggars: French Social Policy in the Age of the Enlightenment.* New York: Oxford University Press, 1990.

Alexander, William, and George Henry Mason. *Views of 18th Century China.* Originally published in 1804 and 1805. New York: Portland House, 1988.

Bao Ying, Zhang Shijie, and Hu Zhenya. *Qing Hong bang mi shi* (Secret history of the Green and Red gangs). Hong Kong: Zhongyuan chubanshe, 1993.

Baum, Vicki. *Shanghai '37.* Hong Kong: Oxford University Press, 1986.

Becker, Jasper. *Hungry Ghost: Mao's Secret Famine.* New York: Henry Holt, 1998.

Beier, A. L. *Masterless Men: The Vagrancy Problem in England, 1560–1640.* London: Methuen, 1985.

Beijing minjian fengsu baitu (One hundred drawings of folk customs in Beijing). Pictures drawn by folk artists during the Qing period preserved in the Beijing Library. Beijing: Shumu wenxian chubanshe, 1983.

Bernhardt, Kathryn. *Rents, Taxes, and Peasant Resistance: The Lower Yangzi Region, 1840–1950.* Stanford, CA: Stanford University Press, 1992.

Biji xiaoshuo daguan (A collection of notes and anecdotes), preface dated 1811. Yangzhou: Jiangsu guanglin, 1984 (reprint).

Billingsley, Phil. *Bandits in Republican China.* Stanford, CA: Stanford University Press, 1988.

Birch, Cyril. *Stories from a Ming Collection: Translations of Chinese Short Stories Published in the Seventeenth Century.* Bloomington: Indiana University Press, 1958.

Birns, Jack. *Assignment Shanghai: Photographs on the Eve of Revolution.* Ed. by Carolyn Wakeman and Ken Light. Berkeley: University of California Press, 2003.

Bredon, Juliet. *Peking: A Historical and Intimate Description of Its Chief Places of Interest.* Shanghai: Kelly & Walsh, 1922.

Buck, David D. *Urban Change in China: Politics and Development in Tsinan, Shantung, 1890–1949.* Madison: University of Wisconsin Press, 1978.

Bun, Kwan Man. "Beggar Gangs in Modern Tianjin: A Discourse on Mendicancy and Strategies of Survival." Paper presented at the annual meeting of the Association for Asian Studies, Apr. 6, 2002, Washington, D.C.

Cahill, James. *Parting at the Shore: Chinese Painting of the Early and Middle Ming Dynasty, 1368–1580.* New York: Weatherhill, 1978.

Candlin, Enid Saunders. *The Breach in the Wall: A Memoir of the Old China.* New York: Macmillan, 1973.

Cao Baoming. *Qigai* (Beggars). Changchun: Jilin University Press, 1999.

Cao Chen. *Yi huan bei chang ji* (A record of the sufferings from a barbarian invasion). Shanghai: Shanghai guji chubanshe, 1989 [1876].

Cen Dali. *Zhongguo qigai shi* (A history of Chinese beggars). Taipei: Wenjin chubanshe, 1992.

Chang, Chung-li. *The Chinese Gentry*. Seattle: University of Washington Press, 1955.

Chang, Chun-shu, and Shelley Hsueh-lun Chang. *Crisis and Transformation in Seventeenth-Century China: Society, Culture, and Modernity in Li Yu's World*. Ann Arbor: University of Michigan Press, 1992.

Chang Renchun. *Lao Beijing de fengsu* (Customs of old Beijing). Beijing: Beijing yanshan chubanshe, 1990.

Changsha wanbao (Changsha evening news), Changsha.

Chen Baoliang. *Zhongguo liumang shi* (A history of Chinese rogues). Beijing: Zhongguo shehui kexue chubanshe, 1993.

Chen Chengren. *Yinyuan shidai shenghuo shi* (A history of life in the era of silver dollars). Shanghai: Shanghai renmin chubanshe, 2000.

Chen Da. *Woguo kangRi zhanzheng shiqi shizhen gongren shenghuo* (The life of urban workers in China during the War of Resistance Against Japan). Beijing: Zhongguo laodong chubanshe, 1993.

Chen Guangzhong. *Huaihe zhuan* (Biography of the Huai River). N.p.: Hebei University Press, 2001.

———. *Liang Huai wenhua* (The culture of the Huai River valley). Shenyang: Liaoning jiaoyu chubanshe, 1995.

Chen Lengseng. "Shanghai de youmin wenti" (The vagabond problem of Shanghai). *Shehui banyuekan* (Social semimonthly), vol. 1, no. 4 (1934): 9–16.

———. "Shanghai qigai wenti de tantao" (Inquiring into the problem of beggars in Shanghai). *Shehui banyuekan*, vol. 1, no. 6 (1934): 13–21.

Chen Que. *Chen Que ji* (Works of Chen Que, 1604–77). Beijing: Zhonghua shuju, 1979.

Chen Yumen. "Jiefang qian Kaifeng Xiangguoshi de xingxing sheshe" (All aspects of Xiangguo Temple in Kaifeng before 1949). *Henan wenshi ziliao* (Cultural and historical materials of Henan), vol. 2 (1985 [1979]): 161–82.

———. "Kaifeng chunjie gouchen" (Reminiscences of Chinese New Year in Kaifeng). *Kaifeng wenshi zhiliao* (Cultural and historical materials of Kaifeng), vol. 5 (1981): 166–94.

Chen Yundun. "Jiu Quanzhou de qigai" (Beggars in old Quanzhou). *Jindai Zhongguo jianghu miwen* (Inside stories of the unorthodox world in modern China), vol. 2: 323–30. Shijiazhuang: Hebei renmin chubanshe, 1997.

Cheng Gang. *Zhongguo qigai da jiemi* (Discovering the secret of Chinese beggars). Changchun: Jilin shiying chubanshe, 1999.

Chengdu wanbao (Chengdu evening news), Chengdu.

Chi Zihua. *Zhongguo jindai liumin* (Vagabonds in modern China). Hangzhou: Zhejiang renmin chubanshe, 1996.

China Daily, Beijing.

Ch'ü, T'ung-tsu. *Local Government in China Under the Ch'ing*. Cambridge, MA: Harvard University Press, 1962.

Cihai (Sea of words). Single-volume edition. Shanghai: Shanghai cishu chubanshe, 1979.

Cochran, Sherman. *Big Business in China: Sino-Foreign Rivalry in the Cigarette Industry, 1890–1930.* Cambridge, MA: Harvard University Press, 1980.

Cohen, Paul. "The Post-Mao Reforms in Historical Perspective." *Journal of Asian Studies*, vol. 47, no. 3 (Aug. 1988): 519–41.

———. "Reflections on a Watershed Date: The 1949 Divide in Chinese History." In Jeffrey N. Wasserstrom, ed., *Twentieth-Century China: New Approaches*, 27–36. London: Routledge, 2003.

Cole, James H. *Shaohsing: Competition and Cooperation in Nineteenth-Century China.* Tucson: University of Arizona Press, 1986.

Conger, Sarah Pike. *Letters from China: With Particular Reference to the Empress Dowager and the Women of China.* Chicago: A. C. McClurg, 1909.

Constable, Nicole, ed. *Guest People: Hakka Identity in China and Abroad.* Seattle: University of Washington Press, 1996.

Cormack, J. G. *Chinese Birthday, Wedding, Funeral, and Other Customs.* Peking: La Librairie française, 1923.

Cotterell, Arthur, and Rachel Storm. *The Ultimate Encyclopedia of Mythology.* New York: Hermes House, 1999.

Covell, Ralph R. *W. A. P. Martin: Pioneer of Progress in China.* Washington, D.C.: Christian University Press, 1978.

Cui Xianchang. "Jiefang qian Sichuan qigai de xingxing sese" (All aspects of the beggars in Sichuan before Liberation). *Chongqing wenshi ziliao* (Cultural and historical materials of Chongqing), vol. 26 (June 1986): 160–227.

Da wanbao (Great evening news), Shanghai.

Dai Zhigong, Tang Zhenbei, and Shi Baozhen. "Tanglao Yizhengzhai yaodian jianshi" (A concise history of the Yizhengzhai Plaster Pharmacy). *Jiangsu wenshi ziliao xuanji* (Selected cultural and historical materials of Jiangsu), vol. 10 (1982): 246–50.

DeGlopper, Donald R. *Lukang: Commerce and Community in a Chinese City.* Albany: State University of New York Press, 1995.

Deng Yunte. *Zhongguo jiuhuang shi* (A history of famine relief in China). Shanghai: Commercial Press, 1937.

Dianshizhai huabao (The Dianshi Study pictorial). 44 volumes, marked in the order of Chinese characters. Shanghai, 1884–98.

Domes, Jürgen. *Peng Te-huai: The Man and the Image.* Stanford, CA: Stanford University Press, 1985.

Doolittle, Justus. *Social Life of the Chinese: With Some Account of Their Religious, Governmental, Educational, and Business Customs and Opinions.* New York: Harper & Brothers, 1865.

Eastman, Lloyd. *Seeds of Destruction: Nationalist China in War and Revolution, 1937–1949.* Stanford, CA: Stanford University Press, 1984.

Eberhard, Wolfram. *A Dictionary of Chinese Symbols: Hidden Symbols in Chinese Life and Thought.* London: Routledge, 1986.

———, trans. and comp. *Chinese Fairy Tales and Folk Tales.* New York: E. P. Dutton, 1938.

————, trans. and comp. *Folktales of China*. Chicago: University of Chicago Press, 1965.

Elman, Benjamin A. *A Cultural History of Civil Examinations in Late Imperial China*. Berkeley: University of California Press, 2000.

Er shi si shi (History of twenty-four dynasties). 20 volumes. Zhonghua shuju reprint version, 1997.

Esherick, Joseph W., ed. *Remaking the Chinese City: Modernity and National Identity, 1900–1950*. Honolulu: University of Hawaii Press, 2000.

————. "Ten Theses on the Chinese Revolution." *Modern China*, vol. 21, no. 1 (Jan. 1995): 44–76.

Fan Zongxiang. "Minguo shiqi Lanzhou de qigai" (Beggars in Lanzhou during the Republican period). *Zhonghua wenshi ziliao wenku* (A compilation of cultural and historical materials of China), vol. 20: 135–38. Beijing: Zhongguo wenshi chubanshe, 1996.

Faure, David. "The Rural Economy of Kiangsu Province, 1870–1911." *Journal of the Institute of Chinese Studies, Hong Kong*, vol. 9, no. 2 (1978): 365–471.

Feng Yinlou. "Gu Bian qigai shengya" (Beggars' lives in Kaifeng). *Kaifeng wenshi ziliao* (Cultural and historical materials of Kaifeng), no. 4 (1984): 152–66.

Fernandez-Stembridge, Leila, and Richard Madsen. "Beggars in the Socialist Market Economy." In Perry Link, Richard Madsen, and Paul Pickowicz, eds., *Popular China: Unofficial Culture in a Globalizing Society*, 207–30. Lanham, MD: Rowman & Littlefield, 2002.

Foster, Arnold. *In the Valley of the Yangtze*. London: London Missionary Society, 1899.

Foster, Portia Billings. *In Pursuit of Justice: Around the World and in the Human Heart*. Eugene, OR: Far Horizons Publishing, 2000.

Fritz, Chester. *China Journey: A Diary of Six Months in Western Inland China, 1917*. Seattle: University of Washington Press, 1982.

Gamble, Sidney D. *Peking: A Social Survey*. New York: George H. Doran, 1921.

————. *Ting Hsien: A North China Rural Community*. Stanford, CA: Stanford University Press, 1968 [1954].

Gao, James Zheng. *The Communist Takeover of Hangzhou: The Transformation of City and Cadre, 1949–1954*. Honolulu: University of Hawaii Press, 2004.

Ge Yuanxi. *Huyou zaji* (Miscellaneous records of a sojourn in Shanghai). Shanghai: Shanghai guji chubanshe, 1989 [1876].

Gee, Nathaniel Gist. *A Class of Social Outcasts: Notes on the Beggars in China*. Peking Leader Reprints, no. 1. Peking: Peking Leader Press, 1925.

Giles, Herbert A. *Historical China and Other Sketches*. London: Thos. De La Rue, 1882.

Giles, Lionel, trans. *A Gallery of Chinese Immortals*. London: John Murray, 1948.

Goldblatt, Howard, ed. *Chairman Mao Would Not Be Amused: Fiction from Today's China*. New York: Grove Press, 1996.

Gray, John Henry. *China: A History of the Laws, Manners, and Customs of the People*. 2 volumes. London: Macmillan, 1878.

Guan Shijie. "Jiu shehui Fuyu de huazifang" (The beggar house in Fuyu county before 1949). *Jindai Zhongguo jianghu miwen* (Inside stories of the unorthodox world in modern China), vol. 2: 291–305. Shijiazhuang: Hebei renmin chuban-she, 1997.

Guanzi. *Guanzi: Political, Economic, and Philosophical Essays from Early China, A Study and Translation by W. Allyn Rickett.* 2 volumes. Princeton, NJ: Princeton University Press, 1985.

Guilinshi difangzhi bianzuan weiyuanhui [Editorial committee for the Guilin city gazetteer], comp. *Guilin shi zhi* (Guilin city gazetteer). 3 volumes. Beijing: Zhonghua shuju, 1997.

Gujin tushu jicheng (A collection of past and present documents). Taipei: Wenxing shudian, 1964 [1728].

Gunde, Richard. *Culture and Customs of China.* Westport, CT: Greenwood Publishing Group, 2002.

Hansson, Anders. *Chinese Outcasts: Discrimination and Emancipation in Late Imperial China.* Leiden: E. J. Brill, 1996.

Hauser, Ernest O. *Shanghai: City for Sale.* New York: Harcourt, Brace, 1940.

Headland, Isaac Taylor. *The Chinese Boy and Girl.* New York: Fleming H. Revell, 1901.

Hengshe lüTai tongren [Colleagues of the Heng Association sojourned in Taiwan]. *Du Yuesheng xiansheng jinian ji* (A symposium in memory of Mr. Du Yuesheng). Taipei: Wenhai chubanshe, 1976.

Henriot, Christian. *Prostitution and Sexuality in Shanghai: A Social History, 1849–1949.* Trans. by Nöel Castelino. Cambridge, UK: Cambridge University Press, 1997.

Hershatter, Gail. *Dangerous Pleasures: Prostitution and Modernity in Twentieth-Century Shanghai.* Berkeley: University of California Press, 1997.

Himmelfarb, Gertrude. *The Idea of Poverty: England in the Early Industrial Age.* New York: Alfred A. Knopf, 1983.

Hinton, William. *Fanshen: A Documentary of Revolution in a Chinese Village.* New York: Vintage, 1968.

Ho Chieh-Shiang. "The Anti-Beggar Movement in Shanghai." *China Weekly Review,* vol. 32, no. 13 (May 30, 1925): 358–60.

Holcombe, Chester. *The Real Chinaman.* New York: Dodd, Mead, 1895.

Honig, Emily. *Creating Chinese Ethnicity: Subei People in Shanghai, 1850–1980.* New Haven, CT: Yale University Press, 1992.

Hosie, Alexander. "Droughts in China, A.D. 620 to 1643." *Journal of North China Branch of the Royal Asiatic Society,* vol. 12 (1878): 51–89.

Hsiao Ch'ien. *Traveller Without a Map.* Trans. by Jeffrey C. Kinkley. London: Hutchinson, 1990.

Hsiao Kung-ch'uan. *Rural China: Imperial Control in the Nineteenth Century.* Seattle: University of Washington Press, 1960.

Hu Huanyong, ed. *Zhongguo renkou, Shanghai fence* (China's population, Shanghai volume). Beijing: Zhongguo caizheng jingji chubanshe, 1987.

Hu Juemin. "Lu Gaojian de yikuai bei" (A stone tablet of Lu Gaojian). *Suzhou wenshi ziliao* (Cultural and historical materials of Suzhou), vols. 1–5 (reprinted, 1990): 425–27.

Hu Pu'an. *Zhonghua quanguo fengsu zhi* (Records of Chinese customs). 2 sections. Shanghai: Shanghai shudian, 1986 [1923].

Hu Xiang. "Wuhu jiu shehui de qigai bang" (Beggars' gangs in Wuhu before 1949). *Wuhu wenshi zhiliao* (Cultural and historical material of Wuhu), no. 2 (n.d.): 278–87.

Huang Junwu. "Bahe huiguan guanshi" (A history of the Bahe Guild). *Guangzhou wenshi ziliao* (Cultural and historical materials of Guangzhou), no. 35 (Aug. 1986): 219–26.

Huang Liu-hung. *A Complete Book Concerning Happiness and Benevolence: A Manual for Local Magistrates in Seventeenth-Century China*. Trans. and ed. by Djang Chu. Tucson: University of Arizona Press, 1984.

Huang, Philip C. C. *The Peasant Economy and Social Change in North China*. Stanford, CA: Stanford University Press, 1985.

———. *The Peasant Family and Rural Development in the Yangzi Delta, 1350–1988*. Stanford, CA: Stanford University Press, 1990.

Huang Qiang. "Huashen wei 'qigai' de laifangshen" (The deities who visit in "beggar" incarnation). *Zhongguo minjian wenhua (di 9 ji)—minjian lisu wenhua yanjiu* (Chinese popular culture [volume 9]: Research on folk rituals), 245–56. Shanghai: Xuelin chubanshe, 1993.

Huang Renyu (Ray Huang). *Jindai Zhongguo de chulu* (The way out for modern China). Taipei: Lianjing chuban shiye gongsi, 1995.

Huntington, Ellsworth. *The Character of Races: Influenced by Physical Environment, Natural Selection and Historical Development*. New York: Ayer, 1977 [1924].

Isaacs, Harold R. *Five Years of Kuomintang Reaction*. Reprinted from the special May 1932 edition of *China Forum*. Shanghai: China Forum Publishing Company, 1932.

Ji Desheng. "Zuchuan sheyao jinxi tan" (A talk on the snake medicines passed down by the ancestors), recorded by Zu Dingyuan, *Jiangsu wenshi ziliao xuanji* (Selected cultural and historical materials of Jiangsu), no. 9 (1982): 154–63.

Ji Han. "Jiefang qian Tianjin shuihuan jilu" (A record of flooding in Tianjin before 1949). *Tianjin wenshi congkan* (Tianjin culture and history series), vol. 6 (n.d.): 210–12.

Jiang Siyi, and Wu Yuanshu. "Shanghai de qigai" (The beggars of Shanghai). *Tianlai* (Sounds of heaven), vol. 22, no. 2 (June 1933): 191–213.

———. *Shanghai qibai ge qigai de shehui diaocha* (A social investigation of 700 beggars in Shanghai). 2 parts. Manuscript. Shanghai: Hujiang University, 1933. Shanghai Municipal Library Special Collections.

Jiangnan shibao (Jiangnan times), Nanjing.

Jiefang ribao she. *Shanghai jiefang yinian* (The first anniversary of the liberation of Shanghai). Shanghai: Jiefang ribao she, 1950.

Jin Feng. "Nantong jiu hunsu shiling" (Miscellaneous notes on old wedding customs in Nantong). *Nantong jin'gu* (Nantong past and present), no. 2 (1991): 25–27.

Jinbao (Crystal), Shanghai.

Jing Junjian. *Qingdai shehui de jianmin dengji* (The mean people category in Qing society). Hangzhou: Zhejiang renmin chubanshe, 1993.

Johnson, Kinchen. *Folksongs and Children-Songs from Peiping*. Taipei: The Oriental Cultural Service, 1971 [prefaced 1932].

Kemp, E. G. *The Face of China*. New York: Duffield, 1909.

Keyserling, Hermann Graf von. *The Travel Diary of A Philosopher.* Trans. by J. Holroyd Reece. 2 volumes. New York: Harcourt, Brace, 1928.

Kinkley, Jeffrey C. *The Odyssey of Shen Congwen.* Stanford, CA: Stanford University Press, 1987.

Kuhn, Philip A. "Chinese Views of Social Classification." In Penelope J. Corfield, ed., *Language, History, and Class,* 227–39. Oxford: Blackwell, 1991.

———. *Rebellion and Its Enemies in Late Imperial China: Militarization and Social Structure, 1796–1864.* Cambridge, MA: Harvard University Press, 1970.

———. *Soulstealers: The Chinese Sorcery Scare of 1768.* Cambridge, MA: Harvard University Press, 1990.

Lai Dongjin. *Qigai jianzai* (Beggar boy). Taipei: Ping'an wenhua, 2000.

———. *Qigai jianzai* (Beggar boy). Mainland version. Beijing: Zhongguo qingnian chubanshe, 2002.

Lai Shuming. *Qigai xianzhang: 921 shizijia xia de Peng Baixian* (The beggar county magistrate: Peng Baixian under the "921 Cross"). Taipei: Peizheng wenhua, 2001.

Lao Tsu. *Tao Te Ching.* Trans. by Stephen Addiss and Stanley Lombardo. Indianapolis: Hackett, 1993.

Lau, D. C., trans. *Mencius.* New York: Penguin, 1970.

Le Roy Ladurie, Emmanuel. *The Beggar and the Professor: A Sixteenth-Century Family Saga.* Trans. by Arthur Goldhammer. Chicago: University of Chicago Press, 1998.

Lee, James Z., and Wang Feng. *One Quarter of Humanity: Malthusian Mythology and Chinese Realities, 1700–2000.* Cambridge, MA: Harvard University Press, 1999.

Legge, James, trans. *The Four Books: Confucian Analects, the Great Learning, the Doctrine of the Mean, and the Works of Mencius.* Shanghai: Commercial Press, 1900.

Leong, Sow-Theng. *Migration and Ethnicity in Chinese History: Hakkas, Pengmin, and Their Neighbors.* Stanford, CA: Stanford University Press, 1997.

Levy, Howard S. *Chinese Footbinding: The History of a Curious Erotic Custom.* Taipei: SMC Publishing, 1980 [1966].

Lewis, Oscar. *La Vida: A Puerto Rican Family in the Culture of Poverty—San Juan and New York.* New York: Vintage, 1965.

———. *A Study of Slum Culture: Background for La Vida.* New York: Random House, 1968.

Li Cishan. "Shanghai laodong qingkuang" (The condition of labor in Shanghai). *Xin qingnian* (New youth), vol. 7, no. 6 (May 1920): 1–83.

Li Jiarui, comp. *Beiping fengsu leizheng* (An assorted collection of Beijing folk customs). 2 volumes. Changsha: Commercial Press, 1937.

Li Qiao. *Zhongguo hangye shen* (Chinese trade deities). 2 volumes. Taipei: Yunlong chubanshe, 1996.

Li Shizhao, and Sun Zhijun. *Wu Xun huazhuan* (An illustrated biography of Wu Xun). Shanghai: Sanlian shudian, 1996 [1950].

Li Shizhen. *Bencao gangmu* (Compendium of *Materia Medica*). Originally published in 1596. 2 volumes. Beijing: Renmin weisheng chubanshe, 1957 (photo-offset copy of the 1885 version).

Li Song'an. "Jiefang qian Guangzhou jizhong guangguai luli de hangdang" (Some bizarre and motley callings in Guangzhou before 1949). *Guangdong wenshi ziliao* (Cultural and historical materials of Guangdong), no. 33 (1981): 230–59.

Li Xiangjun. *Qingdai huangzheng yanjiu* (A study of famine relief administration during the Qing period). Beijing: Nongye chubanshe, 1995.

Li Yu. *Li Liweng xiaoshuo shiwu zhong* (Fifteen stories written by Li Liweng). Hangzhou: Zhejiang renmin chubanshe, 1983.

Li Yuchuan. *Jianghu hangbang quhua* (Intriguing stories about various callings in the unorthodox world). Beijing: Beijing chubanshe, 1995.

Li Zhisui. *The Private Life of Chairman Mao*. New York: Random House, 1994.

Liang Qizi (A. K. C. Leung). "'Pingqiong' yu 'qiongren' guannian zai Zhongguo sushi shehui zhong de lishi yanbian" (The historical changes of the concepts of "poverty" and "the poor" in common Chinese society). In Huang Yinggui (Ying-Kuei Huang), ed., *Renguan, yiyi yu shehui* (English title: *The Concept of the Person, Meaning, and Society*), 129–62. Taipei: Academia Sinica, 1993.

————. *Shishan yu jiaohua: Ming Qing de cishan zuzhi* (Offering and converting: Charity organizations in the Ming-Qing period). Taipei: Liangjing, 1997.

Lin Shu. *Weilu xiaoping* (Essays from the Weilu study). Beijing: Beijing chubanshe, 1998.

Lipkin, Zwia. "Modern Dilemmas: Dealing with Nanjing Beggars, 1927–1937." Paper presented at the annual meeting of the Association for Asian Studies, Apr. 6, 2002, Washington, D.C.

Liu, Frances W. "Woman's [sic] Fight Against Beggary." *China Quarterly* (Shanghai), vol. 1, no. 4 (1935): 99–104.

Liu Hantai. *Zhongguo de qigai qunluo* (The beggars' community in China). N.p.: Jiangsu wenyi, 1987.

Liu Ji. "Zhang Hanhui he ta de 'Songhua jiang shang'" (Zhang Hanhui and his "On the Songhua River"). *Renwu* (Personage), no. 6 (Mar. 1981): 109–15.

Liu, Lydia H. *Translingual Practice: Literature, National Culture, and Translated Modernity—China, 1900–1937*. Stanford, CA: Stanford University Press, 1995.

Liu Yanchi. *The Essential Book of Traditional Chinese Medicine, Volume I: Theory*. Trans. by Fang Tingyu and Chen Laidi. New York: Columbia University Press, 1988.

Liu Yingyuan. "Baotou liumang diceng shehui de 'Liangshan'" ("Mount Liang" in Baotou's underworld of rogues). *Wenshi ziliao xuanji* (Selected cultural and historical materials), no. 38 (1963): 258–69.

Lo, Eileen Yin-Fei. *The Chinese Kitchen*. New York: William Morrow, 1999.

Lo Kuan-Chung (Luo Guanzhong). *Romance of the Three Kingdoms*. Translated by C. H. Brewitt-Taylor. Tokyo: Charles E. Tuttle, 2002.

Lobenstine, E. C., and Warnshuis, A. L., eds. *The China Mission Year Book 1919*. Shanghai: Kwang Hsueh Publishing House, 1920.

Lou Zikuang. *Shanghai xincun nianhua 360 hang* (English title: *Folk Paintings of 360 Workers in Shanghai 1920's New Year*). Originally published by Shanghai weixin meishushe. Taipei: Chinese Association for Folklore, 1984 (reprint).

————. *Xinnian fengsu zhi* (Records of New Year's customs). Shanghai: Commercial Press, 1935.

Lu, Hanchao. "Away from Nanking Road: Small Stores and Neighborhood Life in Modern Shanghai." *Journal of Asian Studies*, vol. 54, no. 1 (Feb. 1995): 92–123.

————. *Beyond the Neon Lights: Everyday Shanghai in the Early Twentieth Century.* Berkeley: University of California Press, 1999.

————. "Creating Urban Outcasts: Shantytowns in Shanghai, 1920–1950." *Journal of Urban History*, vol. 21, no. 5 (July 1995): 563–96.

————. *Hede zhuan* (A biography of Sir Robert Hart). Shanghai: Shanghai renmin Chubanshe, 1986.

Lu, Henry C. *Chinese Natural Cures: Traditional Methods for Remedies and Preventions.* New York: Black Dog & Leventhal Publishers, 1986.

Lu Xun. *Diary of a Madman and Other Stories.* Trans. by William A. Lyell. Honolulu: University of Hawaii Press, 1990.

Lu Yaodong. *Du da neng rong: Zhongguo yinshi wenhua sanji* (Big bellyfuls: Essays on Chinese food culture). Taipei: Dongda tushu, 2001.

Luo Zhiru. *Tongjibiao zhong zhi Shanghai* (Shanghai as shown in statistical tables). Nanjing: Zhongyang yanjiuyuan, 1932.

Ma Wenhan. "Pingxuan liuyangju" (The poorhouse in Pingxuan). *Hebei wenshi ziliao* (Cultural and historical materials of Hebei), no. 30 (Oct. 1989): 169–71.

Macgowan, John. *Men and Manners of Modern China.* London: T. F. Unwin, 1912.

Mallory, Walter H. *China: Land of Famine.* New York: American Geographical Society, 1926.

Mao Tse-tung. *Selected Works of Mao Tse-tung.* 4 volumes. Peking (Beijing): Foreign Languages Press, 1965–75.

Mao Zedong. *Jianguo yilai Mao Zedong wengao* (Mao Zedong's manuscripts after the founding of the PRC). Beijing: Zhongying wenxian chubanshe, 1988.

————. *Report from Xunwu.* Trans. by Roger R. Thompson. Stanford, CA: Stanford University Press, 1990.

Martin, W. A. P. *A Cycle of Cathay; or Chinese, South and North. With Personal Reminiscences.* New York: Fleming H. Revell, 1900.

MeiZhong baodao (English title: *China Tribune*), Los Angeles.

Meng Xin, and Feng Xuemin, comps. *Tong yi shou ge* (The songs we shared). 2 volumes. Beijing: Xiandai chubanshe, 2000.

Moule, Arthur Evans. *New China and Old: Personal Recollections and Observations of Thirty Years.* London: Seeley, 1891.

Murray, Charles. *Losing Ground: American Social Policy, 1950–1980.* New York: Basic Books, 1984.

Na Zhiliang. *Qingming shanghe tu* (Along the river during the Qingming festival). Taipei: Guoli gugong bowuyuan, 1993.

Naquin, Susan. *Peking: Temples and City Life, 1400–1900.* Berkeley: University of California Press, 2000.

Nie Yaodong. *Mao Zedong yu Zhongguo chuantong wenhua* (Mao Zedong and traditional Chinese culture). Fuzhou: Fujian renmin chubanshe, 1992.

Ningjin xian zhi bianweihui [Editorial committee for the Ningjin county gazetteer], comp. "Qiong jia hang" (The company of the poor). *Jindaishi ziliao* (Modern historical materials), no. 58 (1985), 293–300.

North China Herald, weekly, Shanghai.

Obringer, Frederic. "A Song Innovation in Pharmacotherapy: Some Remarks on the Use of White Arsenic and Flowers of Arsenic." In Elisabeth Hsu, ed., *Innovation in Chinese Medicine*, 192–213. New York: Cambridge University Press, 2001.

Ou Yangping. "Jiu Chongqing de gaibang" (Beggars' gangs in old Chongqing). *Jindai Zhongguo jianghu miwen* (Inside stories of the unorthodox world in modern China), vol. 2: 425–36. Shijiazhuang: Hebei renmin chubanshe, 1997.

Pa Chin (Ba Jin). *Family.* Prospect Heights, IL: Waveland Press, 1972.

Peng Dehuai zhuan (A biography of Peng Dehuai). Compiled by Dangdai zhongguo renwu zhuanji congshu bianqibu. N.p.: Dangdai zhongguo chubanshe, 1993.

Perry, Elizabeth J. *Shanghai on Strike: The Politics of Chinese Labor.* Stanford, CA: Stanford University Press, 1993.

Peters, E. W. *Shanghai Policeman.* London: Rich & Cowan, 1937.

Pietz, David Allen. *Engineering the State: The Huai River and Reconstruction in Nationalist China, 1927–1937.* New York: Routledge, 2002.

Pineau, Roger, ed. *The Japan Expedition, 1852–1854: The Personal Journal of Commodore Matthew C. Perry.* Washington, D.C.: Smithsonian Institution Press, 1968.

Pingquan xian zhi bianzuan weiyuanhui [Editorial committee for the Pingquan county gazetteer], comp. *Pingquan xian zhi* (Pingquan county gazetteer). Beijing: Zuojia chubanshe, 2000.

Piven, Frances Fox, and Richard A. Cloward. *Regulating the Poor: The Functions of Public Welfare.* Updated edition. New York: Vintage Books, 1993.

Pruitt, Ida. *A Daughter of Han: The Autobiography of a Chinese Working Woman.* New Haven, CT: Yale University Press, 1945.

Pudong difang zhilüe (Gazetteer of Pudong). Compiled and published by Taibeishi Pudong tongxianghui, 1968.

Qi Ping. "You qigai yueli de hua" (The talk of a person who was a beggar). *Shenghuo* (Life), vol. 1, no. 26 (Apr. 1926): 160–61.

Qian Nairong. *Huyu pandian: Shanghaihua wenhua* (An inventory of the Shanghai vernacular: The culture of the Shanghai dialect). Shanghai: Shanghai wenhua chubanshe, 2002.

———. "Shili yangchang hua fangyan" (Dialects in the foreign concessions of Shanghai). *Dang'an yu lishi* (English title: *Archives and History*), no. 4 (1989): 69–72.

Qin Danhua. "Jiangzhurou he baiyejie" (Braised pork seasoned with soy sauce and twisted dry beancurd sheets). *Shijie ribao* (English title: *World Journal*) (June 22, 1994): D1.

Qu Yanbin. *Zhongguo qigai shi* (A history of Chinese beggars). Shanghai: Shanghai wenyi chubanshe, 1990.

Rattenbury, Harold B. *China, My China.* London: Frederick Muller, 1944.

Ren Ping, comp. *Qishi er hang zushiye de chuanshuo* (Oral traditions concerning the forefathers of the seventy-two callings). Henan: Haiyan chubanshe, 1985.

Renmin ribao (People's daily), Beijing.

Ribton-Turner, C. J. *A History of Vagrants and Vagrancy and Beggars and Begging.* Montclair, NJ: Patterson Smith, 1972 [1887].

Robinson, Lewis Stewart. *Double-Edged Sword: Christianity and 20th Century Chinese Fiction.* Hong Kong: Tao Fong Shan Ecumenical Center, 1986.

Ross, Edward Alsworth. *The Changing Chinese: The Conflict of Oriental and Western Cultures in China.* New York: Century, 1912.

Rowe, William T. *Hankow: Conflict and Community in a Chinese City, 1796–1895.* Stanford, CA: Stanford University Press, 1989.

———. *Saving the World: Chen Hongmou and Elite Consciousness in Eighteenth-Century China*. Stanford, CA: Stanford University Press, 2001.

Sangharakshita. *Who Is the Buddha?* New York: Barnes and Noble, 1995.

Schak, David C. *A Chinese Beggars' Den: Poverty and Mobility in an Underclass Community*. Pittsburgh: University of Pittsburgh Press, 1988.

———. "Images of Beggars in Chinese Culture." In Sarah Allan and Alvin P. Cohen, eds., *Legend, Lore, and Religion in China: Essays in Honor of Wolfram Eberhard on His Seventieth Birthday*, 109–33. San Francisco: Chinese Materials Center, 1979.

Schurmann, Franz. *Ideology and Organization in Communist China*. Berkeley: University of California Press, 1968.

Shandongsheng Ningjinxian shizhi bianzuan weiyuanhui [Editorial committee for the county history and gazetteer of Ningjin, Shandong], comp. *Ningjin xian zhi* (Ningjin county gazetteer). Ji'nan: Qilu shushe, 1992.

Shanghai Jianshe bianji bu [Editorial office of Shanghai Reconstruction], ed. *Shanghai jianshe* (Shanghai reconstruction). Shanghai: Shanghai kexue jishu wenxian chubanshe, 1989.

Shanghai shehui kexueyuan jingji yanjiusuo [Institute of Economics, Shanghai Academy of Social Sciences], ed. *Jiangnan zaochuanchang changshi* (A history of the Jiangnan Shipyard). N.p.: Jiangsu renmin chubanshe, 1983.

Shanghai zhinan (Guide to Shanghai). Compiled and published by the Commercial Press, 1919 edition.

Shanghai zhoubao (Shanghai weekly), Shanghai, 1933.

Shanghaishi lishi bowuguan [Shanghai Municipal Historical Museum], comp. *Ershi shiji chu de Zhongguo yinxiang* (English title: *The Origin of Modern China: Record from an American Photographer*). Shanghai: Shanghai guji chubanshe, 2001.

Shanghaitan heimu (Shady deals in Shanghai). 4 volumes. Originally compiled by Qian Shengbe, under the title *Shanghai heimu*, published in 1917 by *Shanghai shishi xinbao* (Shanghai current affairs news). Beijing: Guoji wenhua, 1992 (reprint).

Shehui ribao (English title: *Social Daily News*), Shanghai, 1934–36.

Shen Congwen. "Teng Huisheng Tang jinxi" (The past and present of the Teng Huisheng Hall). *Guowen zhoubao* (National news weekly), vol. 12, no. 2 (Jan. 7, 1935): 4–5.

Shen Ji, Dong Changqing, and Gan Zhenhu, comps. *Zhongguo mimi shehui* (China's secret society). Shanghai: Shanghai shudian, 1993.

Shen Nianxian. "Jiu Shanghai tan shang de biesan he qigai" (Beggars in old Shanghai). In Shi Fukang, comp., *Shanghai shehui daguan* (All aspects of Shanghai society), 186–91. Shanghai: Shanghai shudian, 2000.

Shenbao (Shanghai daily), Shanghai, 1872–1949.

Shijie ribao (English title: *World Journal*), New York.

Shijie zhoukan (English title: *Supplement to World Journal*), New York.

Siao-Yu. *Mao Tse-Tung and I Were Beggars*. Syracuse, NY: Syracuse University Press, 1959.

Sima Qian. *Records of the Grand Historian: Han Dynasty I*. Revised edition, trans. by Burton Watson. New York: Columbia University Press, 1993.

————. *Records of the Grand Historian: Qin Dynasty*. Trans. by Burton Watson. New York: Columbia University Press, 1993.

————. *Records of the Historian: Chapters from the Shih chi of Ssu-ma Ch'ien*. Trans. by Burton Watson. New York: Columbia University Press, 1969.

Skinner, G. William. "Marketing and Social Structure in Rural China." 3 parts. *Journal of Asian Studies*, vol. 24, no. 1 (Nov. 1964): 3–44, no. 2 (Feb. 1965): 195–228, no. 3 (May 1965): 363–99.

————, ed. *The City in Late Imperial China*. Stanford, CA: Stanford University Press, 1977.

Smith, Arthur Henderson. *Chinese Characteristics*. Edinburgh: Oliphant, Anderson, and Ferrier, 1892.

————. *Proverbs and Common Sayings from the Chinese*. New York: Putnam, 1965 [1914].

————. *Village Life in China: A Study in Sociology*. New York: Fleming H. Revell, 1899.

Smith, Joanna F. Handlin. "Liberating Animals in Ming-Qing China: Buddhist Inspiration and Elite Imagination." *Journal of Asian Studies*, vol. 58, no. 1 (Feb. 1999): 51–84.

Snow, Edgar. *Red China Today*. Revised and updated edition of *The Other Side of the River*. New York: Vintage, 1971.

————. *Red Star Over China*. New York: Grove Press, 1977.

Solinger, Dorothy J. *Contesting Citizenship in Urban China*. Berkeley: University of California Press, 1999.

Song Rulin. *Songjiang fu zhi* (Gazetteer of Songjiang prefecture). 84 volumes (*juan*). 1817.

Soonthorndhammathada, Phra. *Compassion in Buddhism and Puranas*. Delhi: Nag, 1995.

South China Morning Post, Hong Kong.

Spence, Jonathan D. *The Search for Modern China*. New York: W. W. Norton, 1990.

Stapleton, Kristin. *Civilizing Chengdu: Chinese Urban Reform, 1895–1937*. Cambridge, MA: Harvard University Asia Center, 2000.

Stock, Jonathan P. J. *Musical Creativity in Twentieth-Century China: Abing, His Music, and Its Changing Meanings*. Rochester, NY: University of Rochester Press, 1996.

Stott, Amelia O. "Chinese Knights of the Open Palm." *Asia*, vol. 27, no. 10 (Oct. 1927): 830–33.

Strand, David. *Rickshaw Beijing: City People and Politics in the 1920s*. Berkeley: University of California Press, 1989.

Sun Jikang. "Jiushi Yunnan de qigai" (Beggars in old Yunnan). *Jindai Zhongguo jianghu miwen* (Inside stories of the unorthodox world in modern China), vol. 2: 437–41. Shijiazhuang: Hebei renmin chubanshe, 1997.

Sun Mo. "Nantong de 'chi ketuo fan'" (The kowtow rice eaters of Nantong). *Nantong jin'gu* (Nantong past and present), no. 2 (1992): 19–20.

Sun Yunnian. *Jiangnan ganjiu lu* (Memories of Jiangnan). Nanjing: Jiangsu guji chubanshe, 2000.

Tang Youshi. "Qigai" (Beggars). In Zhongguo renmin zhengzhi xieshang huiyi Beijingshi weiyuanhui wenshi ziliao yanjiu weiyuanhui (comp.), *Beijing wangshi tan* (Historical narratives of Beijing), 404–10. Beijing: Beijing chubanshe, 1988.

Tang Zhenchang. *Zhongguo yinshi wenhua sanlun* (Essays on Chinese food culture). Taipei: Commercial Press, 1999.

Tao Juyin. *Tianliang qian de gudao* (The solitary island before dawn). Shanghai: Zhonghua shuju, 1947.

Tian Hua. "Kaibu yihou Shanghai qigai qunti chengyin chutan" (Preliminary research on the formation of Shanghai's beggar community after 1843). *Shanghai yanjiu luncong* (Papers on Shanghai studies), no. 9 (1993): 49–58.

Tianchang xian zhi (Gazetteer of Tianchang county). Shanghai: Guji shudian, 1962 [1550].

Topping, Seymour. *Journey Between Two Chinas.* New York: Harper & Row, 1972.

Tu Shipin. *Shanghai chunqiu* (Annals of Shanghai). Originally published in Shanghai under the title *Shanghaishi daguan* (Overview of Shanghai). Hong Kong: Zhongguo tushu bianyiguan, 1968.

Unschuld, Paul U. *Medicine in China: Historical Artifacts and Images.* Trans. by Sabine Wilms. Munich: Prestel Verlag, 2000.

Vale, J. "Beggar Life in Chentu [Chengdu]." *West China Missionary News*, vol. 9, no. 4 (Apr. 1907): 8–11, and no. 7 (July 1907): 7–10.

Vermeer, Eduard B. *Chinese Local History: Stone Inscriptions from Fukien in the Sung to Ch'ing Periods.* Boulder, CO: Westview Press, 1991.

Wakefield, David. *Fenjia: Household Division and Inheritance in Qing and Republican China.* Honolulu: University of Hawaii Press, 1998.

Wakeman, Frederic, Jr. *Policing Shanghai, 1927–1937.* Berkeley: University of California Press, 1995.

Wang Chufu. "Guangzhou qigai jituan: Guanditing renma" (The Hall of Guandi: Beggar cliques in Guangzhou). *Jindai Zhongguo jianghu miwen* (Inside stories of the unorthodox world in modern China), vol. 2: 356–64. Shijiazhuang: Hebei renmin chubanshe, 1997.

Wang, Di. *Street Culture in Chengdu: Public Space, Urban Commoners, and Local Politics, 1870–1930.* Stanford, CA: Stanford University Press, 2003.

Wang Gungwu. *The Chinese Overseas: From Earthbound China to the Quest for Autonomy.* Cambridge, MA: Harvard University Press, 2000.

Wang Hanmin. *Baxian yu Zhongguo wenhua* (The Eight Immortals and Chinese culture). Beijing: Zhongguo shehui kexue chubanshe, 2000.

Wang Huizu. *Wang Huizu xiansheng ziding nianpu* (The autobiographical chronicle of Mr. Wang Huizu). Originally published in 1796. Taipei: Commercial Press, 1980.

Wang Xiyi, and Lei Zihui. "Wenzhou de xiaceng shehui" (The lower society of Wenzhou). *Jindai Zhongguo jianghu miwen* (Inside stories of the unorthodox world in modern China), vol. 1: 640–43. Shijiazhuang: Hebei renmin chubanshe, 1997.

Wang Xuetai. *Youmin wenhua yu Zhongguo shehui* (Vagrant culture and Chinese society). Beijing: Xueyuan chubanshe, 1999.

———. *Zhongguo liumin* (Chinese vagrants). Hong Kong: Zhonghua shuju, 1992.

Wang Zehua, and Wang He. *Minguo shiqi de lao Chengdu* (Old Chengdu during the Republican period). Chengdu: Sichuan wenyi chubanshe, 1999.

Wang Zhongxian. *Shanghai suyu tushuo* (Illustrated folk adages of Shanghai). Shanghai: Shanghai shehui chubanshe, 1935.

Wang Ziguan. "Yi jiu si er nian da hanzai zhi Sishui" (Sishui in the great drought of 1942). *Henan wenshi ziliao* (Cultural and historical materials of Henan province), vol. 19 (Apr. 1986): 160–65.

Wasserstrom, Jeffrey. *Student Protests in Twentieth-Century China: The View from Shanghai.* Stanford, CA: Stanford University Press, 1991.

Watson, Burton, trans. *The Tso Chuan: Selections from China's Oldest Narrative History.* New York: Columbia University Press, 1989.

Watson, James L. "Funeral Specialists in Cantonese Society: Pollution, Performance, and Social Hierarchy." In James L. Watson and Evelyn S. Rawski, eds., *Death Ritual in Late Imperial and Modern China*, 109–34. Berkeley: University of California Press, 1988.

Wei Shaochang, and Wu Chenghui, comps. *Yuanyang hudie pai yanjiu ziliao* (Research materials on the Mandarin Duck and Butterfly school). 2 volumes. Shanghai: Shanghai wenyi chubanshe, 1984.

Weimin. "Suo heiqi" (On beggars). *Guang Zhao zhoubao* (Cantonese Native Place Association weekly), no. 77 (Sept. 1920).

Werner, E. T. C. *Myths and Legends of China.* New York: Brentano's, 1922.

Whyte, Martin King, and William L. Parish. *Urban Life in Contemporary China.* Chicago: University of Chicago Press, 1984.

Will, Pierre-Etienne. *Bureaucracy and Famine in Eighteenth-Century China.* Trans. by Elborg Forster. Stanford, CA: Stanford University Press, 1990.

Will, Pierre-Etienne, and R. Bin Wong, with James Z. Lee. *Nourish the People: The State Civilian Granary System in China, 1650–1850.* Ann Arbor: University of Michigan Center for Chinese Studies, 1991.

Williams, S. Wells. *The Middle Kingdom: A Survey of the Geography, Government, Literature, Social Life, Arts, and History of the Chinese Empire and Its Inhabitants.* 2 volumes. New York: Charles Scribner's Sons, 1904.

Wilson, William Julius. *The Truly Disadvantaged: The Inner City, the Underclass, and Public Policy.* Chicago: University of Chicago Press, 1990.

Wolf, Arthur P. "Gods, Ghosts and Ancestors." In Arthur P. Wolf, ed., *Religion and Ritual in Chinese Society*, 131–82. Stanford, CA: Stanford University Press,1974.

Wu Han. *Zhu Yuanzhang zhuan* (A biography of Zhu Yuanzhang). Beijing: Sanlian chubanshe, 1980 [1965].

Wu, Hongda Harry, with Carolyn Wakeman. *Bitter Winds: A Memoir of My Years in China's Gulag.* New York: John Wiley and Sons, 1994.

Xiao Qian, ed. *Shehui baixiang* (Society in all its aspects). Taipei: Commercial Press, 1992.

Xiao Xinli, comp. *Wo de xuanze* (My choice). Beijing: Zhonggong zhongyang dangxiao chubanshe, 1998.

Xie Zhaozhi. *Wu za zu* (Five sets of assorted essays). Beijing: Zhonghua shuju, 1959 [1608].

Xin jingbao (New capital news), Beijing.

Xin Ping. *Cong Shanghai faxian lishi* (Discovering history in Shanghai). Shanghai: Shanghai renmin chubanshe, 1996.

Xingxi shibao (Information times), Guangzhou.

Xu Chi, et al. *Shanghai zhongsheng xiang* (All mortals in Shanghai). Shanghai: Xin Zhongguo baoshe, 1943.

Xu Dong, and Ding Richang. *Baojiashu jiyao* (The essence of the *Book of the Baojia System*). Taipei: Chengwen chubanshe, 1968 [1871].

Xu Ke. *Qingbai leichao* (Assorted collection of anecdotes concerning the Qing). Shanghai: Commercial Press, 1917.

Xu Yuanqing. "Diaocha Shanghai qigai zhi jieguo" (Report on an investigation of Shanghai's beggars). *Jiezhi yuekan* (Temperance monthly), (Nov. 1927): 21–22.

Xu Zhiyan. *Xinhua miji* (Confidential notes on the Yuan Shikai regime). Originally published in 1918 (Shanghai: Qinghua shuju). Reprinted in Rong Mengyuan and Zhuang Bofeng, comps., *Jindai baihai* (Unofficial history of modern China), vol. 3: 293–418. Chengdu: Sichuan renmin chubanshe, 1985.

Xue Gengshen. "Wo suo jiechu guo de Shanghai banghui renwu" (The Shanghai gangers I have known). *Shanghai wenshi ziliao xuanji* (Selected cultural and historical materials of Shanghai), no. 54 (1986): 87–107.

Yang Jianyu. *Zhongguo lidai diwang lu* (Biographies of Chinese emperors). Shanghai: Shanghai wenhua chubanshe, 1989.

Yang Jiayou. *Shanghai fengwu gujintan* (Historical narrative on the scenery and relics of Shanghai). Shanghai: Shanghai shudian, 1991.

Yang Jiayou, and He Mingyun. *Ta qiao gujin tan* (Historical narratives on pagodas and bridges). Shanghai: Shanghai huabao chubanshe, 1991.

Yang Wenqi. *Zhongguo yinshi minsu xue* (Folklore in Chinese food). Beijing: Zhongguo zhanwang chubanshe, 1983.

Yangzi wanbao (Yangzi evening news), Nanjing.

Ye Lingfeng. *Nen bu yi Jiangnan* (How can I not be nostalgic about Jiangnan?). Nanjing: Jiangsu guji chubanshe, 2000.

Ye Yonglie. *Hongse de qidian* (The red beginning). Shanghai: Shanghai renmin chubanshe, 1991.

———. *Jiang Qing zhuan* (A biography of Jiang Qing). Changchun: Shidai wenyi chubanshe, 1993.

Yi Jihe, comp. *Anhuisheng Fengyangxian zhilüe* (A concise gazetteer of Fengyang county, Anhui province). Taipei: Chengwen chubanshe, 1975 [1936].

Yi Liyuan. "Qingmo keju tongzishi de xingxing sese" (All aspects of the county-level civil examination in the late Qing). *Wuhan wenshi zhiliao* (Cultural and historical materials of Wuhan), vol. 23 (1986): 153–65.

Yin Dengguo. *Tu shuo 360 hang* (Illustrating the 360 walks of life). 3 volumes. Taipei: Minshengbao she, 1985.

Yiren. "Qigai 'Huangdi'" (Emperor beggars). *Shanghai shenghuo* (Life in Shanghai), vol. 2, no. 1 (June 1938): 14.

Yu Xiu. *Zhongguo qigai diaocha* (Investigations into Chinese beggars). Beijing: Zhonghua gongshang lianhe chubanshe, 1999.

Yuan, L. Z. *Sidelights on Shanghai*. Shanghai: Mercury Press, 1934.

Yuan Xi. *Wu Xun zhuan pipan jishi* (Record of the criticizing *Wu Xun zhuan* campaign). Wuhan: Changjiang wenyi chubanshe, 2000.

Yuan Zheng. "Yi xi tan" (An evening chat). *Shenghuo* (Life), vol. 1, no. 11 (Dec. 20, 1925): 70–71.

Yuhai (Sea of sayings), two volumes. Shanghai: Shanghai wenyi chubanshe, 2000.

Yunyouke. *Jianghu congtan* (Collected accounts of the unorthodox world). Originally published in 3 volumes in 1936 by Beiping shiyanbao she. Beijing: Zhongguo quyi chubanshe, 1988.

Zhang Dai. *Ye hangchuan* (Evening liners). Hangzhou: Zhejiang guji chubanshe, 1987.

Zhang Danian, and Gong Jiang. "Wuxi de qigai yu jiaohua jiatou" (Wuxi's beggars and their headmen). *Jindai Zhongguo jianghu miwen* (Inside stories of the unorthodox world in modern China), vol. 2: 311–15. Shijiazhuang: Hebei renmin chubanshe, 1997.

Zhang Guanding. "Jiefang qian Beijing de zhuangli he gangfangye" (Funerals and funeral services in pre-1949 Beijing). *Wenshi ziliao xuanbian* (Selected cultural and historical materials), no. 14: 214–27. Beijing: Beijing chubanshe, 1989.

Zhang Jiya. "Da jiangjun yan" (The words of the great general). *Shanghai shenghuo* (Life in Shanghai), inaugural issue (Dec. 1926): 20–21.

Zhang Kaiyuan, ed. *Qing tongjian* (Complete chronicles of the Qing dynasty). 4 volumes. Changsha: Yuelu shushe, 2000.

Zhang Ming, comp. *Wu Xun yanjiu ziliao daquan* (A complete collection of research materials on Wu Xun). Ji'nan: Shandong daxue chubanshe, 1991.

Zhang Mosheng. *Yixing zhuan* (Biographies of eccentrics). Chongqing: Chongqing chubanshe, 1987 [1944].

Zhang Runqing. "Qingmo yilai de Shuangcheng fu qigai chu" (The beggars' section in Shuangcheng since the late Qing dynasty). *Heilongjiang wenshi ziliao* (Cultural and historical materials of Heilongjiang), no. 3 (n.d.): 206–10.

Zhang Tao. *Kongzi jia yu zhuye* (An annotated version of the Sayings of the Confucian School). Xi'an: Sanqin chubanshe, 1998.

Zhang Zichen. *Zhongguo gudai chuanshuo* (Ancient Chinese legends). Changchun: Jilin wenshi chubanshe, 1986.

Zhao Yi. *Gaiyu congkao* (Textual research by subject, conducted in a mourning period for mother). Shijiazhuang: Hebei renmin chubanshe, 1990 [1791].

Zhejiang wenyi chubanshe [Zhejiang Literature and Art Press], comp. *Baxian de gushi* (Tales of the Eight Immortals). Hangzhou: Zhejiang wenyi chubanshe, 1983.

Zheng Huanwu. "Cong gaier dao baiwan fuweng de Zhang Songjiao" (Zhang Songjiao: From a beggar boy to a millionaire.) *Wuhan wenshi ziliao* (Cultural and historical materials of Wuhan), vol. 53 (Oct. 1993): 163–65.

Zheng Yuanchuan. "Laohekou de qigai zuzhi" (The beggars' organization in Laohekou). *Hubei wenshi zhiliao* (Cultural and historical materials of Hubei), vol. 28 (Sept. 1989): 232–37.

Zhong Minwen. *Suyan daquan* (A complete book of common adages). Beijing: Dazhong wenyi chubanshe, 1997.

Zhongguo kexueyuan lishi yanjiusuo [Institute of History, Chinese Academy of Sciences], comp. *Wusi aiguo yundong zhiliao* (Materials of the May fourth movement). Beijing: Kexue chubanshe, 1959.

Zhongguo qingnian bao (Chinese youth news), Beijing.

Zhonghua renmin gongheguo guojia tongjiju [Bureau of Statistics of the People's Republic of China], and Zhonghua renmin gongheguo minzhengbu [Ministry of Civil Affairs of the People's Republic of China], comps. *Zhongguo zaiqing baogao*,

1949–1995 (Report of the damage caused by disasters in China). Beijing: Zhong-guo tongji chubanshe, 1995.

Zhou Pei. "Hengyangshi de gaibang" (Beggars' gangs in the city of Hengyang). *Hunan wenshi* (Culture and history of Hunan), no. 39 (Sept. 1990): 210–15.

Zhu Zhenfan. "Fo tiao qiang" (Buddha jumps over the wall). *Shijie ribao* (English title: *World Journal*), Oct. 12–15, 2002.

Zou Yiren. *Jiu Shanghai renkou bianqian de yanjiu* (Research on population change in old Shanghai). Shanghai: Shanghai renmin chubanshe, 1980.